CLEP-6　　COLLEGE-LEVEL EXAMINATION
　　　　　　PROGRAM SERIES

This is your
PASSBOOK for...

College Algebra

Test Preparation Study Guide
Questions & Answers

NATIONAL LEARNING CORPORATION®

COPYRIGHT NOTICE

This book is SOLELY intended for, is sold ONLY to, and its use is RESTRICTED to individual, bona fide applicants or candidates who qualify by virtue of having seriously filed applications for appropriate license, certificate, professional and/or promotional advancement, higher school matriculation, scholarship, or other legitimate requirements of education and/or governmental authorities.

This book is NOT intended for use, class instruction, tutoring, training, duplication, copying, reprinting, excerption, or adaptation, etc., by:

1) Other publishers
2) Proprietors and/or Instructors of "Coaching" and/or Preparatory Courses
3) Personnel and/or Training Divisions of commercial, industrial, and governmental organizations
4) Schools, colleges, or universities and/or their departments and staffs, including teachers and other personnel
5) Testing Agencies or Bureaus
6) Study groups which seek by the purchase of a single volume to copy and/or duplicate and/or adapt this material for use by the group as a whole without having purchased individual volumes for each of the members of the group
7) Et al.

Such persons would be in violation of appropriate Federal and State statutes.

PROVISION OF LICENSING AGREEMENTS – Recognized educational, commercial, industrial, and governmental institutions and organizations, and others legitimately engaged in educational pursuits, including training, testing, and measurement activities, may address request for a licensing agreement to the copyright owners, who will determine whether, and under what conditions, including fees and charges, the materials in this book may be used them. In other words, a licensing facility exists for the legitimate use of the material in this book on other than an individual basis. However, it is asseverated and affirmed here that the material in this book CANNOT be used without the receipt of the express permission of such a licensing agreement from the Publishers. Inquiries re licensing should be addressed to the company, attention rights and permissions department.

All rights reserved, including the right of reproduction in whole or in part, in any form or by any means, electronic or mechanical, including photocopying, recording, or by any information storage and retrieval system, without permission in writing from the Publisher.

Copyright © 2025 by
National Learning Corporation

212 Michael Drive, Syosset, NY 11791
(516) 921-8888 • www.passbooks.com
E-mail: info@passbooks.com

PASSBOOK® SERIES

THE *PASSBOOK® SERIES* has been created to prepare applicants and candidates for the ultimate academic battlefield – the examination room.

At some time in our lives, each and every one of us may be required to take an examination – for validation, matriculation, admission, qualification, registration, certification, or licensure.

Based on the assumption that every applicant or candidate has met the basic formal educational standards, has taken the required number of courses, and read the necessary texts, the *PASSBOOK® SERIES* furnishes the one special preparation which may assure passing with confidence, instead of failing with insecurity. Examination questions – together with answers – are furnished as the basic vehicle for study so that the mysteries of the examination and its compounding difficulties may be eliminated or diminished by a sure method.

This book is meant to help you pass your examination provided that you qualify and are serious in your objective.

The entire field is reviewed through the huge store of content information which is succinctly presented through a provocative and challenging approach – the question-and-answer method.

A climate of success is established by furnishing the correct answers at the end of each test.

You soon learn to recognize types of questions, forms of questions, and patterns of questioning. You may even begin to anticipate expected outcomes.

You perceive that many questions are repeated or adapted so that you can gain acute insights, which may enable you to score many sure points.

You learn how to confront new questions, or types of questions, and to attack them confidently and work out the correct answers.

You note objectives and emphases, and recognize pitfalls and dangers, so that you may make positive educational adjustments.

Moreover, you are kept fully informed in relation to new concepts, methods, practices, and directions in the field.

You discover that you are actually taking the examination all the time: you are preparing for the examination by "taking" an examination, not by reading extraneous and/or supererogatory textbooks.

In short, this PASSBOOK®, used directedly, should be an important factor in helping you to pass your test.

NONTRADITIONAL EDUCATION

Students returning to school as adults bring more varied experience to their studies than do the teenagers who begin college shortly after graduating from high school. As a result, there are numerous programs for students with nontraditional learning curves. Hundreds of colleges and universities grant degrees to people who cannot attend classes at a regular campus or have already learned what the college is supposed to teach.

You can earn nontraditional education credits in many ways:
- Passing standardized exams
- Demonstrating knowledge gained through experience
- Completing campus-based coursework, and
- Taking courses off campus

Some methods of assessing learning for credit are objective, such as standardized tests. Others are more subjective, such as a review of life experiences.

With some help from four hypothetical characters – Alice, Vin, Lynette, and Jorge – this article describes nontraditional ways of earning educational credit. It begins by describing programs in which you can earn a high school diploma without spending 4 years in a classroom. The college picture is more complicated, so it is presented in two parts: one on gaining credit for what you know through course work or experience, and a second on college degree programs. The final section lists resources for locating more information.

Earning High School Credit

People who were prevented from finishing high school as teenagers have several options if they want to do so as adults. Some major cities have back-to-school programs that allow adults to attend high school classes with current students. But the more practical alternatives for most adults are to take the General Educational Development (GED) tests or to earn a high school diploma by demonstrating their skills or taking correspondence classes.

Of course, these options do not match the experience of staying in high school and graduating with one's friends. But they are viable alternatives for adult learners committed to meeting and, often, continuing their educational goals.

GED Program

Alice quit high school her sophomore year and took a job to help support herself, her younger brother, and their newly widowed mother. Now an adult, she wants to earn her high school diploma – and then go on to college. Because her job as head cook and her family responsibilities keep her busy during the day, she plans to get a high school equivalency diploma. She will study for, and take, the GED tests. Every year, about half a million adults earn their high school credentials this way. A GED diploma is accepted in lieu of a high school one by more than 90 percent of employers, colleges, and universities, so it is a good choice for someone like Alice.

The GED testing program is sponsored by the American Council on Education and State and local education departments. It consists of examinations in five subject areas: Writing, science, mathematics, social studies, and literature and the arts. The tests also measure skills such as analytical ability, problem solving, reading comprehension, and ability to understand and apply information. Most of the questions are multiple choice; the writing test includes an essay section on a topic of general interest.

Eligibility rules for taking the exams vary, but some states require that you must be at least 18. Tests are given in English, Spanish, and French. In addition to standard print, versions in large print, Braille, and audiocassette are also available. Total time allotted for the tests is 7 1/2 hours.

The GED tests are not easy. About one-fourth of those who complete the exams every year do not pass. Passing scores are established by administering the tests to a sample of graduating high school seniors. The minimum standard score is set so that about one-third of graduating seniors would not pass the tests if they took them.

Because of the difficulty of the tests, people need to prepare themselves to take them. Often, they start by taking the Official GED Practice Tests, usually available through a local adult education center. Centers are listed in your phone book's blue pages under "Adult Education," "Continuing Education," or "GED." Adult education centers also have information about GED preparation classes and self-study materials. Classes are generally arranged to accommodate adults' work schedules. National Learning Corporation publishes several study guides that aim to thoroughly prepare test-takers for the GED.

School districts, colleges, adult education centers, and community organizations have information about GED testing schedules and practice tests. For more information, contact them, your nearest GED testing center, or:

GED Testing Service
One Dupont Circle, NW, Suite 250
Washington, DC 20036-1163
1(800) 62-MY GED (626-9433)
(202) 939-9490

Skills Demonstration

Adults who have acquired high school level skills through experience might be eligible for the National External Diploma Program. This alternative to the GED does not involve any direct instruction. Instead, adults seeking a high school diploma must demonstrate mastery of 65 competencies in 8 general areas: Communication; computation; occupational preparedness; and self, social, consumer, scientific, and technological awareness.

Mastery is shown through the completion of the tasks. For example, a participant could prove competency in computation by measuring a room for carpeting, figuring out the amount of carpet needed, and computing the cost.

Before being accepted for the program, adults undergo an evaluation. Tests taken at one of the program's offices measure reading, writing, and mathematics abilities. A take-home segment includes a self-assessment of current skills, an individual skill evaluation, and an occupational interest and aptitude test.

Adults accepted for the program have weekly meetings with an assessor. At the meeting, the assessor reviews the participant's work from the previous week. If the task has not been completed properly, the assessor explains the mistake. Participants continue to correct their errors until they master each competency. A high school diploma is awarded upon proven mastery of all 65 competencies.

Fourteen States and the District of Columbia now offer the External Diploma Program. For more information, contact:
External Diploma Program
One Dupont Circle, NW, Suite 250
Washington, DC 20036-1193
(202) 939-9475

Correspondence and Distance Study
Vin dropped out of high school during his junior year because his family's frequent moves made it difficult for him to continue his studies. He promised himself at the time he dropped out that he would someday finish the courses needed for his diploma. For people like Vin, who prefer to earn a traditional diploma in a nontraditional way, there are about a dozen accredited courses of study for earning a high school diploma by correspondence, or distance study. The programs are either privately run, affiliated with a university, or administered by a State education department.

Distance study diploma programs have no residency requirements, allowing students to continue their studies from almost any location. Depending on the course of study, students need not be enrolled full time and usually have more flexible schedules for finishing their work. Selection of courses ranges from vo-tech to college prep, and some programs place different emphasis on the types of diplomas offered. University affiliated schools, for example, allow qualified students to take college courses along with their high school ones. Students can then apply the college credits toward a degree at that university or transfer them to another institution.

Taking courses by distance study is often more challenging and time consuming than attending classes, especially for adults who have other obligations. Success depends on each student's motivation. Students usually do reading assignments on their own. Written exercises, which they complete and send to an instructor for grading, supplement their reading material.

A list of some accredited high schools that offer diplomas by distance study is available free from the Distance Education and Training Council, formerly known as the National Home Study Council. Request the "DETC Directory of Accredited Institutions" from:
The Distance Education and Training Council
1601 18th Street, NW.
Washington, DC 20009-2529
(202) 234-5100

Some publications profiling nontraditional college programs include addresses and descriptions of several high school correspondence ones. See the Resources section at the end of this article for more information.

Getting College Credit For What You Know
Adults can receive college credit for prior coursework, by passing examinations, and documenting experiential learning. With help from a college advisor, nontraditional students should assess their skills, establish their educational goals, and determine the number of college credits they might be eligible for.

Even before you meet with a college advisor, you should collect all your school and training records. Then, make a list of all knowledge and abilities acquired through experience, no matter how irrelevant they seem to your chosen field. Next, determine your educational goals: What specific field do you wish to study? What kind of a degree do you want? Finally, determine how your past work fits into the field of study. Later on, you will evaluate educational programs to find one that's right for you.

People who have complex educational or experiential learning histories might want to have their learning evaluated by the Regents Credit Bank. The Credit Bank, operated by Regents College of the University of the State of New York, allows people to consolidate credits earned through college, experience, or other methods. Special assessments are available for Regents College enrollees whose knowledge in a specific field cannot be adequately evaluated by standardized exams. For more information, contact the Regents Credit Bank at:

Regents College
7 Columbia Circle
Albany, NY 12203-5159
(518) 464-8500

Credit For Prior College Coursework

When Lynette was in college during the 1970s, she attended several different schools and took a variety of courses. She did well in some classes and poorly in others. Now that she is a successful business owner and has more focus, Lynette thinks she should forget about her previous coursework and start from scratch. Instead, she should start from where she is.

Lynette should have all her transcripts sent to the colleges or universities of her choice and let an admissions officer determine which classes are applicable toward a degree. A few credits here and there may not seem like much, but they add up. Even if the subjects do not seem relevant to any major, they might be counted as elective credits toward a degree. And comparing the cost of transcripts with the cost of college courses, it makes sense to spend a few dollars per transcript for a chance to save hundreds, and perhaps thousands, of dollars in books and tuition.

Rules for transferring credits apply to all prior coursework at accredited colleges and universities, whether done on campus or off. Courses completed off campus, often called extended learning, include those available to students through independent study and correspondence. Many schools have extended learning programs; Brigham Young University, for example, offers more than 300 courses through its Department of Independent Study. One type of extended learning is distance learning, a form of correspondence study by technological means such as television, video and audio, CD-ROM, electronic mail, and computer tutorials. See the Resources section at the end of this article for more information about publications available from the National University Continuing Education Association.

Any previously earned college credits should be considered for transfer, no matter what the subject or the grade received. Many schools do not accept the transfer of courses graded below a C or ones taken more than a designated number of years ago. Some colleges and universities also have limits on the number of credits that can be transferred and applied toward a degree. But not all do. For example, Thomas Edison State College, New Jersey's State college for adults, accepts the transfer of all 120 hours of credit required for a baccalaureate degree – provided all the credits are transferred from regionally accredited schools, no more than 80 are at the junior college level, and the student's grades overall and in the field of study average out to C.

To assign credit for prior coursework, most schools require original transcripts. This means you must complete a form or send a written, signed request to have your transcripts released directly to a college or university. Once you have chosen the schools you want to apply to, contact the schools you attended before. Find out how much each transcript costs, and ask them to send your transcripts to the ones you are applying to. Write a letter that includes your name (and names used during attendance, if different) and dates of attendance, along with the names and addresses of the schools to which your transcripts should be sent. Include payment and mail to the registrar at the schools you have attended. The registrar's office will process your request and send an official transcript of your coursework to the colleges or universities you have designated.

Credit For Noncollege Courses

Colleges and universities are not the only ones that offer classes. Volunteer organizations and employers often provide formal training worth college credit. The American Council on Education has two programs that assess thousands of specific courses and make recommendations on the amount of college credit they are worth. Colleges and universities accept the recommendations or use them as guidelines.

One program evaluates educational courses sponsored by government agencies, business and industry, labor unions, and professional and voluntary organizations. It is the Program on Noncollegiate Sponsored Instruction (PONSI). Some of the training seminars Alice has participated in covered topics such as food preparation, kitchen safety, and nutrition. Although she has not yet earned her GED, Alice can earn college credit because of her completion of these formal job-training seminars. The number of credits each seminar is worth does not hinge on Alice's current eligibility for college enrollment.

The other program evaluates courses offered by the Army, Navy, Air Force, Marines, Coast Guard, and Department of Defense. It is the Military Evaluations Program. Jorge has never attended college, but the engineering technology classes he completed as part of his military training are worth college credit. And as an Army veteran, Jorge is eligible for a service that takes the evaluations one step further. The Army/American Council on Education Registry Transcript System (AARTS) will provide Jorge with an individualized transcript of American Council on Education credit recommendations for all courses he completed, the military occupational specialties (MOS's) he held, and examinations he passed while in the Army. All Army and National Guard enlisted personnel and veterans who enlisted after October 1981 are eligible for the transcript. Similar services are being considered by the Navy and Marine Corps.

To obtain a free transcript, see your Army Education Center for a 5454R transcript request form. Include your name, Social Security number, basic active service date, and complete address where you want the transcript sent. Mail your request to:
AARTS Operations Center
415 McPherson Ave.
Fort Leavenworth, KS 66027-1373

Recommendations for PONSI are published in *The National Guide to Educational Credit for Training Programs;* military program recommendations are in *The Guide to the Evaluation of Educational Experiences in the Armed Forces.* See the Resources section at the end of this article for more information about these publications.

Former military personnel who took a foreign language course through the Defense Language Institute may request course transcripts by sending their name, Social Security number, course title, duration of the course, and graduation date to:

Commandant, Defense Language Institute
Attn: ATFL-DAA-AR
Transcripts
Presidio of Monterey
Monterey, CA 93944-5006

Not all of Jorge's and Alice's courses have been assessed by the American Council on Education. Training courses that have no Council credit recommendation should still be assessed by an advisor at the schools they want to attend. Course descriptions, class notes, test scores, and other documentation may be helpful for comparing training courses to their college equivalents. An oral examination or other demonstration of competency might also be required.

There is no guarantee you will receive all the credits you are seeking – but you certainly won't if you make no attempt.

Credit By Examination

Standardized tests are the best-known method of receiving college credit without taking courses. These exams are often taken by high school students seeking advanced placement for college, but they are also available to adult learners. Testing programs and colleges and universities offer exams in a number of subjects. Two U.S. Government institutes have foreign language exams for employees that also may be worth college credit.

It is important to understand that receiving a passing score on these exams does not mean you get college credit automatically. Each school determines which test results it will accept, minimum scores required, how scores are converted for credit, and the amount of credit, if any, to be assigned. Most colleges and universities accept the American Council on Education credit recommendations, published every other year in the 250-page *Guide to Educational Credit by Examination*. For more information, contact:

The American Council on Education
Credit by Examination Program
One Dupont Circle, Suite 250
Washington, DC 20036-1193
(202) 939-9434

Testing programs:

You might know some of the five national testing programs by their acronyms or initials: CLEP, ACT PEP: RCE, DANTES, AP, and NOCTI. (The meanings of these initialisms are explained below.) There is some overlap among programs; for example, four of them have introductory accounting exams. Since you will not be awarded credit more than once for a specific subject, you should carefully evaluate each program for the subject exams you wish to take. And before taking an exam, make sure you will be awarded credit by the college or university you plan to attend.

CLEP (College-Level Examination Program), administered by the College Board, is the most widely accepted of the national testing programs; more than 2,800 accredited schools award credit for passing exam scores. Each test covers material taught in basic

undergraduate courses. There are five general exams – English composition, humanities, college mathematics, natural sciences, and social sciences and history – and many subject exams. Most exams are entirely multiple-choice, but English composition exams may include an essay section. For more information, contact:
    CLEP
    P.O. Box 6600
    Princeton, NJ 08541-6600
    (609) 771-7865

ACT PEP: RCE (American College Testing Proficiency Exam Program: Regents College Examinations) tests are given in 38 subjects within arts and sciences, business, education, and nursing. Each exam is recommended for either lower- or upper-level credit. Exams contain either objective or extended response questions, and are graded according to a standard score, letter grade, or pass/fail. Fees vary, depending on the subject and type of exam. For more information or to request free study guides, contact:
    ACT PEP: Regents College Examinations
    P.O. Box 4014
    Iowa City, IA 52243
    (319) 337-1387
    (New York State residents must contact Regents College directly.)

DANTES (Defense Activity for Nontraditional Education Support) standardized tests are developed by the Educational Testing Service for the Department of Defense. Originally administered only to military personnel, the exams have been available to the public since 1983. About 50 subject tests cover business, mathematics, social science, physical science, humanities, foreign languages, and applied technology. Most of the tests consist entirely of multiple-choice questions. Schools determine their own administering fees and testing schedules. For more information or to request free study sheets, contact:
    DANTES Program Office
    Mail Stop 31-X
    Educational Testing Service
    Princeton, NJ 08541
    1(800) 257-9484

The AP (Advanced Placement) Program is a cooperative effort between secondary schools and colleges and universities. AP exams are developed each year by committees of college and high school faculty appointed by the College Board and assisted by consultants from the Educational Testing Service. Subjects include arts and languages, natural sciences, computer science, social sciences, history, and mathematics. Most tests are 2 or 3 hours long and include both multiple-choice and essay questions. AP courses are available to help students prepare for exams, which are offered in the spring. For more information about the Advanced Placement Program, contact:
    Advanced Placement Services
    P.O. Box 6671
    Princeton, NJ 08541-6671
    (609) 771-7300

NOCTI (National Occupational Competency Testing Institute) assessments are designed for people like Alice, who have vocational-technical skills that cannot be evaluated by other tests. NOCTI assesses competency at two levels: Student/job ready and teacher/experienced worker. Standardized evaluations are available for occupations such as auto-body repair, electronics, mechanical drafting, quantity food preparation, and upholstering. The tests consist of multiple-choice questions and a performance component. Other services include workshops, customized assessments, and pre-testing. For more information, contact:

NOCTI
500 N. Bronson Ave.
Ferris State University
Big Rapids, MI 49307
(616) 796-4699

Colleges and universities:

Many colleges and universities have credit-by-exam programs, through which students earn credit by passing a comprehensive exam for a course offered by the institution. Among the most widely recognized are the programs at Ohio University, the University of North Carolina, Thomas Edison State College, and New York University.

Ohio University offers about 150 examinations for credit. In addition, you may sometimes arrange to take special examinations in non-laboratory courses offered at Ohio University. To take a test for credit, you must enroll in the course. If you plan to transfer the credit earned, you also need written permission from an official at your school. Books and study materials are available, for a cost, through the university. Exams must be taken within 6 months of the enrollment date; most last 3 hours. You may arrange to take the exam off campus if you do not live near the university.

Ohio University is on the quarter-hour system; most courses are worth 4 quarter hours, the equivalent of 3 semester hours. For more information, contact:

Independent Study
Tupper Hall 302
Ohio University
Athens, OH 45701-2979
1(800) 444-2910
(614) 593-2910

The University of North Carolina offers a credit-by-examination option for 140 independent study (correspondence) courses in foreign languages, humanities, social sciences, mathematics, business administration, education, electrical and computer engineering, health administration, and natural sciences. To take an exam, you must request and receive approval from both the course instructor and the independent studies department. Exams must be taken within six months of enrollment, and you may register for no more than two at a time. If you are not near the University's Chapel Hill campus, you may take your exam under supervision at an accredited college, university, community college, or technical institute. For more information, contact:

Independent Studies
CB #1020, The Friday Center
UNC-Chapel Hill
Chapel Hill, NC 27599-1020
1(800) 862-5669 / (919) 962-1134

The Thomas Edison College Examination Program offers more than 50 exams in liberal arts, business, and professional areas. Thomas Edison State College administers tests twice a month in Trenton, New Jersey; however, students may arrange to take their tests with a proctor at any accredited American college or university or U.S. military base. Most of the tests are multiple choice; some also include short answer or essay questions. Time limits range from 90 minutes to 4 hours, depending on the exam. For more information, contact:

Thomas Edison State College
TECEP, Office of Testing and Assessment
101 W. State Street
Trenton, NJ 08608-1176
(609) 633-2844

New York University's Foreign Language Program offers proficiency exams in more than 40 languages, from Albanian to Yiddish. Two exams are available in each language: The 12-point test is equivalent to 4 undergraduate semesters, and the 16-point exam may lead to upper level credit. The tests are given at the university's Foreign Language Department throughout the year.

Proof of foreign language proficiency does not guarantee college credit. Some colleges and universities accept transcripts only for languages commonly taught, such as French and Spanish. Nontraditional programs are more likely than traditional ones to grant credit for proficiency in other languages.

For an informational brochure and registration form for NYU's foreign language proficiency exams, contact:

New York University
Foreign Language Department
48 Cooper Square, Room 107
New York, NY 10003
(212) 998-7030

Government institutes:

The Defense Language Institute and Foreign Service Institute administer foreign language proficiency exams for personnel stationed abroad. Usually, the tests are given at the end of intensive language courses or upon completion of service overseas. But some people -- like Jorge, who knows Spanish -- speak another language fluently and may be allowed to take a proficiency exam in that language before completing their tour of duty. Contact one of the offices listed below to obtain transcripts of those scores. Proof of proficiency does not guarantee college credit, however, as discussed above.

To request score reports from the Defense Language Institute for Defense Language Proficiency Tests, send your name, Social Security number, language for which you were tested, and, most importantly, when and where you took the exam to:

Commandant, Defense Language Institute
Attn: ATFL-ES-T
DLPT Score Report Request
Presidio of Monterey
Monterey, CA 93944-5006

To request transcripts of scores for Foreign Service Institute exams, send your name, Social Security number, language for which you were tested, and dates or year of exams to:

Foreign Service Institute
Arlington Hall
4020 Arlington Boulevard
Rosslyn, VA 22204-1500
Attn: Testing Office (Send your request to the attention of the testing office of the foreign language in which you were tested)

Credit For Experience

Experiential learning credit may be given for knowledge gained through job responsibilities, personal hobbies, volunteer opportunities, homemaking, and other experiences. Colleges and universities base credit awards on the knowledge you have attained, not for the experience alone. In addition, the knowledge must be college level; not just any learning will do. Throwing horseshoes as a hobby is not likely to be worth college credit. But if you've done research on how and where the sport originated, visited blacksmiths, organized tournaments, and written a column for a trade journal – well, that's a horseshoe of a different color.

Adults attempting to get credit for their experience should be forewarned: Having your experience evaluated for college credit is time-consuming, tedious work – not an easy shortcut for people who want quick-fix college credits. And not all experience, no matter how valuable, is the equivalent of college courses.

Requesting college credit for your experiential learning can be tricky. You should get assistance from a credit evaluations officer at the school you plan to attend, but you should also have a general idea of what your knowledge is worth. A common method for converting knowledge into credit is to use a college catalog. Find course titles and descriptions that match what you have learned through experience, and request the number of credits offered for those courses.

Once you know what credit to ask for, you must usually present your case in writing to officials at the college you plan to attend. The most common form of presenting experiential learning for credit is the portfolio. A portfolio is a written record of your knowledge along with a request for equivalent college credit. It includes an identification and description of the knowledge for which you are requesting credit, an explanatory essay of how the knowledge was gained and how it fits into your educational plans, documentation that you have acquired such knowledge, and a request for college credit. Required elements of a portfolio vary by schools but generally follow those guidelines.

In identifying knowledge you have gained, be specific about exactly what you have learned. For example, it is not enough for Lynette to say she runs a business. She must identify the knowledge she has gained from running it, such as personnel management, tax law, marketing strategy, and inventory review. She must also include brief descriptions about her knowledge of each to support her claims of having those skills.

The essay gives you a chance to relay something about who you are. It should address your educational goals, include relevant autobiographical details, and be well organized, neat, and convey confidence. In his essay, Jorge might first state his goal of becoming an engineer. Then he would explain why he joined the Army, where he got hands-on training and experience in developing and servicing electronic equipment.

This, he would say, led to his hobby of creating remote-controlled model cars, of which he has built 20. His conclusion would highlight his accomplishments and tie them to his desire to become an electronic engineer.

Documentation is evidence that you've learned what you claim to have learned. You can show proof of knowledge in a variety of ways, including audio or video recordings, letters from current or former employers describing your specific duties and job performance, blueprints, photographs or artwork, and transcripts of certifying exams for professional licenses and certification – such as Alice's certification from the American Culinary Federation. Although documentation can take many forms, written proof alone is not always enough. If it is impossible to document your knowledge in writing, find out if your experiential learning can be assessed through supplemental oral exams by a faculty expert.

Earning a College Degree

Nontraditional students often have work, family, and financial obligations that prevent them from quitting their jobs to attend school full time. Can they still meet their educational goals? Yes.

More than 150 accredited colleges and universities have nontraditional bachelor's degree programs that require students to spend little or no time on campus; over 300 others have nontraditional campus-based degree programs. Some of those schools, as well as most junior and community colleges, offer associate's degrees nontraditionally. Each school with a nontraditional course of study determines its own rules for awarding credit for prior coursework, exams, or experience, as discussed previously. Most have charges on top of tuition for providing these special services.

Several publications profile nontraditional degree programs; see the Resources section at the end of this article for more information. To determine which school best fits your academic profile and educational goals, first list your criteria. Then, evaluate nontraditional programs based on their accreditation, features, residency requirements, and expenses. Once you have chosen several schools to explore further, write to them for more information. Detailed explanations of school policies should help you decide which ones you want to apply to.

Get beyond the printed word – especially the glowing words each school writes about itself. Check out the schools you are considering with higher education authorities, alumni, employers, family members, and friends. If possible, visit the campus to talk to students and instructors and sit in on a few classes, even if you will be completing most or all of your work off campus. Ask school officials questions about such things as enrollment numbers, graduation rate, faculty qualifications, and confusing details about the application process or academic policies. After you have thoroughly investigated each prospective college or university, you can make an informed decision about which is right for you.

Accreditation

Accreditation is a process colleges and universities submit to voluntarily for getting their credentials. An accredited school has been investigated and visited by teams of observers and has periodic inspections by a private accrediting agency. The initial review can take two years or more.

Regional agencies accredit entire schools, and professional agencies accredit either specialized schools or departments within schools. Although there are no national accrediting standards, not just any accreditation will do. Countless "accreditation associations" have been invented by schools, many of which have no academic programs and sell phony degrees, to accredit themselves. But 6 regional and about 80 professional accrediting associations in the United States are recognized by the U.S. Department of Education or the Commission on Recognition of Postsecondary Accreditation. When checking accreditation, these are the names to look for. For more information about accreditation and accrediting agencies, contact:

> Institutional Participation Oversight Service Accreditation and State Liaison Division
> U.S. Department of Education
> ROB 3, Room 3915
> 600 Independence Ave., SW
> Washington, DC 20202-5244
> (202) 708-7417

Because accreditation is not mandatory, lack of accreditation does not necessarily mean a school or program is bad. Some schools choose not to apply for accreditation, are in the process of applying, or have educational methods too unconventional for an accrediting association's standards. For the nontraditional student, however, earning a degree from a college or university with recognized accreditation is an especially important consideration. Although nontraditional education is becoming more widely accepted, it is not yet mainstream. Employers skeptical of a degree earned in a nontraditional manner are likely to be even less accepting of one from an unaccredited school.

Program Features

Because nontraditional students have diverse educational objectives, nontraditional schools are diverse in what they offer. Some programs are geared toward helping students organize their scattered educational credits to get a degree as quickly as possible. Others cater to those who may have specific credits or experience but need assistance in completing requirements. Whatever your educational profile, you should look for a program that works with you in obtaining your educational goals.

A few nontraditional programs have special admissions policies for adult learners like Alice, who plan to earn their GEDs but want to enroll in college in the meantime. Other features of nontraditional programs include individualized learning agreements, intensive academic counseling, cooperative learning and internship placement, and waiver of some prerequisites or other requirements – as well as college credit for prior coursework, examinations, and experiential learning, all discussed previously.

Lynette, whose primary goal is to finish her degree, wants to earn maximum credits for her business experience. She will look for programs that do not limit the number of credits awarded for equivalency exams and experiential learning. And since well-documented proof of knowledge is essential for earning experiential learning credits, Lynette should make sure the program she chooses provides assistance to students submitting a portfolio.

Jorge, on the other hand, has more credits than he needs in certain areas and is willing to forego some. To become an engineer, he must have a bachelor's degree; but because he is accustomed to hands-on learning, Jorge is interested in getting experience as he gains more technical skills. He will concentrate on finding schools with strong cooperative education, supervised fieldwork, or internship programs.

Residency Requirements

Programs are sometimes deemed nontraditional because of their residency requirements. Many people think of residency for colleges and universities in terms of tuition, with in-state students paying less than out-of-state ones. Residency also may refer to where a student lives, either on or off campus, while attending school.

But in nontraditional education, residency usually refers to how much time students must spend on campus, regardless of whether they attend classes there. In some nontraditional programs, students need not ever step foot on campus. Others require only a very short residency, such as one day or a few weeks. Many schools have standard residency requirements of several semesters but schedule classes for evenings or weekends to accommodate working adults.

Lynette, who previously took courses by independent study, prefers to earn credits by distance study. She will focus on schools that have no residency requirement. Several colleges and universities have nonresident degree completion programs for adults with some college credit. Under the direction of a faculty advisor, students devise a plan for earning their remaining credits. Methods for earning credits include independent study, distance learning, seminars, supervised fieldwork, and group study at arranged sites. Students may have to earn a certain number of credits through the degree-granting institution. But many programs allow students to take courses at accredited schools of their choice for transfer toward their degree.

Alice wants to attend lectures but has an unpredictable schedule. Her best course of action will be to seek out short residency programs that require students to attend seminars once or twice a semester. She can take courses that are televised and videotape them to watch when her schedule permits, with the seminars helping to ensure that she properly completes her coursework. Many colleges and universities with short residency requirements also permit students to earn some credits elsewhere, by whatever means the student chooses.

Some fields of study require classroom instruction. As Jorge will discover, few colleges and universities allow students to earn a bachelor's degree in engineering entirely through independent study. Nontraditional residency programs are designed to accommodate adults' daytime work schedules. Jorge should look for programs offering evening, weekend, summer, and accelerated courses.

Tuition and Other Expenses

The final decisions about which schools Alice, Jorge, and Lynette attend may hinge in large part on a single issue: Cost. And rising tuition is only part of the equation. Beginning with application fees and continuing through graduation fees, college expenses add up.

Traditional and nontraditional students have some expenses in common, such as the cost of books and other materials. Tuition might even be the same for some courses, especially for colleges and universities offering standard ones at unusual times. But for nontraditional programs, students may also pay fees for services such as credit or transcript review, evaluation, advisement, and portfolio assessment.

Students are also responsible for postage and handling or setup expenses for independent study courses, as well as for all examination and transcript fees for transferring credits. Usually, the more nontraditional the program, the more detailed the fees. Some schools charge a yearly enrollment fee rather than tuition for degree completion candidates who want their files to remain active.

Although tuition and fees might seem expensive, most educators tell you not to let money come between you and your educational goals. Talk to someone in the financial aid department of the school you plan to attend or check your library for publications about financial aid sources. The U.S. Department of Education publishes a guide to Federal aid programs such as Pell Grants, student loans, and work-study. To order the free 74-page booklet, *The Student Guide: Financial Aid from the U.S. Department of Education,* contact:

>Federal Student Aid Information Center
>P.O. Box 84
>Washington, DC 20044
>1 (800) 4FED-AID (433-3243)

Resources

Information on how to earn a high school diploma or college degree without following the usual routes is available from several organizations and in numerous publications. Information on nontraditional graduate degree programs, available for master's through doctoral level, though not discussed in this article, can usually be obtained from the same resources that detail bachelor's degree programs.

National Learning Corporation publishes study guides for all of these exams, for both general examinations and tests in specific subject areas. To order study guides, or to browse their catalog featuring more than 5,000 titles, visit NLC online at www.passbooks.com, or contact them by phone at (800) 632-8888.

Organizations

Adult learners should always contact their local school system, community college, or university to learn about programs that are readily available. The following national organizations can also supply information:

>American Council on Education
>One Dupont Circle
>Washington, DC 20036-1193
>(202) 939-9300

Within the American Council on Education, the Center for Adult Learning and Educational Credentials administers the National External Diploma Program, the GED Program, the Program on Noncollegiate Sponsored Instruction, the Credit by Examination Program, and the Military Evaluations Program.

College-Level Examination Program (CLEP)

1. WHAT IS CLEP?

CLEP stands for the College-Level Examination Program, sponsored by the College Board. It is a national program of credit-by-examination that offers you the opportunity to obtain recognition for college-level achievement. No matter when, where, or how you have learned – by means of formal or informal study – you can take CLEP tests. If the results are acceptable to your college, you can receive credit.

You may not realize it, but you probably know more than your academic record reveals. Each day you, like most people, have an opportunity to learn. In private industry and business, as well as at all levels of government, learning opportunities continually occur. If you read widely or intensively in a particular field, think about what you read, discuss it with your family and friends, you are learning. Or you may be learning on a more formal basis by taking a correspondence course, a television or radio course, a course recorded on tape or cassettes, a course assembled into programmed tests, or a course taught in your community adult school or high school.

No matter how, where, or when you gained your knowledge, you may have the opportunity to receive academic credit for your achievement that can be counted toward an undergraduate degree. The College-Level Examination Program (CLEP) enables colleges to evaluate your achievement and give you credit. A wide range of college-level examinations are offered by CLEP to anyone who wishes to take them. Scores on the tests are reported to you and, if you wish, to a college, employer, or individual.

2. WHAT ARE THE PURPOSES OF THE COLLEGE-LEVEL EXAMINATION PROGRAM?

The basic purpose of the College-Level Examination Program is to enable individuals who have acquired their education in nontraditional ways to demonstrate their academic achievement. It is also intended for use by those in higher education, business, industry, government, and other fields who need a reliable method of assessing a person's educational level.

Recognizing that the real issue is not how a person has acquired his education but what education he has, the College Level Examination Program has been designed to serve a variety of purposes. The basic purpose, as listed above, is to enable those who have reached the college level of education in nontraditional ways to assess the level of their achievement and to use the test results in seeking college credit or placement.

In addition, scores on the tests can be used to validate educational experience obtained at a nonaccredited institution or through noncredit college courses.

Some colleges and universities may use the tests to measure the level of educational achievement of their students, and for various institutional research purposes.

Other colleges and universities may wish to use the tests in the admission, placement, and guidance of students who wish to transfer from one institution to another.

Businesses, industries, governmental agencies, and professional groups now accept the results of these tests as a basis for advancement, eligibility for further training, or professional or semi-professional certification.

Many people are interested in the examination simply to assess their own educational progress and attainment.

The college, university, business, industry, or government agency that adopts the tests in the College-Level Examination Program makes its own decision about how it will use and interpret the test scores. The College Board will provide the tests, score them, and report the results either to the individuals who took the tests or the college or agency that administered them. It does NOT, and cannot, award college credit, certify college equivalency, or make recommendations regarding the standards these institutions should establish for the use of the test results.

Therefore, if you are taking the tests to secure credit from an institution, you should FIRST ascertain whether the college or agency involved will accept the scores. Each institution determines which CLEP tests it will accept for credit and the amount of credit it will award. If you want to take tests for college credit, first call, write, or visit the college you wish to attend to inquire about its policy on CLEP scores, as well as its other admission requirements.

The services of the program are also available to people who have been requested to take the tests by an employer, a professional licensing agency, a certifying agency, or by other groups that recognize college equivalency on the basis of satisfactory CLEP scores. You may, of course, take the tests SOLELY for your own information. If you do, your scores will be reported only to you.

While neither CLEP nor the College Board can evaluate previous credentials or award college credit, you will receive, with your scores, basic information to help you interpret your performance on the tests you have taken.

3. WHAT ARE THE COLLEGE-LEVEL EXAMINATIONS?

In order to meet different kinds of curricular organization and testing needs at colleges and universities, the College-Level Examination Program offers 35 different subject tests falling under five separate general categories: Composition and Literature, Foreign Languages, History and Social Sciences, Science and Mathematics, and Business.

4. WHAT ARE THE SUBJECT EXAMINATIONS?

The 35 CLEP tests offered by the College Board are listed below:

COMPOSITION AND LITERATURE:
- American Literature
- Analyzing and Interpreting Literature
- English Composition
- English Composition with Essay
- English Literature
- Freshman College Composition
- Humanities

FOREIGN LANGUAGES
- French
- German
- Spanish

HISTORY AND SOCIAL SCIENCES
- American Government
- Introduction to Educational Psychology
- History of the United States I: Early Colonization to 1877
- History of the United States II: 1865 to the Present
- Human Growth and Development
- Principles of Macroeconomics
- Principles of Microeconomics
- Introductory Psychology
- Social Sciences and History
- Introductory Sociology
- Western Civilization I: Ancient Near East to 1648
- Western Civilization II: 1648 to the Present

SCIENCE AND MATHEMATICS
- College Algebra
- College Algebra-Trigonometry
- Biology
- Calculus
- Chemistry
- College Mathematics
- Natural Sciences
- Trigonometry
- Precalculus

BUSINESS
- Financial Accounting
- Introductory Business Law
- Information Systems and Computer Applications
- Principles of Management
- Principles of Marketing

CLEP Examinations cover material taught in courses that most students take as requirements in the first two years of college. A college usually grants the same amount of credit to students earning satisfactory scores on the CLEP examination as it grants to students successfully completing the equivalent course.

Many examinations are designed to correspond to one-semester courses; some, however, correspond to full-year or two-year courses.

Each exam is 90 minutes long and, except for English Composition with Essay, is made up primarily of multiple-choice questions. Some tests have several other types of questions besides multiple choice. To see a more detailed description of a particular CLEP exam, visit www.collegeboard.com/clep.

The English Composition with Essay exam is the only exam that includes a required essay. This essay is scored by college English faculty designated by CLEP and does not require an additional fee. However, other Composition and Literature tests offer optional essays, which some college and universities require and some do not. These essays are graded by faculty at the individual institutions that require them and require an additional $10 fee. Contact the particular institution to ask about essay requirements, and check with your test center for further details.

All 35 CLEP examinations are administered on computer. If you are unfamiliar with taking a test on a computer, consult the CLEP Sampler online at www.collegeboard.com/clep. The Sampler contains the same tutorials as the actual exams and helps familiarize you with navigation and how to answer different types of questions.

Points are not deducted for wrong or skipped answers – you receive one point for every correct answer. Therefore it is best that an answer is supplied for each exam question, whether it is a guess or not. The number of correct answers is then converted to a formula score. This formula, or "scaled," score is determined by a statistical process called *equating*, which adjusts for slight differences in difficulty between test forms and ensures that your score does not depend on the specific test form you took or how well others did on the same form. The scaled scores range from 20 to 80 – this is the number that will appear on your score report.

To ensure that you complete all questions in the time allotted, you would probably be wise to skip the more difficult or perplexing questions and return to them later. Although the multiple-choice items in these tests are carefully designed so as not to be tricky, misleading, or ambiguous, on the other hand, they are not all direct questions of factual information. They attempt, in their way, to elicit a response that indicates your knowledge or lack of knowledge of the material in question or your ability or inability to use or interpret a fact or idea. Thus, you should concentrate on answering the questions as they appear to be without attempting to out-guess the testmakers.

5. WHAT ARE THE FEES?

The fee for all CLEP examinations is $55. Optional essays required by some institutions are an additional $10.

6. WHEN ARE THE TESTS GIVEN?

CLEP tests are administered year-round. Consult the CLEP website (www.collegeboard.com/clep) and individual test centers for specific information.

7. WHERE ARE THE TESTS GIVEN?

More than 1,300 test centers are located on college and university campuses throughout the country, and additional centers are being established to meet increased needs. Any accredited collegiate institution with an explicit and publicly available policy of credit by examination can become a CLEP test center. To obtain a list of these centers, visit the CLEP website at www.collegeboard.com/clep.

8. HOW DO I REGISTER FOR THE COLLEGE-LEVEL EXAMINATION PROGRAM?

Contact an individual test center for information regarding registration, scheduling and fees. Registration/admission forms can also be obtained on the CLEP website.

9. MAY I REPEAT THE COLLEGE-LEVEL EXAMINATIONS?

You may repeat any examination providing at least six months have passed since you were last administered this test. If you repeat a test within a period of time less than six months, your scores will be cancelled and your fees forfeited. To repeat a test, check the appropriate space on the registration form.

10. WHEN MAY I EXPECT MY SCORE REPORTS?

With the exception of the English Composition with Essay exam, you should receive your score report instantly once the test is complete.

11. HOW SHOULD I PREPARE FOR THE COLLEGE-LEVEL EXAMINATIONS?

This book has been specifically designed to prepare candidates for these examinations. It will help you to consider, study, and review important content, principles, practices, procedures, problems, and techniques in the form of varied and concrete applications.

12. QUESTIONS AND ANSWERS APPEARING IN THIS PUBLICATION

The College-Level Examinations are offered by the College Board. Since copies of past examinations have not been made available, we have used equivalent materials, including questions and answers, which are highly recommended by us as an appropriate means of preparing for these examinations.

If you need additional information about CLEP Examinations, visit www.collegeboard.com/clep.

THE COLLEGE-LEVEL EXAMINATION PROGRAM

How The Program Works

CLEP examinations are administered at many colleges and universities across the country, and most institutions award college credit to those who do well on them. The examinations provide people who have acquired knowledge outside the usual educational settings the opportunity to show that they have learned college-level material without taking certain college courses.

The CLEP examinations cover material that is taught in introductory-level courses at many colleges and universities. Faculties at individual colleges review the tests to ensure that they cover the important material taught in their courses. Colleges differ in the examinations they accept; some colleges accept only two or three of the examinations while others accept nearly all of them.

Although CLEP is sponsored by the College Board and the examinations are scored by Educational Testing Service (ETS), neither of these organizations can award college credit. Only accredited colleges may grant credit toward a degree. When you take a CLEP examination, you may request that a copy of your score report be sent to the college you are attending or plan to attend. After evaluating your scores, the college will decide whether or not to award you credit for a certain course or courses, or to exempt you from them. If the college gives you credit, it will record the number of credits on your permanent record, thereby indicating that you have completed work equivalent to a course in that subject. If the college decides to grant exemption without giving you credit for a course, you will be permitted to omit a course that would normally be required of you and to take a course of your choice instead.

What the Examinations Are Like

The examinations consist mostly of multiple-choice questions to be answered within a 90-minute time limit. Additional information about each CLEP examination is given in the examination guide and on the CLEP website.

Where To Take the Examinations

CLEP examinations are administered throughout the year at the test centers of approximately 1,300 colleges and universities. On the CLEP website, you will find a list of institutions that award credit for satisfactory scores on CLEP examinations. Some colleges administer CLEP examinations to their own students only. Other institutions administer the tests to anyone who registers to take them. If your college does not administer the tests, contact the test centers in your area for information about its testing schedule.

Once you have been tested, your score report will be available instantly. CLEP scores are kept on file at ETS for 20 years; and during this period, for a small fee, you may have your transcript sent to another college or to anyone else you specify. (Your scores will never be sent to anyone without your approval.)

APPROACHING A COLLEGE ABOUT CLEP

The following sections provide a step-by-step approach to learning about the CLEP policy at a particular college or university. The person or office that can best assist students desiring CLEP credit may have a different title at each institution, but the following guidelines will lead you to information about CLEP at any institution.

Adults returning to college often benefit from special assistance when they approach a college. Opportunities for adults to return to formal learning in the classroom are now widespread, and colleges and universities have worked hard to make this a smooth process for older students. Many colleges have established special service offices that are staffed with trained professionals who understand the kinds of problems facing adults returning to college. If you think you might benefit from such assistance, be sure to find out whether these services are available at your college.

How to Apply for College Credit

STEP 1. Obtain the General Information Catalog and a copy of the CLEP policy from the colleges you are considering. If you have not yet applied for admission, ask for an admissions application form too.

Information about admissions and CLEP policies can be obtained by contacting college admissions offices or finding admissions information on the school websites. Tell the admissions officer that you are a prospective student and that you are interested in applying for admission and CLEP credit. Ask for a copy of the publication in which the college's complete CLEP policy is explained. Also get the name and the telephone number of the person to contact in case you have further questions about CLEP.

At this step, you may wish to obtain information from external degree colleges. Many adults find that such colleges suit their needs exceptionally well.

STEP 2. If you have not already been admitted to the college you are considering, look at its admission requirements for undergraduate students to see if you can qualify.

This is an important step because if you can't get into college, you can't get college credit for CLEP. Nearly all colleges require students to be admitted and to enroll in one or more courses before granting the students CLEP credit.

Virtually all public community colleges and a number of four-year state colleges have open admission policies for in-state students. This usually means that they admit anyone who has graduated from high school or has earned a high school equivalency diploma.

If you think you do not meet the admission requirements, contact the admissions office for an interview with a counselor. Colleges do sometimes make exceptions, particularly for adult applicants. State why you want the interview and ask what documents you should bring with you or send in advance. (These materials may include a high school transcript, transcript of previous college work, completed application for admission, etc.) Make an extra effort to have all the information requested in time for the interview.

During the interview, relax and be yourself. Be prepared to state honestly why you think you are ready and able to do college work. If you have already taken CLEP examinations and scored high enough to earn credit, you have shown that you are able to do college work. Mention this achievement to the admissions counselor because it may increase your chances of being accepted. If you have not taken a CLEP examination, you can still improve your chances of being accepted by describing how your job training or independent study has helped prepare you for college-level work. Tell the counselor what you have learned from your work and personal experiences.

STEP 3. Evaluate the college's CLEP policy.

Typically, a college lists all its academic policies, including CLEP policies, in its general catalog. You will probably find the CLEP policy statement under a heading such as Credit-by-Examination, Advanced Standing, Advanced Placement, or External Degree Program. These sections can usually be found in the front of the catalog.

Many colleges publish their credit-by-examination policies in a separate brochure, which is distributed through the campus testing office, counseling center, admissions office, or registrar's office. If you find a very general policy statement in the college catalog, seek clarification from one of these offices.

Review the material in the section of this guide entitled Questions to Ask About a College's CLEP Policy. Use these guidelines to evaluate the college's CLEP policy. If you have not yet taken a CLEP examination, this evaluation will help you decide which examinations to take and whether or not to take the free-response or essay portion. Because individual colleges have different CLEP policies, a review of several policies may help you decide which college to attend.

STEP 4. If you have not yet applied for admission, do so early.

Most colleges expect you to apply for admission several months before you enroll, and it is essential that you meet the published application deadlines. It takes time to process your application for admission; and if you have yet to take a CLEP examination, it will be some time before the college receives and reviews your score report. You will probably want to take some, if not all, of the CLEP examinations you are interested in before you enroll so you know which courses you need not register for. In fact, some colleges require that all CLEP scores be submitted before a student registers.

Complete all forms and include all documents requested with your application(s) for admission. Normally, an admissions decision cannot be reached until all documents have been submitted and evaluated. Unless told to do so, do not send your CLEP scores until you have been officially admitted.

STEP 5. Arrange to take CLEP examination(s) or to submit your CLEP score(s).

You may want to wait to take your CLEP examinations until you know definitely which college you will be attending. Then you can make sure you are taking tests your college will accept for credit. You will also be able to request that your scores be sent to the college, free of charge, when you take the tests.

If you have already taken CLEP examinations, but did not have a copy of your score report sent to your college, you may request the College Board to send an official transcript at any time for a small fee. Use the Transcript Request Form that was sent to you with your score report. If you do not have the form, you may find it online at www.collegeboard.com/clep.

Your CLEP scores will be evaluated, probably by someone in the admissions office, and sent to the registrar's office to be posted on your permanent record once you are enrolled. Procedures vary from college to college, but the process usually begins in the admissions office.

STEP 6. Ask to receive a written notice of the credit you receive for your CLEP score(s).

A written notice may save you problems later, when you submit your degree plan or file for graduation. In the event that there is a question about whether or not you earned CLEP credit, you will have an official record of what credit was awarded. You may also need this verification of course credit if you go for academic counseling before the credit is posted on your permanent record.

STEP 7. Before you register for courses, seek academic counseling.

A discussion with your academic advisor can prevent you from taking unnecessary courses and can tell you specifically what your CLEP credit will mean to you. This step may be accomplished at the time you enroll. Most colleges have orientation sessions for new students prior to each enrollment period. During orientation, students are usually assigned an academic advisor who then gives them individual help in developing long-range plans and a course schedule for the next semester. In conjunction with this counseling, you may be asked to take some additional tests so that you can be placed at the proper course level.

External Degree Programs

If you have acquired a considerable amount of college-level knowledge through job experience, reading, or noncredit courses, if you have accumulated college credits at a variety of colleges over a period of years, or if you prefer studying on your own rather than in a classroom setting, you may want to investigate the possibility of enrolling in an external degree program. Many colleges offer external degree programs that allow you to earn a degree by passing examinations (including CLEP), transferring credit from other colleges, and demonstrating in other ways that you have satisfied the educational requirements. No classroom attendance is required, and the programs are open to out-of-state candidates as well as residents. Thomas A. Edison State College in New Jersey and Charter Oaks College in Connecticut are fully accredited independent state colleges; the New York program is part of the state university system and is also fully accredited. If you are interested in exploring an external degree, you can write for more information to:

Charter Oak College
The Exchange, Suite 171
270 Farmington Avenue
Farmington, CT 06032-1909

Regents External Degree Program
Cultural Education Center
Empire State Plaza
Albany, New York 12230

Thomas A. Edison State College
101 West State Street
Trenton, New Jersey 08608

Many other colleges also have external degree or weekend programs. While they often require that a number of courses be taken on campus, the external degree programs tend to be more flexible in transferring credit, granting credit-by-examination, and allowing independent study than other traditional programs. When applying to a college, you may wish to ask whether it has an external degree or weekend program.

Questions to Ask About a College's CLEP Policy

Before taking CLEP examinations for the purpose of earning college credit, try to find the answers to these questions:

1. Which CLEP examinations are accepted by this college?

A college may accept some CLEP examinations for credit and not others - possibly not the one you are considering. The English faculty may decide to grant college English credit based on the CLEP English Composition examination, but not on the Freshman College Composition examination. Or, the mathematics faculty may decide to grant credit based on the College Mathematics to non-mathematics majors only, requiring majors to take an examination in algebra, trigonometry, or calculus to earn credit. For these reasons, it is important that you know the specific CLEP tests for which you can receive credit.

2. Does the college require the optional free-response (essay) section as well as the objective portion of the CLEP examination you are considering?

Knowing the answer to this question ahead of time will permit you to schedule the optional essay examination when you register to take your CLEP examination.

3. Is credit granted for specific courses? If so, which ones?

You are likely to find that credit will be granted for specific courses and the course titles will be designated in the college's CLEP policy. It is not necessary, however, that credit be granted for a specific course in order for you to benefit from your CLEP credit. For instance, at many liberal arts colleges, all students must take certain types of courses; these courses may be labeled the core curriculum, general education requirements, distribution requirements, or liberal arts requirements. The requirements are often expressed in terms of credit hours. For example, all students may be required to take at least six hours of humanities, six hours of English, three hours of mathematics, six hours of natural science, and six hours of social science, with no particular courses in these disciplines specified. In these instances, CLEP credit may be given as 6 hrs. English credit or 3 hrs. Math credit without specifying for which English or mathematics courses credit has been awarded. In order to avoid possible disappointment, you should know before taking a CLEP examination what type of credit you can receive and whether you will only be exempted from a required course but receive no credit.

4. How much credit is granted for each examination you are considering, and does the college place a limit on the total amount of CLEP credit you can earn toward your degree?

Not all colleges that grant CLEP credit award the same amount for individual tests. Furthermore, some colleges place a limit on the total amount of credit you can earn through CLEP or other examinations. Other colleges may grant you exemption but no credit toward your degree. Knowing several colleges' policies concerning these issues may help you decide which college you will attend. If you think you are capable of passing a number of CLEP examinations, you may want to attend a college that will allow you to earn credit for all or most of them. For example, the state external degree programs grant credit for most CLEP examinations (and other tests as well).

5. What is the required score for earning CLEP credit for each test you are considering?

Most colleges publish the required scores or percentile ranks for earning CLEP credit in their general catalog or in a brochure. The required score may vary from test to test, so find out the required score for each test you are considering.

6. What is the college's policy regarding prior course work in the subject in which you are considering taking a CLEP test?

Some colleges will not grant credit for a CLEP test if the student has already attempted a college-level course closely aligned with that test. For example, if you successfully completed English 101 or a comparable course on another campus, you will probably not be permitted to receive CLEP credit in that subject, too. Some colleges will not permit you to earn CLEP credit for a course that you failed.

7. Does the college make additional stipulations before credit will be granted?

It is common practice for colleges to award CLEP credit only to their enrolled students. There are other stipulations, however, that vary from college to college. For example, does the college require you to formally apply for or accept CLEP credit by completing and signing a form? Or does the college require you to validate your CLEP score by successfully completing a more advanced course in the subject? Answers to these and other questions will help to smooth the process of earning college credit through CLEP.

The above questions and the discussions that follow them indicate some of the ways in which colleges' CLEP policies can vary. Find out as much as possible about the CLEP policies at the colleges you are interested in so you can choose a college with a policy that is compatible with your educational goals. Once you have selected the college you will attend, you can find out which CLEP examinations your college recognizes and the requirements for earning CLEP credit.

DECIDING WHICH EXAMINATIONS TO TAKE

If You're Taking the Examinations for College Credit or Career Advancement:

Most people who take CLEP examinations do so in order to earn credit for college courses. Others take the examinations in order to qualify for job promotions or for professional certification or licensing. It is vital to most candidates who are taking the tests for any of these reasons that they be well prepared for the tests they are taking so that they can advance as rapidly as possible toward their educational or career goals.

It is usually advisable that those who have limited knowledge in the subjects covered by the tests they are considering enroll in the college courses in which that material is taught. Those who are uncertain about whether or not they know enough about a subject to do well on a particular CLEP test will find the following guidelines helpful.

There is no way to predict if you will pass a particular CLEP examination, but answers to the questions under the seven headings below should give you an indication of whether or not you are likely to succeed.

1. Test Descriptions

Read the description of the test provided. Are you familiar with most of the topics and terminology in the outline?

2. Textbooks

Examine the suggested textbooks and other resource materials following the test descriptions in this guide. Have you recently read one or more of these books, or have you read similar college-level books on this subject? If you have not, read through one or more of the textbooks listed, or through the textbook used for this course at your college. Are you familiar with most of the topics and terminology in the book?

3. Sample Questions

The sample questions provided are intended to be typical of the content and difficulty of the questions on the test. Although they are not an exact miniature of the test, the proportion of the sample questions you can answer correctly should be a rough estimate of the proportion of questions you will be able to answer correctly on the test.

Answer as many of the sample questions for this test as you can. Check your answers against the correct answers. Did you answer more than half the questions correctly?

Because of variations in course content at different institutions, and because questions on CLEP tests vary from easy to difficult - with most being of moderate difficulty - the average student who passes a course in a subject can usually answer correctly about half the questions on the corresponding CLEP examination. Most colleges set their passing scores near this level, but some set them higher. If your college has set its required score above the level required by most colleges, you may need to answer a larger proportion of questions on the test correctly.

4. Previous Study

Have you taken noncredit courses in this subject offered by an adult school or a private school, through correspondence, or in connection with your job? Did you do exceptionally well in this subject in high school, or did you take an honors course in this subject?

5. Experience

Have you learned or used the knowledge or skills included in this test in your job or life experience? For example, if you lived in a Spanish-speaking country and spoke the language for a year or more, you might consider taking the Spanish examination. Or, if you have worked at a job in which you used accounting and finance skills, Principles of Accounting would be a likely test for you to take. Or, if you have read a considerable amount of literature and attended many art exhibits, concerts, and plays, you might expect to do well on the Humanities exam.

6. Other Examinations

Have you done well on other standardized tests in subjects related to the one you want to take? For example, did you score well above average on a portion of a college entrance examination covering similar skills, or did you obtain an exceptionally high score on a high school equivalency test or a licensing examination in this subject? Although such tests do not cover exactly the same material as the CLEP examinations and may be easier, persons who do well on these tests often do well on CLEP examinations, too.

7. Advice

Has a college counselor, professor, or some other professional person familiar with your ability advised you to take a CLEP examination?

If your answer was yes to questions under several of the above headings, you probably have a good chance of passing the CLEP examination you are considering. It is unlikely that you would have acquired sufficient background from experience alone. Learning gained through reading and study is essential, and you will probably find some additional study helpful before taking a CLEP examination.

If You're Taking the Examinations to Prepare for College

Many people entering college, particularly adults returning to college after several years away from formal education, are uncertain about their ability to compete with other college students. They wonder whether they have sufficient background for college study, and those who have been away from formal study for some time wonder whether they have forgotten how to study, how to take tests, and how to write papers. Such people may wish to improve their test-taking and study skills prior to enrolling in courses.

One way to assess your ability to perform at the college level and to improve your test-taking and study skills at the same time is to prepare for and take one or more CLEP examinations. You need not be enrolled in a college to take a CLEP examination, and you may have your scores sent only to yourself and later request that a transcript be sent to a college if you then decide to apply for credit. By reviewing the test descriptions and sample questions, you may find one or several subject areas in which you think you have substantial knowledge. Select one examination, or more if you like, and carefully read at least one of the textbooks listed in the bibliography for the test. By doing this, you will get a better idea of how much you know of what is usually taught in a college-level course in that subject. Study as much material as you can, until you think you have a good grasp of the subject matter. Then take the test at a college in your area. It will be several weeks before you receive your results, and you may wish to begin reviewing for another test in the meantime.

To find out if you are eligible for credit for your CLEP score, you must compare your score with the score required by the college you plan to attend. If you are not yet sure which college you will attend, or whether you will enroll in college at all, you should begin to follow the steps outlined. It is best that you do this before taking a CLEP test, but if you are taking the test only for the experience and to familiarize yourself with college-level material and requirements, you might take the test before you approach a college. Even if the college you decide to attend does not accept the test you took, the experience of taking such a test will enable you to meet with greater confidence the requirements of courses you will take.

You will find information about how to interpret your scores in WHAT YOUR SCORES MEAN, which you will receive with your score report, and which can also be found online at the CLEP website. Many colleges follow the recommendations of the American Council on Education (ACE) for setting their required scores, so you can use this information as a guide in determining how well you did. The ACE recommendations are included in the booklet.

If you do not do well enough on the test to earn college credit, don't be discouraged. Usually, it is the best college students who are exempted from courses or receive credit-by-examination. The fact that you cannot get credit for your score means that you should probably enroll in a college course to learn the material. However, if your score was close to the required score, or if you feel you could do better on a second try or after some additional study, you may retake the test after six months. Do not take it sooner or your score will not be reported and your fee will be forfeited.

If you do earn the score required to earn credit, you will have demonstrated that you already have some college-level knowledge. You will also have a better idea whether you should take additional CLEP examinations. And, what is most important, you can enroll in college with confidence, knowing that you do have the ability to succeed.

PREPARING TO TAKE CLEP EXAMINATIONS

Having made the decision to take one or more CLEP examinations, most people then want to know if it is worthwhile to prepare for them - how much, how long, when, and how should they go about it? The precise answers to these questions vary greatly from individual to individual. However, most candidates find that some type of test preparation is helpful.

Most people who take CLEP examinations do so to show that they have already learned the important material that is taught in a college course. Many of them need only a quick review to assure themselves that they have not forgotten some of what they once studied, and to fill in some of the gaps in their knowledge of the subject. Others feel that they need a thorough review and spend several weeks studying for a test. A few wish to take a CLEP examination as a kind of final examination for independent study of a subject instead of the college course. This last group requires significantly more study than those who only need to review, and they may need some guidance from professors of the subjects they are studying.

The key to how you prepare for CLEP examinations often lies in locating those skills and areas of prior learning in which you are strong and deciding where to focus your energies. Some people may know a great deal about a certain subject area, but may not test well. These individuals would probably be just as concerned about strengthening their test-taking skills as they are about studying for a specific test. Many mental and physical skills are used in preparing for a test. It is important not only to review or study for the examinations, but to make certain that you are alert, relatively free of anxiety, and aware of how to approach standardized tests. Suggestions on developing test-taking skills and preparing psychologically and physically for a test are given. The following section suggests ways of assessing your knowledge of the content of a test and then reviewing and studying the material.

Using This Study Guide

Begin by carefully reading the test description and outline of knowledge and skills required for the examination, if given. As you read through the topics listed there, ask yourself how much you know about each one. Also note the terms, names, and symbols that are mentioned, and ask yourself whether you are familiar with them. This will give you a quick overview of how much you know about the subject. If you are familiar with nearly all the material, you will probably need a minimum of review; however, if less than half of it is familiar, you will probably require substantial study to do well on the test.

If, after reviewing the test description, you find that you need extensive review, delay answering the sample question until you have done some reading in the subject. If you complete them before reviewing the material, you will probably look for the answers as you study, and then they will not be a good assessment of your ability at a later date.

If you think you are familiar with most of the test material, try to answer the sample questions.

Apply the test-taking strategies given. Keeping within the time limit suggested will give you a rough idea of how quickly you should work in order to complete the actual test.

Check your answers against the answer key. If you answered nearly all the questions correctly, you probably do not need to study the subject extensively. If you got about half the questions correct, you ought o review at least one textbook or other suggested materials on the subject. If you answered less than half the questions correctly, you will probably benefit from more extensive reading in the subject and thorough study of one or more textbooks. The textbooks listed are used at many colleges but they are not the only good texts. You will find helpful almost any standard text available to you., such as the textbook used at your college, or earlier editions of texts listed. For some examinations, topic outlines and textbooks may not be available. Take the sample tests in this book and check your answers at the end of each test. Check wrong answers.

Suggestions for Studying

The following suggestions have been gathered from people who have prepared for CLEP examinations or other college-level tests.

1. Define your goals and locate study materials

First, determine your study goals. Set aside a block of time to review the material provided in this book, and then decide which test(s) you will take. Using the suggestions, locate suitable resource materials. If a preparation course is offered by an adult school or college in your area, you might find it helpful to enroll.

2. Find a good place to study

To determine what kind of place you need for studying, ask yourself questions such as: Do I need a quiet place? Does the telephone distract me? Do objects I see in this place remind me of things I should do? Is it too warm? Is it well lit? Am I too comfortable here? Do I have space to spread out my materials? You may find the library more conducive to studying than your home. If you decide to study at home, you might prevent interruptions by other household members by putting a sign on the door of your study room to indicate when you will be available.

3. Schedule time to study

To help you determine where studying best fits into your schedule, try this exercise: Make a list of your daily activities (for example, sleeping, working, and eating) and estimate how many hours per day you spend on each activity. Now, rate all the activities on your list in order of their importance and evaluate your use of time. Often people are astonished at how an average day appears from this perspective. They may discover that they were unaware how large portions of time are spent, or they learn their time can be scheduled in alternative ways. For example, they can remove the least important activities from their day and devote that time to studying or another important activity.

4. Establish a study routine and a set of goals

In order to study effectively, you should establish specific goals and a schedule for accomplishing them. Some people find it helpful to write out a weekly schedule and cross out each study period when it is completed. Others maintain their concentration better by writing down the time when they expect to complete a study task. Most people find short periods of intense study more productive than long stretches of time. For example, they may follow a regular schedule of several 20- or 30-minute study periods with short breaks between them. Some people like to allow themselves rewards as they complete each study goal. It is not essential that you accomplish every goal exactly within your schedule; the point is to be committed to your task.

5. Learn how to take an active role in studying.

If you have not done much studying for some time, you may find it difficult to concentrate at first. Try a method of studying, such as the one outlined below, that will help you concentrate on and remember what you read.

    a. First, read the chapter summary and the introduction. Then you will know what to look for in your reading.

    b. Next, convert the section or paragraph headlines into questions. For example, if you are reading a section entitled, The Causes of the American Revolution, ask yourself: *What were the causes of the American Revolution?* Compose the answer as you read the paragraph. Reading and answering questions aloud will help you understand and remember the material.

c. Take notes on key ideas or concepts as you read. Writing will also help you fix concepts more firmly in your mind. Underlining key ideas or writing notes in your book can be helpful and will be useful for review. Underline only important points. If you underline more than a third of each paragraph, you are probably underlining too much.

d. If there are questions or problems at the end of a chapter, answer or solve them on paper as if you were asked to do them for homework. Mathematics textbooks (and some other books) sometimes include answers to some or all of the exercises. If you have such a book, write your answers before looking at the ones given. When problem-solving is involved, work enough problems to master the required methods and concepts. If you have difficulty with problems, review any sample problems or explanations in the chapter.

e. To retain knowledge, most people have to review the material periodically. If you are preparing for a test over an extended period of time, review key concepts and notes each week or so. Do not wait for weeks to review the material or you will need to relearn much of it.

Psychological and Physical Preparation

Most people feel at least some nervousness before taking a test. Adults who are returning to college may not have taken a test in many years or they may have had little experience with standardized tests. Some younger students, as well, are uncomfortable with testing situations. People who received their education in countries outside the United States may find that many tests given in this country are quite different from the ones they are accustomed to taking.

Not only might candidates find the types of tests and the kinds of questions on them unfamiliar, but other aspects of the testing environment may be strange as well. The physical and mental stress that results from meeting this new experience can hinder a candidate's ability to demonstrate his or her true degree of knowledge in the subject area being tested. For this reason, it is important to go to the test center well prepared, both mentally and physically, for taking the test. You may find the following suggestions helpful.

1. Familiarize yourself, as much as possible, with the test and the test situation before the day of the examination. It will be helpful for you to know ahead of time:

a. How much time will be allowed for the test and whether there are timed subsections.

b. What types of questions and directions appear on the examination.

c. How your test score will be computed.

d. How to properly answer the questions on the computer (See the CLEP Sample on the CLEP website)

  e. In which building and room the examination will be administered. If you don't know where the building is, locate it or get directions ahead of time.

  f. The time of the test administration. You might wish to confirm this information a day or two before the examination and find out what time the building and room will be open so that you can plan to arrive early.

  g. Where to park your car or, if you wish to take public transportation, which bus or train to take and the location of the nearest stop.

  h. Whether smoking will be permitted during the test.

  i. Whether there will be a break between examinations (if you will be taking more than one on the same day), and whether there is a place nearby where you can get something to eat or drink.

2. Go to the test situation relaxed and alert. In order to prepare for the test:

  a. Get a good night's sleep. Last minute cramming, particularly late the night before, is usually counterproductive.

  b. Eat normally. It is usually not wise to skip breakfast or lunch on the day of the test or to eat a big meal just before the test.

  c. Avoid tranquilizers and stimulants. If you follow the other directions in this book, you won't need artificial aids. It's better to be a little tense than to be drowsy, but stimulants such as coffee and cola can make you nervous and interfere with your concentration.

  d. Don't drink a lot of liquids before the test. Having to leave the room during the test will disturb your concentration and take valuable time away from the test.

  e. If you are inclined to be nervous or tense, learn some relaxation exercises and use them before and perhaps during the test.

3. Arrive for the test early and prepared. Be sure to:

  a. Arrive early enough so that you can find a parking place, locate the test center, and get settled comfortably before testing begins. Allow some extra time in case you are delayed unexpectedly.

  b. Take the following with you:

- Your completed Registration/Admission Form
- Two forms of identification – one being a government-issued photo ID with signature, such as a driver's license or passport
- Non-mechanical pencil
- A watch so that you can time your progress (digital watches are prohibited)
- Your glasses if you need them for reading or seeing the chalkboard or wall clock

c. Leave all books, papers, and notes outside the test center. You will not be permitted to use your own scratch paper; it will be provided. Also prohibited are calculators, cell phones, beepers, pagers, photo/copy devices, radios, headphones, food, beverages, and several other items.

d. Be prepared for any temperature in the testing room. Wear layers of clothing that can be removed if the room is too hot but will keep you warm if it is too cold.

4. When you enter the test room:

a. Sit in a seat that provides a maximum of comfort and freedom from distraction.

b. Read directions carefully, and listen to all instructions given by the test administrator. If you don't understand the directions, ask for help before test timing begins. If you must ask a question after the test has begun, raise your hand and a proctor will assist you. The proctor can answer certain kinds of questions but cannot help you with the test.

c. Know your rights as a test taker. You can expect to be given the full working time allowed for the test(s) and a reasonably quiet and comfortable place in which to work. If a poor test situation is preventing you from doing your best, ask if the situation can be remedied. If bad test conditions cannot be remedied, ask the person in charge to report the problem in the Irregularity Report that will be sent to ETS with the answer sheets. You may also wish to contact CLEP. Describe the exact circumstances as completely as you can. Be sure to include the test date and name(s) of the test(s) you took. ETS will investigate the problem to make sure it does not happen again, and, if the problem is serious enough, may arrange for you to retake the test without charge.

TAKING THE EXAMINATIONS

A person may know a great deal about the subject being tested, but not do as well as he or she is capable of on the test. Knowing how to approach a test is an important part of the testing process. While a command of test-taking skills cannot substitute for knowledge of the subject matter, it can be a significant factor in successful testing.

Test-taking skills enable a person to use all available information to earn a score that truly reflects his or her ability. There are different strategies for approaching different kinds of test questions. For example, free-response questions require a very different tack than do multiple-choice questions. Other factors, such as how the test will be graded, may also influence your approach to the test and your use of test time. Thus, your preparation for a test should include finding out all you can about the test so that you can use the most effective test-taking strategies.

Before taking a test, you should know approximately how many questions are on the test, how much time you will be allowed, how the test will be scored or graded, what types of questions and directions are on the test, and how you will be required to record your answers.

Taking Multiple-Choice Tests

1. Listen carefully to the instructions given by the test administrator and read carefully all directions before you begin to answer the questions.

2. Note the time that the test administrator starts timing the test. As you proceed, make sure that you are not working too slowly. You should have answered at least half the questions in a section when half the time for that section has passed. If you have not reached that point in the section, speed up your pace on the remaining questions.

3. Before answering a question, read the entire question, including all the answer choices. Don't think that because the first or second answer choice looks good to you, it isn't necessary to read the remaining options. Instructions usually tell you to select the best answer. Sometimes one answer choice is partially correct, but another option is better; therefore, it is usually a good idea to read all the answers before you choose one.

4. Read and consider every question. Questions that look complicated at first glance may not actually be so difficult once you have read them carefully.

5. Do not puzzle too long over any one question. If you don't know the answer after you've considered it briefly, go on to the next question. Make sure you return to the question later.

6. Make sure you record your response properly.

7. In trying to determine the correct answer, you may find it helpful to cross out those options that you know are incorrect, and to make marks next to those you think might be correct. If you decide to skip the question and come back to it later, you will save yourself the time of reconsidering all the options.

8. Watch for the following key words in test questions:

all	generally	never	perhaps
always	however	none	rarely
but	may	not	seldom
except	must	often	sometimes
every	necessary	only	usually

When a question or answer option contains words such as always, every, only, never, and none, there can be no exceptions to the answer you choose. Use of words such as often, rarely, sometimes, and generally indicates that there may be some exceptions to the answer.

9. Do not waste your time looking for clues to right answers based on flaws in question wording or patterns in correct answers. Professionals at the College Board and ETS put

a great deal of effort into developing valid, reliable, fair tests. CLEP test development committees are composed of college faculty who are experts in the subject covered by the test and are appointed by the College Board to write test questions and to scrutinize each question that is included on a CLEP test. Committee members make every effort to ensure that the questions are not ambiguous, that they have only one correct answer, and that they cover college-level topics. These committees do not intentionally include trick questions. If you think a question is flawed, ask the test administrator to report it, or contact CLEP immediately.

Taking Free-Response or Essay Tests

If your college requires the optional free-response or essay portion of a CLEP Composition and Literature exams, you should do some additional preparation for your CLEP test. Taking an essay test is very different from taking a multiple-choice test, so you will need to use some other strategies.

The essay written as part of the English Composition and Essay exam is graded by English professors from a variety of colleges and universities. A process called holistic scoring is used to rate your writing ability.

The optional free-response essays, on the other hand, are graded by the faculty of the college you designate as a score recipient. Guidelines and criteria for grading essays are not specified by the College Board or ETS. You may find it helpful, therefore, to talk with someone at your college to find out what criteria will be used to determine whether you will get credit. If the test requires essay responses, ask how much emphasis will be placed on your writing ability and your ability to organize your thoughts as opposed to your knowledge of subject matter. Find out how much weight will be given to your multiple-choice test score in comparison with your free-response grade in determining whether you will get credit. This will give you an idea where you should expend the greatest effort in preparing for and taking the test.

Here are some strategies you will find useful in taking any essay test:

1. Before you begin to write, read all questions carefully and take a few minutes to jot down some ideas you might include in each answer.

2. If you are given a choice of questions to answer, choose the questions you think you can answer most clearly and knowledgeably.

3. Determine in what order you will answer the questions. Answer those you find the easiest first so that any extra time can be spent on the more difficult questions.

4. When you know which questions you will answer and in what order, determine how much testing time remains and estimate how many minutes you will devote to each question. Unless suggested times are given for the questions or one question appears to require more or less time than the others, allot an equal amount of time to each question.

5. Before answering each question, indicate the number of the question as it is given in the test book. You need not copy the entire question from the question sheet, but it will be helpful to you and to the person grading your test if you indicate briefly the topic you are addressing – particularly if you are not answering the questions in the order in which they appear on the test.

6. Before answering each question, read it again carefully to make sure you are interpreting it correctly. Underline key words, such as those listed below, that often appear in free-response questions. Be sure you know the exact meaning of these words before taking the test.

analyze	demonstrate	enumerate	list
apply	derive	explain	outline
assess	describe	generalize	prove
compare	determine	illustrate	rank
contrast	discuss	interpret	show
define	distinguish	justify	summarize

If a question asks you to outline, define, or summarize, do not write a detailed explanation; if a question asks you to analyze, explain, illustrate, interpret, or show, you must do more than briefly describe the topic.

For a current listing of CLEP Colleges

where you can get credit and be tested, write:

CLEP, P.O. Box 6600, Princeton, NJ 08541-6600

Or e-mail: clep@ets.org, or call: (609) 771-7865

COLLEGE ALGEBRA

Description of the Examination
The College Algebra examination covers material that is usually taught in a one-semester college course in algebra. Nearly half of the test is made up of routine problems requiring basic algebraic skills; the remainder involves solving nonroutine problems in which candidates must demonstrate their understanding of concepts. The test includes questions on basic algebraic operations; linear and quadratic equations, inequalities, and graphs; algebraic, exponential, and logarithmic functions; and miscellaneous other topics.

It is assumed that candidates are familiar with currently taught algebraic vocabulary, symbols, and notation. The test places little emphasis on arithmetic calculations. However, an online scientific calculator (nongraphing) will be available during the examination.

The examination contains approximately 60 questions to be answered in 90 minutes. Some of these are pretest questions that will not be scored. Any time candidates spend on tutorials and providing personal information is in addition to the actual testing time.

Knowledge and Skills Required
Questions on the College Algebra examination require candidates to demonstrate the following abilities in the approximate proportions indicated.

- Solving routine, straightforward problems (about 50 percent of the examination)

- Solving nonroutine problems requiring an understanding of concepts and the application of skills and concepts (about 50 percent of the examination)

The subject matter of the College Algebra examination is drawn from the following topics. The percentages next to the main topics indicate the approximate percentage of exam questions on that topic.

25%   Algebraic operations
- Factoring and expanding polynomials
- Operations with algebraic expressions
- Operations with exponents
- Properties of logarithms

25%   Equations and inequalities
- Linear equations and inequalities
- Quadratic equations and inequalities
- Absolute value equations and inequalities
- Systems of equations and inequalities

30%   Functions and their properties
- Definition and interpretation
- Representation/modeling (graphical, numerical, symbolic, and verbal representations of functions)
- Domain and range
- Algebra of functions
- Graphs and their properties (including intercepts, symmetry, and transformations)
- Inverse functions

20% Number systems and operations
- Real numbers
- Complex numbers
- Sequences and series
- Factorials and Binomial Theorem
- Determinants of 2-by-2 matrices

HOW TO TAKE A TEST

You have studied long, hard and conscientiously.

With your official admission card in hand, and your heart pounding, you have been admitted to the examination room.

You note that there are several hundred other applicants in the examination room waiting to take the same test.

They all appear to be equally well prepared.

You know that nothing but your best effort will suffice. The "moment of truth" is at hand: you now have to demonstrate objectively, in writing, your knowledge of content and your understanding of subject matter.

You are fighting the most important battle of your life—to pass and/or score high on an examination which will determine your career and provide the economic basis for your livelihood.

What extra, special things should you know and should you do in taking the examination?

I. YOU MUST PASS AN EXAMINATION

A. WHAT EVERY CANDIDATE SHOULD KNOW
Examination applicants often ask us for help in preparing for the written test. What can I study in advance? What kinds of questions will be asked? How will the test be given? How will the papers be graded?

B. HOW ARE EXAMS DEVELOPED?
Examinations are carefully written by trained technicians who are specialists in the field known as "psychological measurement," in consultation with recognized authorities in the field of work that the test will cover. These experts recommend the subject matter areas or skills to be tested; only those knowledges or skills important to your success on the job are included. The most reliable books and source materials available are used as references. Together, the experts and technicians judge the difficulty level of the questions.
Test technicians know how to phrase questions so that the problem is clearly stated. Their ethics do not permit "trick" or "catch" questions. Questions may have been tried out on sample groups, or subjected to statistical analysis, to determine their usefulness.
Written tests are often used in combination with performance tests, ratings of training and experience, and oral interviews. All of these measures combine to form the best-known means of finding the right person for the right job.

II. HOW TO PASS THE WRITTEN TEST

A. BASIC STEPS

1) Study the announcement

How, then, can you know what subjects to study? Our best answer is: "Learn as much as possible about the class of positions for which you've applied." The exam will test the knowledge, skills and abilities needed to do the work.

Your most valuable source of information about the position you want is the official exam announcement. This announcement lists the training and experience qualifications. Check these standards and apply only if you come reasonably close to meeting them. Many jurisdictions preview the written test in the exam announcement by including a section called "Knowledge and Abilities Required," "Scope of the Examination," or some similar heading. Here you will find out specifically what fields will be tested.

2) Choose appropriate study materials

If the position for which you are applying is technical or advanced, you will read more advanced, specialized material. If you are already familiar with the basic principles of your field, elementary textbooks would waste your time. Concentrate on advanced textbooks and technical periodicals. Think through the concepts and review difficult problems in your field.

These are all general sources. You can get more ideas on your own initiative, following these leads. For example, training manuals and publications of the government agency which employs workers in your field can be useful, particularly for technical and professional positions. A letter or visit to the government department involved may result in more specific study suggestions, and certainly will provide you with a more definite idea of the exact nature of the position you are seeking.

3) Study this book!

III. KINDS OF TESTS

Tests are used for purposes other than measuring knowledge and ability to perform specified duties. For some positions, it is equally important to test ability to make adjustments to new situations or to profit from training. In others, basic mental abilities not dependent on information are essential. Questions which test these things may not appear as pertinent to the duties of the position as those which test for knowledge and information. Yet they are often highly important parts of a fair examination. For very general questions, it is almost impossible to help you direct your study efforts. What we can do is to point out some of the more common of these general abilities needed in public service positions and describe some typical questions.

1) General information

Broad, general information has been found useful for predicting job success in some kinds of work. This is tested in a variety of ways, from vocabulary lists to questions about current events. Basic background in some field of work, such as sociology or economics, may be sampled in a group of questions. Often these are principles which have become familiar to most persons through exposure rather than through formal training. It is difficult to advise you how to study for these questions; being alert to the world around you is our best suggestion.

2) Verbal ability

An example of an ability needed in many positions is verbal or language ability. Verbal ability is, in brief, the ability to use and understand words. Vocabulary and grammar tests are typical measures of this ability. Reading comprehension or paragraph interpretation questions are common in many kinds of civil service tests. You are given a paragraph of written material and asked to find its central meaning.

IV. KINDS OF QUESTIONS

1. Multiple-choice Questions

Most popular of the short-answer questions is the "multiple choice" or "best answer" question. It can be used, for example, to test for factual knowledge, ability to solve problems or judgment in meeting situations found at work.

A multiple-choice question is normally one of three types:
- It can begin with an incomplete statement followed by several possible endings. You are to find the one ending which best completes the statement, although some of the others may not be entirely wrong.
- It can also be a complete statement in the form of a question which is answered by choosing one of the statements listed.
- It can be in the form of a problem – again you select the best answer.

Here is an example of a multiple-choice question with a discussion which should give you some clues as to the method for choosing the right answer:

When an employee has a complaint about his assignment, the action which will best help him overcome his difficulty is to
- A. discuss his difficulty with his coworkers
- B. take the problem to the head of the organization
- C. take the problem to the person who gave him the assignment
- D. say nothing to anyone about his complaint

In answering this question, you should study each of the choices to find which is best. Consider choice "A" – Certainly an employee may discuss his complaint with fellow employees, but no change or improvement can result, and the complaint remains unresolved. Choice "B" is a poor choice since the head of the organization probably does not know what assignment you have been given, and taking your problem to him is known as "going over the head" of the supervisor. The supervisor, or person who made the assignment, is the person who can clarify it or correct any injustice. Choice "C" is, therefore, correct. To say nothing, as in choice "D," is unwise. Supervisors have and interest in knowing the problems employees are facing, and the employee is seeking a solution to his problem.

2. True/False

3. Matching Questions

Matching an answer from a column of choices within another column.

V. RECORDING YOUR ANSWERS

Computer terminals are used more and more today for many different kinds of exams.

For an examination with very few applicants, you may be told to record your answers in the test booklet itself. Separate answer sheets are much more common. If this separate answer sheet is to be scored by machine – and this is often the case – it is highly important that you mark your answers correctly in order to get credit.

VI. BEFORE THE TEST

YOUR PHYSICAL CONDITION IS IMPORTANT

If you are not well, you can't do your best work on tests. If you are half asleep, you can't do your best either. Here are some tips:

1) Get about the same amount of sleep you usually get. Don't stay up all night before the test, either partying or worrying—DON'T DO IT!
2) If you wear glasses, be sure to wear them when you go to take the test. This goes for hearing aids, too.
3) If you have any physical problems that may keep you from doing your best, be sure to tell the person giving the test. If you are sick or in poor health, you relay cannot do your best on any test. You can always come back and take the test some other time.

Common sense will help you find procedures to follow to get ready for an examination. Too many of us, however, overlook these sensible measures. Indeed, nervousness and fatigue have been found to be the most serious reasons why applicants fail to do their best on civil service tests. Here is a list of reminders:

- Begin your preparation early – Don't wait until the last minute to go scurrying around for books and materials or to find out what the position is all about.
- Prepare continuously – An hour a night for a week is better than an all-night cram session. This has been definitely established. What is more, a night a week for a month will return better dividends than crowding your study into a shorter period of time.
- Locate the place of the exam – You have been sent a notice telling you when and where to report for the examination. If the location is in a different town or otherwise unfamiliar to you, it would be well to inquire the best route and learn something about the building.
- Relax the night before the test – Allow your mind to rest. Do not study at all that night. Plan some mild recreation or diversion; then go to bed early and get a good night's sleep.
- Get up early enough to make a leisurely trip to the place for the test – This way unforeseen events, traffic snarls, unfamiliar buildings, etc. will not upset you.
- Dress comfortably – A written test is not a fashion show. You will be known by number and not by name, so wear something comfortable.
- Leave excess paraphernalia at home – Shopping bags and odd bundles will get in your way. You need bring only the items mentioned in the official notice you received; usually everything you need is provided. Do not bring reference books to the exam. They will only confuse those last minutes and be taken away from you when in the test room.

- Arrive somewhat ahead of time – If because of transportation schedules you must get there very early, bring a newspaper or magazine to take your mind off yourself while waiting.
- Locate the examination room – When you have found the proper room, you will be directed to the seat or part of the room where you will sit. Sometimes you are given a sheet of instructions to read while you are waiting. Do not fill out any forms until you are told to do so; just read them and be prepared.
- Relax and prepare to listen to the instructions
- If you have any physical problem that may keep you from doing your best, be sure to tell the test administrator. If you are sick or in poor health, you really cannot do your best on the exam. You can come back and take the test some other time.

VII. AT THE TEST

The day of the test is here and you have the test booklet in your hand. The temptation to get going is very strong. Caution! There is more to success than knowing the right answers. You must know how to identify your papers and understand variations in the type of short-answer question used in this particular examination. Follow these suggestions for maximum results from your efforts:

1) Cooperate with the monitor

The test administrator has a duty to create a situation in which you can be as much at ease as possible. He will give instructions, tell you when to begin, check to see that you are marking your answer sheet correctly, and so on. He is not there to guard you, although he will see that your competitors do not take unfair advantage. He wants to help you do your best.

2) Listen to all instructions

Don't jump the gun! Wait until you understand all directions. In most civil service tests you get more time than you need to answer the questions. So don't be in a hurry. Read each word of instructions until you clearly understand the meaning. Study the examples, listen to all announcements and follow directions. Ask questions if you do not understand what to do.

3) Identify your papers

Civil service exams are usually identified by number only. You will be assigned a number; you must not put your name on your test papers. Be sure to copy your number correctly. Since more than one exam may be given, copy your exact examination title.

4) Plan your time

Unless you are told that a test is a "speed" or "rate of work" test, speed itself is usually not important. Time enough to answer all the questions will be provided, but this does not mean that you have all day. An overall time limit has been set. Divide the total time (in minutes) by the number of questions to determine the approximate time you have for each question.

5) Do not linger over difficult questions

If you come across a difficult question, mark it with a paper clip (useful to have along) and come back to it when you have been through the booklet. One caution if you do this – be sure to skip a number on your answer sheet as well. Check often to be sure that you have not lost your place and that you are marking in the row numbered the same as the question you are answering.

6) Read the questions

Be sure you know what the question asks! Many capable people are unsuccessful because they failed to read the questions correctly.

7) Answer all questions

Unless you have been instructed that a penalty will be deducted for incorrect answers, it is better to guess than to omit a question.

8) Speed tests

It is often better NOT to guess on speed tests. It has been found that on timed tests people are tempted to spend the last few seconds before time is called in marking answers at random – without even reading them – in the hope of picking up a few extra points. To discourage this practice, the instructions may warn you that your score will be "corrected" for guessing. That is, a penalty will be applied. The incorrect answers will be deducted from the correct ones, or some other penalty formula will be used.

9) Review your answers

If you finish before time is called, go back to the questions you guessed or omitted to give them further thought. Review other answers if you have time.

10) Return your test materials

If you are ready to leave before others have finished or time is called, take ALL your materials to the monitor and leave quietly. Never take any test material with you. The monitor can discover whose papers are not complete, and taking a test booklet may be grounds for disqualification.

VIII. EXAMINATION TECHNIQUES

1) Read the general instructions carefully. These are usually printed on the first page of the exam booklet. As a rule, these instructions refer to the timing of the examination; the fact that you should not start work until the signal and must stop work at a signal, etc. If there are any special instructions, such as a choice of questions to be answered, make sure that you note this instruction carefully.

2) When you are ready to start work on the examination, that is as soon as the signal has been given, read the instructions to each question booklet, underline any key words or phrases, such as least, best, outline, describe and the like. In this way you will tend to answer as requested rather than discover on reviewing your paper that you listed without describing, that you selected the worst choice rather than the best choice, etc.

3) If the examination is of the objective or multiple-choice type – that is, each question will also give a series of possible answers: A, B, C or D, and you are called upon to select the best answer and write the letter next to that answer on your answer paper – it is advisable to start answering each question in turn. There may be anywhere from 50 to 100 such questions in the three or four hours allotted and you can see how much time would be taken if you read through all the questions before beginning to answer any. Furthermore, if you

come across a question or group of questions which you know would be difficult to answer, it would undoubtedly affect your handling of all the other questions.

4) If the examination is of the essay type and contains but a few questions, it is a moot point as to whether you should read all the questions before starting to answer any one. Of course, if you are given a choice – say five out of seven and the like – then it is essential to read all the questions so you can eliminate the two that are most difficult. If, however, you are asked to answer all the questions, there may be danger in trying to answer the easiest one first because you may find that you will spend too much time on it. The best technique is to answer the first question, then proceed to the second, etc.

5) Time your answers. Before the exam begins, write down the time it started, then add the time allowed for the examination and write down the time it must be completed, then divide the time available somewhat as follows:
    - If 3-1/2 hours are allowed, that would be 210 minutes. If you have 80 objective-type questions, that would be an average of 2-1/2 minutes per question. Allow yourself no more than 2 minutes per question, or a total of 160 minutes, which will permit about 50 minutes to review.
    - If for the time allotment of 210 minutes there are 7 essay questions to answer, that would average about 30 minutes a question. Give yourself only 25 minutes per question so that you have about 35 minutes to review.

6) The most important instruction is to read each question and make sure you know what is wanted. The second most important instruction is to time yourself properly so that you answer every question. The third most important instruction is to answer every question. Guess if you have to but include something for each question. Remember that you will receive no credit for a blank and will probably receive some credit if you write something in answer to an essay question. If you guess a letter – say "B" for a multiple-choice question – you may have guessed right. If you leave a blank as an answer to a multiple-choice question, the examiners may respect your feelings but it will not add a point to your score. Some exams may penalize you for wrong answers, so in such cases only, you may not want to guess unless you have some basis for your answer.

7) Suggestions
    a. Objective-type questions
        1. Examine the question booklet for proper sequence of pages and questions
        2. Read all instructions carefully
        3. Skip any question which seems too difficult; return to it after all other questions have been answered
        4. Apportion your time properly; do not spend too much time on any single question or group of questions
        5. Note and underline key words – all, most, fewest, least, best, worst, same, opposite, etc.
        6. Pay particular attention to negatives
        7. Note unusual option, e.g., unduly long, short, complex, different or similar in content to the body of the question
        8. Observe the use of "hedging" words – probably, may, most likely, etc.

9. Make sure that your answer is put next to the same number as the question
10. Do not second-guess unless you have good reason to believe the second answer is definitely more correct
11. Cross out original answer if you decide another answer is more accurate; do not erase until you are ready to hand your paper in
12. Answer all questions; guess unless instructed otherwise
13. Leave time for review

b. Essay questions
1. Read each question carefully
2. Determine exactly what is wanted. Underline key words or phrases.
3. Decide on outline or paragraph answer
4. Include many different points and elements unless asked to develop any one or two points or elements
5. Show impartiality by giving pros and cons unless directed to select one side only
6. Make and write down any assumptions you find necessary to answer the questions
7. Watch your English, grammar, punctuation and choice of words
8. Time your answers; don't crowd material

8) Answering the essay question

Most essay questions can be answered by framing the specific response around several key words or ideas. Here are a few such key words or ideas:

M's: manpower, materials, methods, money, management
P's: purpose, program, policy, plan, procedure, practice, problems, pitfalls, personnel, public relations

a. Six basic steps in handling problems:
1. Preliminary plan and background development
2. Collect information, data and facts
3. Analyze and interpret information, data and facts
4. Analyze and develop solutions as well as make recommendations
5. Prepare report and sell recommendations
6. Install recommendations and follow up effectiveness

b. Pitfalls to avoid
1. Taking things for granted – A statement of the situation does not necessarily imply that each of the elements is necessarily true; for example, a complaint may be invalid and biased so that all that can be taken for granted is that a complaint has been registered
2. Considering only one side of a situation – Wherever possible, indicate several alternatives and then point out the reasons you selected the best one
3. Failing to indicate follow up – Whenever your answer indicates action on your part, make certain that you will take proper follow-up action to see how successful your recommendations, procedures or actions turn out to be
4. Taking too long in answering any single question – Remember to time your answers properly

EXAMINATION SECTION

EXAMINATION SECTION
TEST 1

DIRECTIONS: Each question or incomplete statement is followed by several suggested answers or completions. Select the one that BEST answers the question or completes the statement. *PRINT THE LETTER OF THE CORRECT ANSWER IN THE SPACE AT THE RIGHT.*

1. Monday I read *a* pages of a book, Tuesday I read *b* pages, Wednesday I read *c* pages. How many pages did I read altogether?   1._____

    A. abc B. a+b+c C. 3abc D. Not given

2. If the number of days in March is represented by *d*, indicate the number of days in January.   2._____

    A. d-1 B. d-2 C. d-3 D. Not given

3. A man 45 years old has a son who is *y* years younger. Indicate the age of the son.   3._____

    A. y-45 B. 45-y C. 45y D. Not given

4. Ray wants to buy a gun which costs *x* dollars. He has *y* dollars, but that is NOT enough. How many dollars more does he need?   4._____

    A. y-x B. xy C. x-y D. Not given

5. Represent the integer next greater than the one represented by *m*.   5._____

    A. m B. m+1 C. 1-m D. Not given

6. What is the volume of a room which is *r* feet wide, *s* feet long, and *t* feet high?   6._____

    A. rst B. r+s+t C. r+st D. Not given

7. One day a boy caught *f* fish, then gave away *a* of them. The next day, he caught *b* more, but sold half of them. How many fish had he left?   7._____

    A. fa-b B. fa-1/2b C. f-a+1/2b D. Not given

8. Indicate the number of days in *r* weeks.   8._____

    A. 7r B. $\frac{r}{7}$ C. r+7 D. Not given

9. John and James have *x* marbles between them, and each has as many as the other. How many has each?   9._____

    A. 2x B. $\frac{2}{x}$ C. $\frac{x}{2}$ D. Not given

2 (#1)

10. If a certain number is represented by x and we give x a value of 5, what would be the value of $x + 2$?

    A. 10   B. 5x+2   C. 7   D. Not given

10.____

Questions 11-15.

DIRECTIONS: Use the following code to answer Questions 11 to 15.

⌋ = 1, ⌊ = 2, L = 3, ⌐ = 4, □ = 5, ⊏ = 6,
⌝ = 7, ⊓ = 8, ⌜ = 9. (Therefore, ⌝ L ⌊ is 673.2.)

11. ⌋ ⌜ ⊓ ⊏ =

    A. 1927   B. 1986   C. 3784   D. 3926   E. 9683

11.____

12. ⌋ □ × L =

    A. L □   B. ⌐ □   C. ⌜ L

    D. ⌋ ⌋ □   E. ⌋ ⌊ L

12.____

13. □ ⌐ + ⌊ □ =

    A. 63   B. 65   C. 74   D. 79   E. 141

13.____

14. ⌊ ⊓ ÷ ⌝ =

    A. L   B. ⊓   C. ⌜   D. ⌐   E. ⌊

14.____

15. 45 ÷ 18 =

    A. ⌋.□   B. □.⌊   C. L.L

    D. ⌊.⌊   E. ⌊.□

15.____

16. $\dfrac{5}{7} \div \dfrac{2}{3} =$

    A. $\dfrac{7}{10}$ B. $\dfrac{10}{21}$ C. $1\dfrac{8}{21}$ D. $1\dfrac{1}{14}$ E. $3\dfrac{1}{3}$

16.____

17. The lowest common denominator for $\frac{2}{3}, \frac{1}{4}, \frac{7}{9}$ is

    A. 9   B. 12   C. 16   D. 36   E. 108

18. The basic formula for the volume of a box is V =

    A. lwh   B. $\frac{1}{3}$ lw h

    C. 6lwh   D. $\pi r^2 h$

    E. 2(lw+lh+wh)

19. 24 yards =

    A. 72 ft.   B. 72 in   C. 8 yds   D. 8 ft   E. 1 rod

20. $\sqrt{36}$ =

    A. 1   B. 6   C. 18   D. 36   E. 136

21. Subtract $9x^2y^3$ from $4x^2y^3$.

    A. -5   B. -5xy   C. $-5x^2y^3$
    D. $-5x^4y^6$ E. Not given

22. The equation 5x + 7 = 2 + 3x is equivalent to which of the following?

    A. 8x = 9   B. 8x = -9   C. 5x = -5   D. 2x = 5   E. 2x = -5

23. Multiply: (x+7)(x-2).

    A. x^2-14 B. x^2+x-14 C. $x^2+5x+14$
    D. $x^2+9x-14$ E. $x^2-9x+14$

24. Solve for x: 5x + 7 = 9.

    A. $\frac{2}{5}$ B. $\frac{5}{2}$ C. $\frac{16}{5}$
    D. -3   E. Not given

25. A quantity, P, is determined by the formula $1/2h(a^2+b)$. If h = 5, a = 3, and b = 7, what does P equal?

    A. 40   B. 52   C. 80
    D. 160   E. Not given

KEY (CORRECT ANSWERS)

1.	B	11.	B
2.	D	12.	B
3.	B	13.	D
4.	C	14.	D
5.	B	15.	E
6.	A	16.	D
7.	C	17.	D
8.	A	18.	A
9.	C	19.	A
10.	C	20.	B

21. C
22. E
23. B
24. A
25. A

SOLUTIONS TO PROBLEMS

1. The sum of a, b, and c is represented as a + b + c
2. d = number of days in March = number of days in January
3. The son's age is 45 - y
4. If x is larger than y, their difference is shown as x-y
5. If x is an integer, the next integer must be m+1
6. Volume = (width)x(length)x height = rst
7. After one day, the boy had f-a fish. On the second day, he caught b fish but, after giving away 1/2b fish, had 1/2b fish left for that day. His 2-day total was f - a + 1/2b
8. r weeks means (r)(7) = 7r days
9. Each of them has half of x = $\dfrac{x}{2}$ marbles
10. x + 2 = 5 + 2 = 7
11. ⌋⌈⌉⌊ = 1986
12. ⌋☐×⌊ = 15 × 3 = 45 = ⌉☐
13. ☐⌉+⌊☐ = 54 + 25 = 79
14. ⌊⌈ ÷ 7 = 28 ÷ 7 = 4 = ⌉
16. $\dfrac{5}{7} \div \dfrac{2}{3} = \left(\dfrac{5}{7}\right)\left(\dfrac{3}{2}\right) = \dfrac{15}{14} = 1\dfrac{1}{14}$
15. 45 ÷ 18 = 2.5 = ⌊ · ☐
17. The lowest common denominator for 3, 4, and 9 is 36
18. The volume of a box V = Lwh, where L = length, w = width, and h = height
19. 24 yards = (24)(3) = 72 feet
20. $\sqrt{36}$ = 6, Since 6^2
21. $4x^2y^3 - 9x^2y^3 = -5x^2y^3$
22. 5x + 7 = 2 + 3x can be written as 2x = -5 by subtracting 3x + 7 from both sides of the equation
23. $(x+7)(x-2) = x^2 + 7x - 2x - 14 = x^2 + 5x - 14$
24. 5x + 7 = 9. Then, 5x = 2, so x = $\dfrac{2}{5}$
25. $P = \dfrac{1}{2}h(a^2 + b) = \left(\dfrac{1}{2}\right)(5)(9+7) = \dfrac{5}{2}(16) = 40$

TEST 2

DIRECTIONS: Each question or incomplete statement is followed by several suggested answers or completions. Select the one that BEST answers the question or completes the statement. *PRINT THE LETTER OF THE CORRECT ANSWER IN THE SPACE AT THE RIGHT.*

1. 2.4 x 6 =

   A. 1.8　　　B. 8.4　　　C. 14.4　　　D. 40　　　E. 144

2. In the problem 2 + 9 + 12 + 24 = 47, 47 is called the

   A. addend　　　B. subtrahend　　　C. dividend
   D. sum　　　E. difference

3. In the fraction $\frac{21}{26}$,

   A. 21 is the denominator
   B. 26 is the numerator
   C. both are numerators
   D. neither is the denominator
   E. 26 is the denominator

4. To cut a board into 5 equal lengths would require _____ separate cuts.

   A. 3　　　B. 3 1/2　　　C. 4　　　D. 5　　　E. 6

5. In the problem 21 - 3 = 18, 18 is called the

   A. subtrahend　　　B. minuend　　　C. difference
   D. quotient　　　E. product

6. $\frac{5}{7} - \frac{2}{3} =$

   A. $\frac{3}{4}$　　　B. $\frac{3}{10}$　　　C. $\frac{7}{10}$　　　D. $\frac{1}{21}$　　　E. $\frac{3}{21}$

7. The LOWEST common denominator of $\frac{3}{5}, \frac{4}{5},$ and $\frac{2}{5}$ is

   A. 120　　　B. 24　　　C. 15　　　D. 10　　　E. 5

8. In the problem 7 x 8 = 56, 56 is called the

   A. product　　　B. quotient　　　C. multiplier
   D. multiplicand　　　E. sum

9. _____ are both factors of 10.

   A. 10, 0　　　B. 8, 2　　　C. 2, 5　　　D. 6, 4　　　E. 7, 3

10. $\sqrt{64} =$

    A. 0   B. 1   C. 8   D. 32   E. 128

11. Which number is SMALLEST?

    A. 4.5   B. 4.449   C. .459
    D. .057399   E. 1.000

12. Of these two formulas: A = 1/2bh and A = bh, the

    A. first gives the area of a rectangle
    B. first gives the area of a triangle
    C. first gives the area of a trapezoid
    D. second gives the perimeter of a rectangle
    E. second gives the perimeter of a triangle

13. If you earn $40.00 and save $8.00 of it, what percent do you save?

    A. $\frac{1}{5}$ B. 5   C. 8   D. 20   E. 32

14. Reduce $\dfrac{\frac{36}{2}}{\frac{12}{4}}$ to simplest terms.

    A. 5   B. $\frac{15}{3}$ C. $\frac{1}{5}$ D. $\frac{3}{15}$ E. 6

15. I = PRT is a formula for

    A. increment   B. investment   C. interest
    D. insurance   E. none of the above

16. Take any number (your age will do); add ten to it; double the answer; subtract the number you started with; add twenty to that answer; again subtract your starting number; square that answer. The final answer is

    A. your age   B. 80   C. 160
    D. 1600   E. 1960

Questions 17-18.

DIRECTIONS: Use the following code to answer Questions 17 and 18.

    Let □ stand for the number of boys in the class. Let o stand for the number of girls in the class.

17. ☐ - o = the

    A. sum of boys and girls
    B. total of boys and girls
    C. total ages of the class
    D. excess of boys over girls
    E. excess of girls over boys

18. The ratio of boys to the TOTAL enrollment in the class would be

    A. $\dfrac{o}{\square}$ B. $\dfrac{\square}{o}$ C. $o \div \square$

    D. $\dfrac{\square}{o + \square}$ E. $\dfrac{o}{\square + o}$

19. Perimeters are ALWAYS measured in

    A. volume   B. area   C. linear measure
    D. square measure   E. cubic measure

20. 5 × 30% of 30 =

    A. 30   B. 40   C. 45   D. 50   E. 150

Questions 21-30.

DIRECTIONS: Each of Questions 21 to 30 presents a TRUE statement about counting numbers which are represented by the letters x, y, k, m, or s. You are to tell what MUST happen to x if certain changes are made in y, k, m, or s and the statement is to remain TRUE. If there is not enough information given to decide what happens to x, choose answer D, "cannot tell".

21. x = y + 8
    If y were made greater, what MUST happen to x?

    A. Remain the same   B. Become greater
    C. Become less   D. Cannot tell

22. x = y + m
    If m were to be made 1 greater and y were to be made 1 less, what MUST happen to x?

    A. Remain the same   B. Become greater
    C. Become less   D. Cannot tell

23. y = x + m
    If m were made greater, what MUST happen to x so that y would remain the same?

    A. Remain the same   B. Become greater
    C. Become less   D. Cannot tell

24. x = ym

If y were made greater and m were made less, what MUST happen to x?

   A. Remain the same
   B. Become greater
   C. Become less
   D. Cannot tell

25. $x = y + \dfrac{m}{s}$

If m were made less and y and s did not change, what MUST happen to x?

   A. Remain the same
   B. Become greater
   C. Become less
   D. Cannot tell

26. k = xm

If m were made less and k remained the same, what MUST happen to x?

   A. Remain the same
   B. Become greater
   C. Become less
   D. Cannot tell

27. x = y - m

If m were made greater and y remained the same, what MUST happen to x?

   A. Remain the same
   B. Become greater
   C. Become less
   D. Cannot tell

28. x = y + m - k

If y, m, and k were made equal to each other, what MUST happen to x?

   A. Remain the same
   B. Become greater
   C. Become less
   D. Cannot tell

29. $x = y + \dfrac{m}{s}$

If s were made less and y and m did not change, what MUST happen to x?

   A. Remain the same
   B. Become greater
   C. Become less
   D. Cannot tell

30. $x = \dfrac{y}{m}$

Given that y and m are always equal, what MUST happen to x if y and m are made greater in the same proportion?

   A. Remain the same
   B. Become greater
   C. Become less
   D. Cannot tell

KEY (CORRECT ANSWERS)

1.	C	16.	D
2.	D	17.	D
3.	E	18.	D
4.	C	19.	C
5.	C	20.	C
6.	D	21.	B
7.	E	22.	A
8.	A	23.	C
9.	C	24.	D
10.	C	25.	C
11.	D	26.	B
12.	B	27.	C
13.	D	28.	D
14.	E	29.	B
15.	C	30.	A

SOLUTIONS TO PROBLEMS

1. $2.4 \times 6 = 14.4$
2. In $2 + 9 + 12 + 24 = 47$, 47 is called the sum
3. In $\dfrac{21}{26}$, 26 is the denominator
4. Since 1 cut makes 2 equal lengths, 4 cuts would make 5 equal lengths
5. In $21 - 3 = 18$, 18 is called the difference
6. $\dfrac{5}{7} - \dfrac{2}{3} = \dfrac{15}{21} - \dfrac{14}{21} = \dfrac{1}{21}$
7. Since all fractions have a denominator of 5, then 5 is the lowest common denominator
8. In $7 \times 8 = 56$, 56 is called the product
9. 2 and 5 are both factors of 10 since 10 divides evenly by each of them
10. $\sqrt{64} = 8$, since $8^2 = 64$
11. .057399 is the smallest in this group of numbers
12. The formula $A = 1/2\, bh$ represents the area of a triangle
13. $\$8 / \$40 = \dfrac{1}{5} = 20\%$
14. $\dfrac{36}{2} \div \dfrac{12}{4} = 18 \div 3 = 6$
15. $I = PRT$ is a formula for interest. (Incidentally, P = principal, R = rate, and T = time)
16. Let x = initial number. Following directions, we get: $x + 10$, $2x + 20$, $x + 20$, $x + 40$, 40, 1600
17. □ - ○ = the difference between number of boys and the number of girls = excess of boys over girls
18. Total enrollment is □ + ○. The ratio of boys to this total = $\dfrac{\square}{\bigcirc + \square}$
19. Perimeters are always a linear measure
20. $5 \times 30\%$ of $30 = (5)(9) = 45$
21. $x = y + 8$. As y increases, so will x increase
22. $x = y + m$. By changing m to m+1 and y to y-1, $x = y-1 + m+1 = y + m$. Thus, x remains the same
23. $y = x + m$. If m is increased and x were decreased, by the same amount, then y remains the same
24. $x = ym$. If y increases and m decreases, the change in x is unknown
25. $x = y + \dfrac{m}{s}$. By decreasing m and leaving y and s alone, x becomes o less

26. k = xm. If m decreases and k remains unchanged, then x becomes greater
27. x = y - m. If m increases and y remains unchanged, then x becomes less
28. x = y + m - k. If y = m = k, x = y = m = k, but the change in x is unknown
29. $x = y + \frac{m}{s}$. If s decreases and y, m remain unchanged, x becomes S greater.
30. $x = \frac{y}{m}$. If m = y, and both m and y change equally, then x remains the same. (In fact, x = 1)

TEST 3

DIRECTIONS: Each question or incomplete statement is followed by several suggested answers or completions. Select the one that BEST answers the question or completes the statement. *PRINT THE LETTER OF THE CORRECT ANSWER IN THE SPACE AT THE RIGHT.*

1. 24 ft. =

    A. 72 ft.   B. 72 in.   C. 8 yds.   D. 8 ft.   E. 1 rod

2. The formula for the area of a circle is A =

    A. πr^2
    B. $1/2 \pi r^2$
    C. $2\pi r$
    D. $2\pi r^2$
    E. none of the above

3. $\frac{24}{124}$ reduces to

    A. $\frac{1}{6}$ B. $\frac{2}{12}$ C. $\frac{6}{31}$ D. $\frac{6}{1}$ E. $\frac{1}{5}$

4. Of these two formulas: P = a+b+c and P = 2a+2b, the

    A. first gives the area of a rectangle
    B. first gives the area of a triangle
    C. first gives the perimeter of a triangle
    D. second gives the perimeter of a trapezoid
    E. second gives the area of a trapezoid

5. 4 x 20% of 25 =

    A. 10   B. 20   C. 4.8   D. 80   E. 200

6. Distances are measured in units of

    A. volume   B. area   C. linear measure
    D. square measure   E. cubic measure

7. In the problem 56 ÷ 7 = 8, 8 is called the

    A. quotient   B. dividend   C. divisor
    D. product   E. sum

8. If $\frac{x}{2} = 12$, x =

    A. 1/6   B. 1/2   C. 2   D. 6   E. 24

9. Melons are selling at 3 for 25¢. Each weighs 2 lbs. How much would 54 lbs. cost?

    A. 75¢   B. $1.62   C. $2.25   D. $4.50   E. $9.00

2 (#3)

10. Take any number; double it; add ten; subtract twice the number you started with; double the answer; square this answer; subtract one hundred. The answer is   10.___

    A. 90   B. 100   C. 300
    D. 500   E. impossible

Questions 11-14.

DIRECTIONS: Use the following code and rules to answer Questions 11 to 14.

```
    0 = 0           Rules for addition:
    I = 1           0 + 0 = 0
   10 = 2           0 + I = I
   II = 3           I + I = 10 (Put down 0, carry I to the next
  100 = 4                       column left.)
  101 = 5
  110 = 6           Example:
  III = 7                        10  (2)
 1000 = 8                       +II  (3)
                                 101 (5)
```

11. 3+4 can then be written   11.___

    A. I+II   B. II+100   C. 0+100
    D. 101+III   E. 1000+10

12. 100 + I =   12.___

    A. 3   B. 4   C. 5   D. 6   E. 7

13. 9 would be   13.___

    A. 1000   B. 1001   C. 1011   D. IIII   E. 10000

14. III + 101 =   14.___

    A. 1000   B. 1001   C. 1011   D. 1100   E. 1101

15. Reduce $\dfrac{\frac{24}{4}}{\frac{18}{9}}$ to simplest terms.   15.___

    A. $\dfrac{1}{3}$ B. 3   C. $\dfrac{6}{2}$ D. 4   E. $1\dfrac{1}{6}$

16. If you spend $21.00 from your savings account of $28.00, what percent have you spent?   16.___

    A. $\dfrac{3}{4}$ B. 21   C. 25   D. 70   E. 75

17. A cube has 6 sides that are squares. Besides, it has _____ edges and _____ corners.   17.___

    A. 6; 6   B. 8; 8   C. 6; 8
    D. 8; 6   E. none of the above

18. $\dfrac{2}{3} \div \dfrac{3}{2}$

    A. $\dfrac{4}{9}$ B. $\dfrac{9}{4}$ C. 1   D. $\dfrac{4}{6}$ E. $\dfrac{2}{3}$

19. The formula for the area of a sphere (ball) is A =

    A. lwh   B. πr^2 C. 1/2bh   D. prt   E. $4\pi r^2$

20. If y represents an even number, represent the next greater even number.

    A. y+2   B. y+1   C. 2y+l   D. Not given

21. If one load of coal costs o dollars, what will be the cost of b loads of such coal?

    A. b-c   B. b+c   C. b/c   D. Not given

22. How much money is in Joe's bank account when y dollars are deposited and x dollars withdrawn if the previous balance was k dollars?

23. Three boys decide to run a refreshment stand. The equipment costs r dollars. The father of one of the boys gave them $20.00.
    Indicate how many dollars each boy will have to pay if the remaining expense is to be divided evenly among them.

    A. $\dfrac{r-20}{3}$ B. $\dfrac{r-20}{3}$ C. $\dfrac{20r}{3}$ D. Not given

24. How many hours will it take a person to go m miles if he goes r miles in one hour?

    A. mr   B. $\dfrac{r}{m}$ C. $\dfrac{m}{r}$ D. Not given

25. If the product of two numbers is 24 and one of the numbers is m, what is the other number?

    A. 24m   B. 24+m   C. 24-m   D. Not given

26. If the quotient of two numbers is y and the divisor is m, represent the dividend.

    A. $\dfrac{y}{m}$ B. my   C. $\dfrac{m}{c}$ D. Not given

27. Indicate the number of cents in m dimes and 2 pennies.

    A. 12   B. m+2   C. 10m   D. Not given

28. A book, a pencil, and a tablet together cost y cents. The pencil cost m cents, and the tablet cost twice as much as the pencil. What did the book cost?

    A. y-3m   B. 2m-y   C. 3m   D. Not given

29. One roll of telephone wire will reach *f* feet.
    How many rolls of such wire are needed to reach *t* feet?

    A. t-f   B. $\dfrac{t}{f}$ C. tf   D. Not given

30. One number is 7 less than another number. If 5 times the greater number is subtracted from 8 times the other, the difference is 25.
    What is the GREATER number?

    A. 27   B. 20   C. 9
    D. 2   E. Not given

KEY (CORRECT ANSWERS)

1. C		16. E	
2. A		17. E	
3. C		18. A	
4. C		19. E	
5. B		20. A	
6. C		21. D	
7. A		22. B	
8. E		23. A	
9. C		24. C	
10. C		25. D	
11. B		26. B	
12. C		27. D	
13. B		28. A	
14. D		29. B	
15. B		30. A	

5 (#3)

SOLUTIONS TO PROBLEMS

1. 24 ft = 24 ÷ 3 = 8 yds

2. The area of a circle is given by A = πr^2, where $\pi \approx \dfrac{22}{7}$ and r = radius

3. $\dfrac{24}{124}$ reduces to $\dfrac{6}{124}$ by dividing numerator and denominator by 4

4. P=a+b+c represents the perimeter of a triangle, where a, b, and c represent the sides

5. 4 x 20% of 25 = (4)(.20)(25) = 20

6. Distances are measured in units of linear measure

7. In 56 ÷ 7 = 8, 8 is called the quotient

8. $\dfrac{x}{2}$ = 12. Multiply both sides by 2 to get x = 24

9. 54 ÷ 2 = 27. If 3 melons cost 25¢, then 27 melons cost (9)(.25) = $2.25

10. Let x = original number. Following instructions, we get: 2x, 2x+10, 10, 20, 400, 300

11. 3 + 4 = II + 100

12. 100 + I = 4+1=5

13. 9 would be written as IOOI

14. III + IOI = 7 + 5 = I2 = IIOO

15. $\dfrac{24}{4} \div \dfrac{18}{9} = 6 \div 2 = 3$

16. $21 ÷ $28 = .75 = 75%

17. A cube has 12 edges and 8 corners

18. $\dfrac{2}{3} \div \dfrac{3}{2} = \dfrac{2}{3} \cdot \dfrac{2}{3} = \dfrac{4}{9}$

19. The formula for the area of a sphere is A = 4 π r2, where r = radius. Incidentally, this area is called surface area.

20. If y is an even number, the next largest even number is y + 2

21. One load costs c dollars. Thus, b loads cost bc dollars

22. Starting with a balance of k dollars, depositing y dollars, and withdrawing x dollars, yields a result of k + y - x dollars

23. The remaining expense is r-20. If this is divided evenly 3 ways, each boy will have to pay (r-20)/3

24. A rate of r miles per hour means a distance of m miles, requires $\dfrac{m}{r}$ hours

25. If m is one number and two numbers multiply to give 24, then the other number is $\dfrac{24}{m}$

26. If y = quotient, m = divisor, then my = dividend

6 (#3)

27. m dines and 2 pennies is equivalent to 10m+2 cents

28. Since the pencil costs m cents, the tablet costs 2m cents. Now, the book must have cost y - m - 2m = y - 3m cents

29. If one roll of wire reaches f feet, then $\dfrac{t}{f}$ rolls are needed to reach t feet

30. Let x = larger number, x-7 = smaller number. Then, we get 8(x-7) - 5x = 25. Simplifying, 8x - 56 - 5x = 25. This reduces to 3x = 81, so x = 27

EXAMINATION SECTION
TEST 1

DIRECTIONS: Each question or incomplete statement is followed by several suggested answers or completions. Select the one that BEST answers the question or completes the statement. *PRINT THE LETTER OF THE CORRECT ANSWER IN THE SPACE AT THE RIGHT.*

1. What is the sum of 7 and -8?   1.____
   - A. -56
   - B. -15
   - C. 1
   - D. 15
   - E. Not given

2. Multiply -3 by -15.   2.____
   - A. 45
   - B. 12
   - C. -12
   - D. -18
   - E. -45

3. Two integers differ by 3. Their sum is 51. One of the integers is   3.____
   - A. 21
   - B. 23
   - C. 24
   - D. 25
   - E. 26

4. Solve for t: $12(\frac{7}{3}) = \frac{1}{3}(t)$ 4.____
   - A. $\frac{7}{12}$
   - B. 19
   - C. 43
   - D. 84
   - E. 252

5. What quantity is one-half of x?   5.____
   - A. $2x$
   - B. $\frac{1}{2} \cdot x$
   - C. $\frac{1}{2} + x$
   - D. $\frac{1}{2x}$
   - E. Not given

6. When does 3 - b equal b - 3?   6.____
   - A. Only when b = -3
   - B. Only when b = 3
   - C. Only when b = 0
   - D. For all values of b
   - E. For no values of b

7. 3 - (-8) =   7.____
   - A. 11
   - B. 5
   - C. -5
   - D. -11
   - E. -24

8. If x > 7, what is TRUE about the quantity (x+2)? It is   8.____
   - A. equal to 5
   - B. greater than 9
   - C. equal to 9
   - D. greater than 14
   - E. equal to 14

9. What is the sum of $a^2 + 3b^2 + 3a^2 + b^2$?   9.____
   - A. $15a^2b^2$
   - B. $8a^2b^2$
   - C. $8a^4b^4$
   - D. $4(a^2+b^2)$
   - E. $4a^4 + 4b^4$

10. One number plus one-half of a SECOND number equals 36. What is the second number?

   A. 27
   B. 18
   C. 12
   D. 9
   E. Cannot be determined without more information

11. Bananas are 10 cents a pound. For p pounds and q ounces of bananas, Mary MUST pay _____ cents.

   A. $10(p+\frac{q}{16})$
   B. $10(p + 16q)$
   C. $10(16p + q)$
   D. $10p + \frac{q}{16}$
   E. $10(p+q)$

12. In the problem 11 + 8 + 23 = 42, 8 is called a(n)

   A. addend
   B. subtrahend
   C. dividend
   D. sum
   E. difference

13. $\frac{2}{3} \div \frac{2}{3} =$

   A. $\frac{4}{9}$
   B. $\frac{9}{4}$
   C. 1
   D. $\frac{4}{6}$
   E. $\frac{2}{3}$

14. Which number is the LARGEST?

   A. 4.5
   B. 4.4449
   C. .459
   D. .057399
   E. 1.000

15. $2.4 \div 6 =$

   A. .4
   B. 2.8
   C. 8.4
   D. 14.4
   E. 40

16. In the fraction $\frac{11}{16}$,

   A. 11 is the denominator
   B. 16 is the numerator
   C. 11 and 16 are both numerators
   D. both are denominators
   E. 16 is the denominator

17. $-8 - (-7) =$

   A. -15
   B. -1
   C. 1
   D. 15

18. $5x^3 - 2x^3 + 3x^3 =$

    A. $-30x^3$ B. $3x^3$ C. $6x^3$ D. $3 + 3x^3$

19. If $16 * \frac{1}{2} = 8$ the operation * could be which operation?

    A. Addition B. Subtraction
    C. Multiplication D. Division

20. If $3y - 6 = 5y$, then $y =$

    A. -3 B. -2 C. 2 D. 3

21. If $p = 0$, the expression $r + p(r+s) + 1 =$

    A. r B. r+1 C. r+s+1 D. 2r+l

22. $6x^2 - 8xy$ is the product of $2x$ and

    A. 3x-4y B. 3x-4 C. 4x-6y D. 3x-8xy

23. $(x+2y)(2x-y) =$

    A. $2x^2 - 2y^2$ B. $2x^2 + 3xy - 2y^2$
    C. $2x^2 + 3xy + 2y^2$ D. $2x^2 + 5xy + 2y^2$

24. For which of the following values of x is $\sqrt{x^2-1}$ NOT a real number?

    A. -3 B. -2 C. -1 D. 0

25.

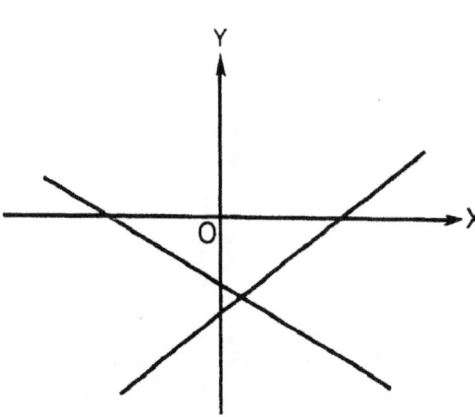

In the figure above, which of these (x,y) pairs could be the common solution of the two linear equations represented on the graph?

A. (1, -4) B. (1, 4) C. (-1, -4) D. (4, 1)

KEY (CORRECT ANSWERS)

1.	E	11.	A
2.	A	12.	A
3.	C	13.	C
4.	D	14.	A
5.	E	15.	A
6.	B	16.	E
7.	A	17.	B
8.	B	18.	C
9.	D	19.	C
10.	E	20.	A

21. B
22. A
23. B
24. D
25. A

SOLUTIONS TO PROBLEMS

1. $7 + (-8) = -1$

2. $(-3)(-15) = 45$

3. Let x = 1st integer, x + 3 = 2nd integer. Then, x + x + 3 = 51. Solving, x = 24 (The other integer is 27)

4. $12(\frac{7}{3}) = \frac{1}{3}t$. $28 = \frac{1}{3}t$. So, t = (28)(3) = 84

5. One-half of x is written as $\frac{1}{2}x$ or $\frac{x}{2}$

6. If 3-b=b-3, then -2b = -6. Solving, b = 3

7. $3 - (-8) = 3 + 8 = 11$

8. Since x > 7, then x + 2 > 9

9. $a^2 + 3b^2 + 3a^2 + b^2 = 4a^2 + 4b^2 = 4(a^2+b^2)$

10. The given statement can be written as $x + \frac{1}{2}y = 36$. Neither number can be found solely from this equation.

11. The cost of p pounds = 10p. The cost of q ounces = 10·q/16.
    Total cost is 10p + 10q/16 = $10p + \frac{q}{16}$

12. In 11 + 8 + 23 = 42, 8 is an addend.

13. $\frac{2}{3} \div \frac{2}{3} = \frac{2}{3} \cdot \frac{3}{2} = 1$

14. 4.5 is larger than the other selections.

15. $2.4 \div 6 = .4$

16. For the fraction $\frac{11}{16}$, 16 is the denominator.

17. $-8 - (-7) = -8 + 7 = -1$

18. $5x^3 - 2x^3 + 3x^3 = 6x^3$

19. Since $(16)(\frac{1}{2}) = 8$, the * could be a multiplication operation.

20. $3y - 6 = 5y$. Then, $-6 = 2y$, so $y = -3$

21. $r + p(r+s) + 1 = r + 0(r+s) + 1 = r + 1$

22. $6x^2 - 8xy$ can be written as $(2x)(3x-4y)$

23. $(x+2y)(2x-y) = 2x^2 + 4xy - xy - 2y^2 = 2x^2 + 3xy - 2y^2$

24. For $\sqrt{x^2-1}$ NOT to be a real number, $x^2 - 1 < 0$. Then, $x^2 < 1$, so $-1 < x < 1$. Choice D, with $x = 0$, satisifes this inequality.

25. Since the intersection occurs where x is positive and y is negative, only choice A (1,-4) would be correct.

TEST 2

DIRECTIONS: Each question or incomplete statement is followed by several suggested answers or completions. Select the one that BEST answers the question or completes the statement. *PRINT THE LETTER OF THE CORRECT ANSWER IN THE SPACE AT THE RIGHT.*

Questions 1-4.

DIRECTIONS: In answering Questions 1 to 4, use the following information.

An operation involves the addition of integers 1, 2, 3, ... up to some final integer A. This operation we might represent by the special symbol A*. From this definition A*, we can see that 4* =1+2+3+4= 10.

1. What is the value of 3*?   1._____
   A. 3   B. 5   C. 7   D. Not given

2. What is the sum of 5* and 7*?   2._____
   A. 24   B. 42   C. 43   D. Not given

3. If B* - 5* = 13, what does B* equal?   3._____
   A. 28   B. 18   C. 8   D. Not given

4. What is another way of representing 8+7+6?   4._____
   A. 8*   B. 8* - 5* C. 8* - 6* D. Not given

Questions 5-8.

DIRECTIONS: Use the definition below in answering Questions 5 to 8.
The symbol means A times D minus B times C. That is, the product of B and C is subtracted from the product of A and D

5. What is the value of $\begin{vmatrix} 3 & 1 \\ 2 & 3 \end{vmatrix}$?   5._____
   A. 2   B. 3   C. 7   D. Not given

6. If $\begin{vmatrix} 1 & 2 \\ 3 & 6 \end{vmatrix} = \begin{vmatrix} 2 & 2 \\ 3 & A \end{vmatrix}$, what does A equal?   6._____
   A. 3   B. 5   C. 6   D. Not given

7. If $\begin{vmatrix} 4 & D \\ D & 5 \end{vmatrix} = 11$, what does D equal?   7._____

   A. 3   B. 6   C. 9   D. Not given

25

8. What is the value of $\begin{vmatrix} 3 & H \\ 2 & H \end{vmatrix}$?

   A. 1 B. 5 C. H D. Not given

9. Solve for y: 6 - y = 10.

   A. 16 B. 4 C. -4
   D. -16 E. Not given

10. What is the sum of $8a^3$ and $6a^3$?

    A. $14a^3$ B. $14a^6$ C. $48a^3$ D. $48a^6$ E. $48a^9$

11. One-fourth of the quantity (2r+12) equals 25. Find the value of r.

    A. 6 1/2 B. 26 C. 44
    D. 56 E. Not given

12. Divide $15m^2n^4$ by $3mn^2$.

    A. $5mn$ B. $5mn^2$ C. $5m^2n^2$
    D. $5m^3n^6$ E. Not given

13. Subtract: $6a^2 + 5b^3 - 3c$
    $5a^2 + 4b^3 - 2c$

    A. $a^2 + b^3 - 5c$ B. $a^2 + 9b^3 - c$ C. $a^2 + 9b^3 - 5c$
    D. $11a^2 + 9b^3 - 5c$ E. Not given

14. What is the value of 5(7b-9) + 3?

    A. 12b - 11 B. 12b +17 C. 35b + 48
    D. 35b - 42 E. Not given

15. Mr. Smith leaves home on a business trip at 8 A.M. He averages 45 miles an hour. Mr. Smith's son, John, leaves home at 9 A.M. trying to catch him.
    The MINIMUM speed John can average and still catch his father by noon is _____ miles per hour.

    A. 70 B. 60 C. 55 D. 50 E. 40

16. What is the sum of $3x^2$ and $5y^2$?

    A. $8xy^2$ B. $8x^2y^2$ C. $15x^2y^2$
    D. $3x^2 + 5y^2$ E. Not given

17. Write in simplified form: a(2x-7y+1) + a.

    A. 2ax - 7ay + 2a B. 2ax - 7ay C. 2ax - 7ay + 1 + a
    D. -5axy + 2a E. 2a + 2x - 7y + 1

18. -3 is a solution for which of these equations?

    A. $x^2 = -9$ B. $x^3 = 27$ C. $-5x = -15$
    D. $5x^2 + 3x = 36$ E. $2x^2 + 6x + 1 = 0$

19. $a^2 + b^2 - a(a-b) =$

    A. $a^2 + b^2 + ab$ B. $2a^2 + b^2 - ab$ C. $2a^2 + b^2 + ab$
    D. $b^2 - ab$ E. $b^2 + ab$

20.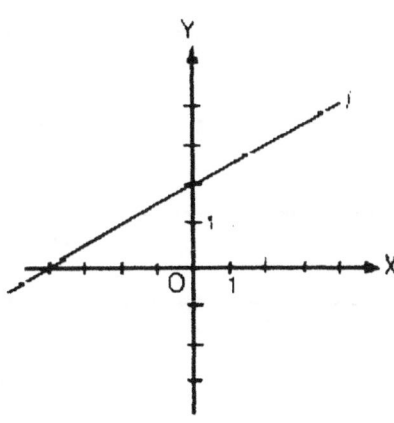

    What is the slope of line l above?

    A. 2   B. 1/2   C. -1/2   D. -2

21. In which diagram could the shaded region represent $\{(x,y): x > 2 \text{ and } y < -1\}$?

    A. 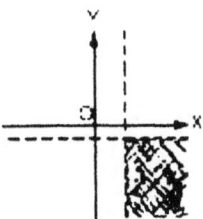   B.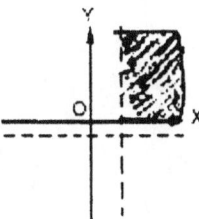

    C. 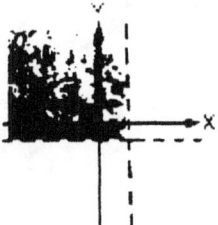   D.

22. If $x > 1$ and $\dfrac{x^n}{x^2} = x^3$ for all x, then n =

    A. 1   B. 2   C. 5   D. 6

23. What is the solution set of the equation $x^2 - x = 0$?

    A. $\{0\}$ B. $\{0, 1\}$ C. $\{0, 1, 2\}$ D. $\{-1, 0, 1\}$

24. John states that $\dfrac{x^2 - 1}{x - 1} = x + 1$ for all numbers x.
    Which value of x shows that John is WRONG?

    A. $x = 0$ B. $x = 1/2$ C. $x = 1$ D. $x = 2$

25. Which of these is the graph of the inequality $x - 2 \geq 0$?

    A. [number line with closed dot at -2, arrow extending right]

    B. [number line with closed dot at 2, arrow extending left]

    C. [number line with closed dot at 0, arrow extending left]

    D. [number line with closed dot at 2, arrow extending right]

KEY (CORRECT ANSWERS)

1.	D	11.	C
2.	C	12.	B
3.	A	13.	E
4.	B	14.	D
5.	C	15.	B
6.	A	16.	D
7.	A	17.	A
8.	C	18.	D
9.	C	19.	E
10.	A	20.	B

21. A
22. C
23. B
24. C
25. D

SOLUTIONS TO PROBLEMS

1. $3^* = 3+2+1 = 6$

2. $5^* + 7^* = (1+2+3+4+5) + (1+2+3+4+5+6+7) = 15 + 28 = 43$

3. $B^* - 5^* = 13$. Since $5^* = 15$, $B^* = 13 + 15 = 28$

4. $8 + 7 + 6 = (8+7+6+5+4+3+2+1) - (5+4+3+2+1) = 8^* - 5^*$

5. $\begin{vmatrix} 3 & 1 \\ 2 & 3 \end{vmatrix} = (3)(3) - (2)(1) = 9 - 2 = 7$

6. $\begin{vmatrix} 1 & 2 \\ 3 & 6 \end{vmatrix} = \begin{vmatrix} 2 & 2 \\ 3 & A \end{vmatrix}$ Then, $6-6 = 2A - 6$, $0 = 2A - 6$. Solving, $A = 3$

7. $\begin{vmatrix} 4 & D \\ D & 5 \end{vmatrix} = 11$ Then, $2D - D^2 = 11$. So, $D^2 = 9$ and D could equal 3 or -3

8. $\begin{vmatrix} 3 & H \\ 2 & H \end{vmatrix} = 3H - 2H = H$

9. $6 - y = 10$. Then, $-y = 4$, so $y = -4$

10. $8a^3 + 6a^3 = 14a^3$

11. $\frac{1}{4}(2r+12) = 25$. Then, $2r + 12 = 100$. Simplifying, $2r = 88$. Solving, $r = 44$.

12. $15m^2n^4 \div 3mn^2 = 5mn^2$

13. $(6a^2+5b^3-3c) - (5a^2+4b^3-2c) = a^2 + b^3 - c$

14. $5(7b-9) + 3 = 35b - 45 + 3 = 35b - 42$

15. Mr. Smith travels a total of $(45)(4) = 180$ miles. Since John must cover the same distance in 3 hours, his minimum speed must be $180 \div 3 = 60$ mph.

16. Since $3x^2$ and $5y^2$ are unlike terms, their sum can only be written as $3x^2 + 5y^2$

17. $a(2x-7y+1) + a = 2ax - 7ay + a + a = 2ax - 7ay + 2a$

18. -3 is a solution of $5x^2 + 3x = 36$, since $5(-3)^2 + 3(-3) = 45 - 9 = 36$

19. $a^2 + b^2 - a(a-b) = a^2 + b^2 - a^2 + ab = b^2 + ab$

20. From the points (0,2) and (-4,0), the slope is $\dfrac{0-2}{-4-0} = \dfrac{1}{2}$

21. The graph of x > 2 and y < -1 must lie to the right of x = 2 and below y = -1, as in choice A.

22. $X^n \div X^2 = X^3$ Then, n - 2 = 3, so n = 5

23. $x^2 - x = 0$. Then, x(x-1) = 0. Solving, x = 0 or x = 1

24. If x = 1, then , $\dfrac{x^2-1}{x-1} = \dfrac{0}{0}$ = undefined

25. If x - 2 ≥ 0, then x ≥ 2. The single variable graph would be a dot on 2 and an arrow to the right of 2.

TEST 3

DIRECTIONS: Each question or incomplete statement is followed by several suggested answers or completions. Select the one that BEST answers the question or completes the statement. *PRINT THE LETTER OF THE CORRECT ANSWER IN THE SPACE AT THE RIGHT.*

Questions 1-3.

DIRECTIONS: In answering Questions 1 to 3, use the following definitions.

A vector may be represented by a row of numbers inside parentheses. An example of a vector is (1, 3, 7). The numbers 1, 3, and 7 are called the elements of the vector. A vector may have any number of elements.

The following is an example of vector addition: (4, 5, 6) + (1, 2, 3) = (5, 7, 9). The first elements of the added vectors are 4 and 1, and the first element of the sum vector is 4 + 1 = 5. The other elements of the sum vector are found in the same manner. Vector subtraction is performed by subtracting comparable elements.

1. What vector is obtained by subtracting (14, 42, 18) from (67, 59, 83)? 1._____

    A. (53, 17, 65) B. (53, 17, 75)
    C. (53, 27, 75) D. Not given

2. Which of these operations is NOT defined in the introductory material? 2._____

    A. (7, 8, 3) - (7, 8, 3) B. (4, 10, 3) - (0, 0, 0)
    C. (9, 5, 2, 1) - (3, 4, 1, 1) D. (4, 6, 2) - (5, 3, 1, 7)

3. Which of these defines in symbolic form the addition of vectors with three elements? 3._____

    A. (a, b, c) + (d, e, f) = (a+b+c,d+e+f)
    B. (a, b, c) + (d, e, f) = (a, b, c, d, e, f)
    C. (a, b, c) + (d, e, f) = (a+b+c+d+e+f)
    D. (a, b, c) + (d, e, f) = (a+d, b+e, c+f)

Questions 4-8.

DIRECTIONS: Questions 4 to 8 are based on the following:

Vector multiplication is shown by an example. (1, 2, 3) x (4, 6, 5) = 1x4+2x6+3x5=4+ 12 +15 =31. Another example is (1, 1) x (2, 2) = 4

4. What is the product of (3, 7, 11) and (1, 2, 2)? 4._____

    A. 28 B. 39 C. 40 D. Not given

5. What is the product of (3, 3, 3, 3) and (4, 5, 4, 3)? 5._____

    A. 38 B. 48 C. 53 D. Not given

6. What is the product of (17, 4) and (0, 0)? 6._____

    A. 21 B. 1 C. 0 D. Not given

31

7. When D = 4, what does (D, 7) x (1, D) equal?

   A. 4 B. 28 C. 32 D. Not given

8. If (2, 4) x (3, C) = 18, what does C equal?

   A. 3 B. 6 C. 9 D. Not given

9. What value of m makes 6 - 3m = 15 a TRUE statement?

   A. -9 B. -7 C. -3 D. 3 E. 7

10. Let $y = \dfrac{2}{1+x}$, where x > 0. Then,

    A. as x increases, y increases
    B. as x decreases, y decreases
    C. as x increases, y decreases
    D. when 0 < x < 1, y is less than 1
    E. when x > 1, y is greater than 1

11. $(x^3)^2$ equals

    A. x^5 B. x^6 C. x^8 D. x^9 E. x^{32}

12. What is $7 + \dfrac{1}{4-y}$ when y = -4?

    A. 7
    B. $7\dfrac{1}{8}$
    C. $7\dfrac{1}{4}$
    D. 8
    E. Not defined

13. What is the value of $3a^2$ when a = -6?

    A. -18 B. -36 C. 36 D. 108 E. -108

14. The perimeter of a square is 4e.
    What is the area of another square whose sides are twice as long as the sides of the first square?

    A. 8e
    B. $4e^2$
    C. $16e^2$
    D. $64e^2$
    E. Not given

15. If x > 3 and y < 0, then the value of is

    A. greater than 3
    B. 3
    C. between 0 and 3
    D. 0
    E. less than 0

16. One-third of a certain number minus one-eighth of the same number equals 5. What is the number?

    A. 1
    B. 8
    C. 24
    D. 48
    E. Not given

17. Solve for y: 5 - 4y = 2.

    A. $-\dfrac{7}{4}$
    B. $-\dfrac{2}{5}$
    C. $\dfrac{2}{5}$
    D. $\dfrac{3}{4}$
    E. Not given

18. What is the value of $d^2 d^x$ when x is an integer and d is any real number?

    A. $d^{(x+2)}$
    B. d^{x^2}
    C. d^{2^x}
    D. d^{2x}
    E. Not given

19. What is $\dfrac{5}{3-x}$ when x = 3?

    A. 0
    B. $\dfrac{5}{6}$
    C. $\dfrac{5}{3}$
    D. 5
    E. Not defined

20. The sum of three numbers is 50, and x is the average of the first two numbers. Identify the BEST expression for the third number.

    A. 25 - x
    B. 50 - x
    C. 50 - 2x
    D. $\dfrac{50+x}{2}$

21. $\dfrac{3}{x-1} - \dfrac{2}{x} =$

    A. $\dfrac{1}{x-1}$
    B. $\dfrac{1}{x(x-1)}$
    C. $\dfrac{x-2}{x(x-1)}$
    D. $\dfrac{x+2}{x(x-1)}$

22. The meter in a certain taxi registers a minimum fare for distances up to 0.5 kilometer and $0.30 for each 0.5 kilometer thereafter. The *total* fare for a 4-kilometer ride is $2.85. What is the fare for the FIRST 0.5 kilometer?

    A. $0.45
    B. $0.65
    C. $0.75
    D. $0.85

23. The annual income of a corporation increased 70 percent during the past year. What is the ratio of its present income to its income a year ago?

    A. $\dfrac{1}{70}$
    B. $\dfrac{7}{70}$
    C. $\dfrac{10}{7}$
    D. $\dfrac{17}{10}$

24. $(x^2-5x+3) - (x^2-6x+4) =$

    A. x - 1
    B. x + 7
    C. -11x - 7
    D. $x^2 - 11x + 7$

25.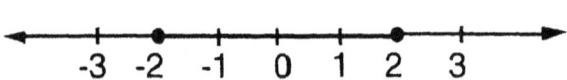

If the graph above represents $\{x : x^2 - k \leq 0\}$, then k =

A. 4 B. 2 C. -2 D. -4

KEY (CORRECT ANSWERS)

1. A
2. D
3. D
4. B
5. B

6. C
7. C
8. A
9. C
10. C

11. B
12. B
13. D
14. B
15. E

16. C
17. D
18. A
19. E
20. C

21. D
22. C
23. D
24. A
25. A

SOLUTIONS TO PROBLEMS

1. (67, 59, 83) - (14, 42, 18) = (53, 17, 65)

2. (4, 6, 2) - (5, 3, 1, 7) is undefined since the two vectors do not have the same number of elements.

3. (a, b, c) + (d, e, f) = (a+d, b+e, c+f)

4. (3, 7, 11) x (1, 2, 2) = 3 + 14 + 22 = 39

5. (3, 3, 3, 3) x (4, 5, 4, 3) = 12 + 15 + 12 + 9 = 48

6. (17, 4) x (0, 0) = 0 + 0 = 0

7. (4, 7) x (1, 4) = 4 + 28 = 32

8. 6 + 4C = 18. Then, 4C = 12. Solving, C = 3

9. 6 - 3M = 15. Then, -3M = 9. Solving, M = -3

10. With $y = \dfrac{2}{1+x}$ x > 0, as x increases, y decreases. For example, when x = 1, y = 1. When x = 2, $y = \dfrac{2}{3}$

11. $\left(x^3\right)^2 = x^3 \cdot x^3 = x^6$

12. $7 + \dfrac{1}{4-(-4)} = 7 + \dfrac{1}{8} = 7\dfrac{1}{8}$

13. $3(-6)^2 = (3)(36) = 108$

14. If perimeter is 4e, each side of the original square is e. The new square will have each side of length 2e. Thus, the area of the new square is $(2e)^2 = 4e^2$

15. If x > 3 and y < 0, then must be negative (positive * negative = negative). Thus $\dfrac{x}{y} < 0$

16. Let x = number. Then, $\dfrac{1}{3}x - \dfrac{1}{8}x = 5$. Simplifying, $\dfrac{5}{24}x = 5$. So, $x = 5 \div \dfrac{5}{24} = 24$

17. 5 - 4y = 2. Then, -4y = -3. Solving, $y = \dfrac{3}{4}$

18. $d^2 \cdot d^x = d^{2+x}$ or $d^{(x+2)}$

19. If $x = 3$, $\dfrac{5}{3-x} = \dfrac{5}{0}$ undefined

20. If x = average of two numbers, their sum must be 2x. Since all three numbers add up to 50, the 3rd number is 50 - 2x.

21. $\dfrac{3}{x-1} - \dfrac{2}{x} = \dfrac{3x}{x(x-1)} - \dfrac{2(x-1)}{x(x-1)} = \dfrac{x+2}{x(x-1)}$

22. Let x = fare for the first .5 km. Then, x + .30(7) = 2.85. Solving, x = .75

23. Let x = income one year ago, so that x + .70x = 1.70x = current income. Then, 1.70x/x = 1.7/1 = $\dfrac{17}{10}$

24. $(x^2-5x+3) - (x^2-6x+4) = x - 1$

25. For $x^2 - 4 \leq 0$, the solution is $-2 \leq x \leq 2$, which is the given graph. So, k = 4

TEST 4

DIRECTIONS: Each question or incomplete statement is followed by several suggested answers or completions. Select the one that BEST answers the question or completes the statement. *PRINT THE LETTER OF THE CORRECT ANSWER IN THE SPACE AT THE RIGHT.*

1. Factor $t^2 - 8t + 16$. 1._____

    A. (t-8)(t-2)   B. (t-4)(t-4)   C. (t-4)(t+4)
    D. (t+4)(t+4)   E. Not given

2. Rich and Drew have 11 marbles to share. Rich takes more than 4. How many does Drew get? 2._____

    A. More than 7   B. 7   C. Less than 7
    D. 6   E. Less than 6

3. $(5x-3)(7x+4) =$ 3._____

    A. $12x + 1$ B. $35x^2 - 12$ C. $12x + 2x + 1$
    D. $35x^2 - x - 12$ E. $35x^2 - 41x - 12$

4. For any real number p, which of the following is TRUE? 4._____

    A. $p^2 \leq 0$ B. $p^2 \geq 0$ C. $p^3 \geq 0$
    D. $p^2 \leq p$ E. $p^2 \geq p$

5. A track star practices t hours each day. He alternates running and walking, spending one-half his time on each.
   He runs at 16 miles per hour and walks at 3 miles per hour.
   During practice, he covers _____ miles. 5._____

    A. 9.5t   B. 11t   C. 19t   D. 22t   E. 38t

6. $\dfrac{5u}{4} = 2 - \dfrac{u}{3}$. what is the value of u? 6._____

    A. $\dfrac{2}{19}$ B. $\dfrac{1}{3}$ C. $1\dfrac{5}{19}$
    D. $1\dfrac{11}{19}$ E. Not given

7. For non-zero x and y, when does $x \div y = y \div x$? 7._____

    A. Only when y = 1
    B. Only when x = -y
    C. When x = y or x = -y
    D. For all non-zero values of x and y
    E. For no values of x and y

8. If $5 + x < 3$, then 8._____

    A. $x > 8$ B. $x < 8$ C. $x < 2$ D. $x > -2$ E. $x < -2$

9. The quantity $\dfrac{1}{-x}$, where $x \neq 0$, is the same as

   A. $\dfrac{1}{x}$ B. $\dfrac{-1}{x}$ C. $-x$ D. x E. $-\left(\dfrac{1}{-x}\right)$

10. Which is a solution to the equation $x^4 = 625$?

    A. -5 B. 25 C. 125 D. $156\dfrac{1}{4}$ E. 2500

11. To cut a ribbon into 7 equal lengths would require _____ separate cuts.

    A. $3\dfrac{1}{2}$ B. 6 C. 7 D. 8 E. 14

12. _____ are both factors of 12.

    A. 10, 2   B. 9, 3   C. 4, 3   D. 12, 0   E. 8, 4

13. In the problem $63 \div 7 = 9$, 7 is called the

    A. quotient   B. dividend   C. divisor
    D. product   E. sum

14. $\dfrac{124}{24}$ reduces completely to

    A. $\dfrac{12}{2}$ B. 6 C. $5\dfrac{1}{6}$ D. $5\dfrac{4}{24}$ E. $\dfrac{1}{6}$

15. If $\dfrac{x}{4} = 12$, $x = $

    A. 48   B. 4   C. 3   D. $\dfrac{1}{3}$ E. $\dfrac{1}{4}$

16. Solve the formula $T = b + \dfrac{km}{3}$ for k.

    A. $k = 3T - 3b - m$
    B. $k = \dfrac{T-b-m}{3}$
    C. $k = \dfrac{T-b}{3} - m$
    D. $k = \dfrac{3(T-b)}{m}$
    E. $k = \dfrac{3T+3b}{m}$

17. If $\dfrac{2x-1}{3} = 5$, then $2x+1 =$

   A. 7   B. 13   C. 16   D. 17

18. A shelf contains a total of 180 science, math and English books. There are twice as many English books as math books and three times as many math books as science books. How many English books are on the shelf?

   A. 60   B. 72   C. 108   D. 120

19. If $|x-3| = 4$, then the solution set of x is

   A. $\{-1\}$ B. $\{7\}$ C. $\{-1, 7\}$ D. $\{1, -1\}$

20. If 2 is a root of the equation $3x^2 + ax - 12 = 0$, then $a =$

   A. -12   B. 0   C. 6   D. 12

21. $\begin{cases} x - 8y = 2 \\ x + 4y = 5 \end{cases}$

   What is the value of x that satisfies the system of equations above?

   A. 0   B. 2   C. 4   D. 6

22. $(y-3)(y+2) - (y-3) =$

   A. $(y+3)(y-1)$ B. $(y-3)(y+1)$ C. $(y-3)(y+3)$ D. $(y+3)(y+1)$

23. $\sqrt{16^3} =$

   A. $4\sqrt{3}$ B. 24   C. 64   D. 512

24. If $x \neq 0$, then $\dfrac{15x^3 + 3x}{3x} =$

   A. $15x^3$ B. $15x^3 + 1$ C. $5x^2 + 3x$ D. $5x^2 + 1$

25. Line *l* shown at the right is the graph of the equation $y =$

   A. $-\dfrac{3}{2}x - 3$ B. $-\dfrac{3}{2}x + 2$

   C. $\dfrac{3}{2}x - 3$ D. $\dfrac{3}{2}x + 2$

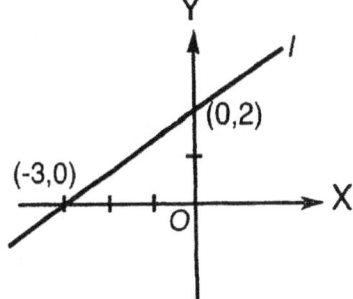

KEY (CORRECT ANSWERS)

1. B
2. C
3. D
4. B
5. A

6. C
7. C
8. E
9. B
10. A

11. B
12. C
13. C
14. C
15. A

16. D
17. D
18. C
19. C
20. B

21. C
22. B
23. C
24. D
25. D

___

SOLUTIONS TO PROBLEMS

1. The factoring of $t^2 - 8t + 16$ is $(t-4)(t-4)$

2. Since Rich takes more than 4 marbles, Drew will have less than 11 - 4 or less than 7 marbles.

3. $(5x-3)(7x+4) = 35x^2 + 20x - 21x - 12 = 35x^2 - x - 12$

4. For any real p, $p^2 \geq 0$ always

5. t/2 hours are spent running and t/2 hours are spent walking. Total distance (in miles) is $16(t/2) + 3(t/2) = 9.5t$

6. $5u/4 = 2 - u/3$. Multiply equation by 12 to get: $15u = 24 - 4u$. Then, $19u = 24$, so $u = 24/19 = 1\ 5/19$.

7. If $x \div y = y \div x$, then $x^2 = y^2$. This is true if $x = y$ or if $x = -y$

8. $5 + x < 3$. Then, $x < -2$

9. $\dfrac{1}{-x} = \dfrac{-1}{x}$ provided $x \neq 0$

10. $x^4 = 625$. Then, $x = \pm \sqrt[4]{625} = 5$ or -5

11. Since the first cut would provide 2 equal lengths, 6 cuts would be needed for 7 equal lengths.

12. 4 and 3 are both factors of 12, since both divide evenly into 12.

13. $63 \div 7 = 9$. The 7 is called the divisor.

14. $\dfrac{124}{24}$ can be reduced to $5\dfrac{1}{6}$

15. $\dfrac{x}{4} = 12$. Multiply both sides by 4 to get $x = 48$

16. $T = b + \dfrac{km}{3}$. Then, $3T = 3b + Km$. Subtracting 3b, $3T - 3b = Km$
    Finally, $K = (3T-3b)/m$ or $3(T-b)/m$

17. $\dfrac{2x-1}{3} = 5$ Then, $2x - 1 = 15$, so $x = 8$. Thus, $2x + 1 = 2(8) + 1 = 17$

18. Let x = number of science books, 3x = number of math books, and 6x = number of English books. Then, x + 3x + 6x = 180. Solving, x = 18. The number of English books is 6(18) = 108

19. If |x-3| = 4, then x-3=4 or x-3=-4. The solution set is {7,-1}

20. $3(2^2)$ + 2a - 12 = 0. Then, 12 + 2a - 12 = 0. Thus, a = 0

21. Double the 2nd equation to read 2x + 8y = 10 and now add the 1st equation. The result is 3x = 12, so x = 4

22. (y-3)(y+2) - (y-3) = y^2-y-6-y+3=y2-2y-3= (y-3)(y+1)

23. $\sqrt{16^3} = \left(\sqrt{16}\right)^3 = 4^3 = 64$

24. $(15x^3 + 3x)/3x = 5x^2 + 1$, provided x ≠ 0

25. The slope is (2-0)/(0-(-3)) = and the y-intercept is (0,2). Thus, $y = \frac{2}{3}x + 2$

EXAMINATION SECTION
TEST 1

DIRECTIONS: Each question or incomplete statement is followed by several suggested answers or completions. Select the one that BEST answers the question or completes the statement. *PRINT THE LETTER OF THE CORRECT ANSWER IN THE SPACE AT THE RIGHT.*

1. What is(are) the value(s) of x in the equation $\dfrac{(4x-7)}{(x-2)} = 3 + \dfrac{1}{(x-2)}$

   A. 2
   B. 0
   C. 0, 2
   D. no solution

2. By factoring $x^3 - 3x^2 - 10x = 0$, what are the values of x?

   A. 0, -5, -2   B. 0, 5, 2   C. 0, 5, -2   D. 0, -5, 2

3. By completing the square, what are the values of x in the equation $3x^2 - 6x + 2 = 0$?

   A. $1 \pm \sqrt{3}$ B. $1 \pm \sqrt{\dfrac{1}{3}}$ C. $-1 \pm \sqrt{\dfrac{1}{3}}$ D. $-1 \pm \sqrt{3}$

4. Using the quadratic formula, what are the values of x in the equation $x^2 + 5x + 6 = 0$?

   A. -3, 2   B. -3, -2   C. 3, 2   D. 3, -2

5. What are the values of x in the equation $\sqrt{3-2x} = 3 - \sqrt{2x+2}$?

   A. $-\dfrac{1}{2}, -1$ B. $\dfrac{1}{2}, 1$ C. $\dfrac{1}{2}, -1$ D. $-\dfrac{1}{2}, 1$

Questions 6-10.

DIRECTIONS: In answering Questions 6 through 10, use the quadratic equation $2x^2 - 7x + k = kx^2$.

6. What is the sum of the roots?

   A. $\dfrac{7}{2-k}$ B. $\dfrac{2}{7-k}$ C. $\dfrac{7}{k-2}$ D. $\dfrac{2}{k-7}$

7. What is the product of the roots?

   A. $\dfrac{k-2}{k}$ B. $\dfrac{k}{k-2}$ C. $\dfrac{k}{2-k}$ D. $\dfrac{2-k}{k}$

8. Which of the following ACCURATELY describes the nature of the roots if k = -5?

   A. Real, unequal, rational
   B. Real, unequal, irrational
   C. Real, equal, rational
   D. Real, equal, irrational

9. What is the value of k when one root is equal to zero?

   A. 2   B. 14   C. 7   D. 0

10. What value is NOT permissible for k if this equation is quadratic?

    A. 7   B. 5   C. 0   D. 2

KEY (CORRECT ANSWERS)

1. D
2. C
3. B
4. B
5. D

6. A
7. C
8. B
9. D
10. D

SOLUTIONS TO PROBLEMS

1. $\dfrac{4x-7}{x-2} = 3 + \dfrac{1}{x-2}$ Multiply the equation by x-2 to get

   4x-7 = 3x - 6 + 1. Simplifying, x = 2. However, since a value of x = 2 renders the fractional expressions meaningless, there is no solution.

2. $x^3 - 3x^2 - 10x = 0$ becomes (x)(x-5)(x+2) = 0. Setting each factor equal to zero, x=0, x=5, x = -2.

3. $3x^2 - 6x + 2 = 0$. Write as $x^2 - 2x = -\dfrac{2}{3}$. Now add 1 to both sides to get

   $x^2 - 2x + 1 = -\dfrac{2}{3} + 1 = \dfrac{1}{3}$. Then we have $(x-1)^2 = \dfrac{1}{3}$, so x-1 = and x-1 = $\sqrt{\dfrac{1}{3}}$. Solving,

   $x = 1 + \sqrt{\dfrac{1}{3}}$ and $1 - \sqrt{\dfrac{1}{3}}$.

4. $x^2 + 5x + 6 = 0$. Then, $x = \dfrac{-5 \pm \sqrt{25 - (4)(1)(6)}}{2} = \dfrac{-5 \pm 1}{2}$ So, $x = \dfrac{(-5-1)}{2} = -3$, and

   $x = \dfrac{(-5+1)}{2} = -2$.

5. $\sqrt{3-2x} = 3 - \sqrt{2x+2}$. Square both sides to get:

   $3 - 2x = 9 - 6\sqrt{2x+2} + 2x + 2$. Simplifying, $-4x - 8 = -6\sqrt{2x+2}$, which reduces to 2x+4 = $3\sqrt{2x+2}$. Square this equation to get $4x^2 + 16x + 16 = 9(2x+2)$. Simplifying, $4x^2 - 2x - 2 = 0$. This becomes $2x^2 - x - 1 = 0$ or (2x+1)(x-1) = 0. Thus, and x = 1.

6. Write the equation as $(2-k)x^2 - 7x + k = 0$. For any equation $Ax^2 + Bx + C = 0$, the sum of the roots is $-\dfrac{B}{A}$. Thus, the sum of the roots is $\dfrac{7}{2-k}$.

7. For $Ax^2 + Bx + C = 0$, the product of the roots is $\dfrac{C}{A}$. Thus, the product of the roots is $\dfrac{K}{2-K}$.

8. If k = -5, then $7x^2 - 7x - 5 = 0$. For any $Ax^2 + Bx + C = 0$, the nature of the roots is determined by the value of $B^2 - 4AC$. If $B^2 - 4AC = 0$, the 2 roots are identical and real. If $B^2 - 4AC < 0$, there are no real roots. If $B^2 - 4AC$ is a perfect square (and positive of course), the 2 roots are rational. Finally, if $B^2 - 4AC > 0$ but not a perfect square, the 2 roots are irrational. For our present example, $(-7)^2 - (4)(7)(-5) = 189$. Since 189 is not a perfect square, the 2 roots are real and irrational.

9. If one root is zero, then $(2-k)(0) - 7(0) + k = 0$. So, $k = 0$.

10. If the equation is quadratic, then the coefficient of x^2 must not be zero. Thus, $2 - k \neq 0$. So, $k \neq 2$.

TEST 2

DIRECTIONS: Each question or incomplete statement is followed by several suggested answers or completions. Select the one that BEST answers the question or completes the statement. *PRINT THE LETTER OF THE CORRECT ANSWER IN THE SPACE AT THE RIGHT.*

1. What is the simplified form of $(2^7 \cdot 3^3 \cdot 4^5)^2 (2^5 \cdot 3^8 \cdot 4^7)^3$?   1._____

   A. $2^{29} \cdot 3^{30} \cdot 4^{31}$ B. $2^{17} \cdot 3^{16} \cdot 4^{17}$
   C. $2^{18} \cdot 3^{17} \cdot 4^{18}$ D. $2^{30} \cdot 3^{31} \cdot 4^{29}$

2. What is the simplified form of $(3a^n b^m)^2 \cdot (3a^x b^y)^p$?   2._____

   A. $3^{2+p} a^{2n+xp} b^{2m+yp}$ B. $3^p a^{2nxp} b^{2myp}$
   C. $3^{1+p} a^{n2+xp} b^{m2+yp}$ D. $(9a^{nx} b^{my})^{2+p}$

3. What is the expanded form of $(x+y+z)^2$?   3._____

   A. $x^2 + y^2 + z^2 + 2x + 2y + 2z$
   B. $x^2 + 2xy + 2xz + 2yz + y^2 + z^2$
   C. $x^2 + xy + y^2 + xz + z^2 + yz$
   D. $x^2 + x + y^2 + y + z^2 + z$

4. What is the expanded form of $(-x+3+c)^2$?   4._____

   A. $x^2 + 9 + c^2 - x + 3x + c$
   B. $x^2 + 9 + c^2 - 2x + xc + 2c$
   C. $c^2 + 6c - 2cx - 6x + 9 + x^2$
   D. $c^2 + 6c - 2cx - 3x + 6 + x^2$

5. What is the simplified form of $-3a(2x-7)$?   5._____

   A. $6ax - 21a$ B. $5ax - 10a$
   C. $-6ax + 21a$ D. $-5ax + 10a$

6. What is the simplified form of $4a(3a^2 - a - 1)$?   6._____

   A. $12a^3 - 4a^2 - 4a$ B. $7a^3 - 5a^2 - 4a$
   C. $12a^3 - 4a^2 - 1$ D. $7a^3 - 5a - 1$

7. Write the simplified form of $(x^4 + x^2 + x + 2)(x^3 - 2x - 1)$.   7._____

   A. $x^7 + x^5 - 3x^2 + 5x - 2$ B. $x^7 - x^5 - 3x^2 - 5x - 2$
   C. $x^7 + x^5 + 3x^2 - 5x - 2$ D. $x^7 - x^5 + 3x^2 + 5x - 2$

8. What is the quotient of $(2^7 \cdot 3^3 \cdot a^5 \cdot b^2)$ divided by $(2^4 \, 3^6 \cdot a \cdot b^5)$?   8._____

   A. $\dfrac{8a^4 b^3}{27}$ B. $\dfrac{8b^3}{27a^4}$ C. $\dfrac{8}{27a^4 b^3}$ D. $\dfrac{8a^4}{27b^3}$

47

9. What is the reduced form of $(x^2y^3) \div (x^5y^2)$

    A. yx^3 B. $\dfrac{x^3}{y}$ C. $\dfrac{y}{x^3}$ D. $\dfrac{1}{yx^3}$

10. What is the product of $(x^m-y^m)(x^m+y^m)$?

    A. $x^{2m} - x^my^m + y^{2m}$
    B. $x^{2m} + y^{2m}$
    C. $x^{2m} + x^my^m - y^{2m}$
    D. $x^{2m} - y^{2m}$

11. What is the factoring for $x(x-1) + 3(x-1)$?

    A. $(x-1)(x+3)$
    B. $(x-1)(x-3)$
    C. $(x+1)(x-1)(x+3)$
    D. $(x+1)(x-1)(x-3)$

12. What is the factoring for $x(x+4) + 2x + 8$?

    A. $(x+4)(x+2)$
    B. $(x+4)(x+8)$
    C. $(x+2)(x+4)(x+8)$
    D. $(x+2)(x+8)$

13. What is the factoring for $y^2 + 2y + 3y + 6$?

    A. $(y+3)(y+6)$
    B. $(y+2)(y+3)(y+6)$
    C. $(y+3)(y+2)$
    D. $(y+1)(y+6)$

14. What is the factoring for $x^2 + 5x + 6$?

    A. $(x-3)(x-2)$
    B. $(x-6)(x-1)$
    C. $(x+6)(x+1)$
    D. $(x+3)(x+2)$

15. What is the factoring for $m^2 - 7m + 10$?

    A. $(m-2)(m+5)$
    B. $(m-2)(m-5)$
    C. $(m+2)(m+5)$
    D. $(m+2)(m-5)$

16. What is the factoring for $c^2 + 14c + 24$?

    A. $(c+10)(c+4)$
    B. $(c+12)(c-2)$
    C. $(c+6)(c+4)$
    D. $(c+12)(c+2)$

17. What is the factoring for $-6y^2 - 7y + 3$?

    A. $-(2y-3)(3y+1)$
    B. $-(6y-1)(y+3)$
    C. $-(2y+3)(3y-1)$
    D. $-(6y+1)(y-3)$

18. What is the factoring for $(x+1)^2 + 5(x+1) + 4$?

    A. $(x+2)(x+5)$
    B. $(x+1)(x+4)$
    C. $(x+2)(x+3)$
    D. $(x+1)(x+3)$

19. What is the factoring for $3 - 7(x+5) - 6(x+5)^2$?

    A. $-(3x+14)(2x+13)$
    B. $-(3x+11)(2x+15)$
    C. $-(6x+14)(x+13)$
    D. $-(6x+11)(x+15)$

20. What is the factoring for $4x^2 - 25$?   20.____

    A. $(4x+5)(x-5)$ B. $(2x+5)(2x-5)$
    C. $(2x+25)(2x-1)$ D. $(4x+25)(x-1)$

21. What is the sum $\dfrac{2}{a} + \dfrac{b}{3}$?   21.____

    A. $\dfrac{6+b}{3ab}$ B. $\dfrac{6+ab}{3a}$ C. $\dfrac{2b}{a+3}$ D. $\dfrac{2+b}{a+3}$

22. What is the sum $\dfrac{2}{u-v} + \dfrac{3}{v-u}$ 22.____

    A. $\dfrac{1}{u-v}$ B. $\dfrac{5}{v-u}$ C. $\dfrac{1}{v-u}$ D. $\dfrac{5}{u-v}$

23. What is the difference $\dfrac{7}{c^2-7c+12} - \dfrac{3}{c-4}$?   23.____

    A. $\dfrac{(16-3c)}{[(c-4)(c-3)]}$ B. $\dfrac{(12-7c)}{[(c-4)(c-3)]}$

    C. $\dfrac{(2-3c)}{[(c-4)(c-3)]}$ D. $\dfrac{(4-7c)}{[(c-4)(c-3)]}$

24. What is the quotient $(y - \dfrac{y}{3}) \div (y + \dfrac{y}{3})$?   24.____

    A. 1   B. $\dfrac{1}{3}$ C. 2   D. $\dfrac{1}{2}$

25. What is the quotient $(d - \dfrac{20}{d} - 1) \div (d + 2 - \dfrac{8}{d})$?   25.____

    A. $\dfrac{d-8}{d-5}$ B. $\dfrac{d-5}{d-2}$ C. $\dfrac{d-20}{d-8}$ D. $\dfrac{d-5}{d-20}$

KEY (CORRECT ANSWERS)

1. A
2. A
3. B
4. C
5. C

6. A
7. B
8. D
9. C
10. D

11. A
12. A
13. C
14. D
15. B

16. D
17. C
18. A
19. A
20. B

21. B
22. C
23. A
24. D
25. B

———

SOLUTIONS TO PROBLEMS

1. $(2^7 \cdot 3^3 \cdot 4^5)^2 \cdot (2^5 \cdot 3^8 \cdot 4^7)^3 = 2^{14} \cdot 3^6 \cdot 4^{10} \cdot 2^{15} \cdot 3^{24} \cdot 4^{21} = 2^{29} \cdot 3^{30} \cdot 4^{31}$

2. $(3a^n b^m)^2 \cdot (3a^x b^y)p = 3^2 a^{2n} b^{2m} \cdot 3^p a^{xp} b^{yp} = 3^{2+p} a^{2n+xp} b^{2m+yp}$

3. $(x+y+z)^2 = x^2 + xy + xz + xy + y^2 + yz + xz + yz + z^2 = x^2 + 2xy + 2xz + 2yz + y^2 + z^2$

4. $(-x+3+c)^2 = x^2 - 3x - xc - 3x + 9 + 3c - xc + 3c + c^2 = x^2 - 6x - 2xc + 6c + 9 + c^2$

5. $-3a(2x-7) = -6ax + 21a$

6. $4a(3a^2 - a - 1) = 12a^3 - 4a^2 - 4a$

7. $(x^4+x^2+x+2)(x^3-2x-1) = x^7 + x^5 + x^4 + 2x^3 - 2x^5 - 2x^3 - 2x^2 - 4x - x^4 - x^2 - x - 2 = x^7 - x^5 - 3x^2 - 5x - 2$

8. $(2^7 \cdot 3^3 \cdot a^5 \cdot b^2) \div (2^4 \cdot 3^6 \cdot a \cdot b^5) = \dfrac{2^3 a^4}{3^3 b^3} = \dfrac{8a^4}{27b^3}$

9. $x^2 y^3 \div x^5 y^2 = \dfrac{y}{x^3}$

10. $(x^m - y^m)(x^m + y^m) = x^{2m} + x^m y^m - x^m y^m - y^{2m} = x^{2m} - y^{2m}$

11. $x(x-1) + 3(x-1) = (x-1)(x+3)$

12. $x(x+4) + 2x + 8 = x(x+4) + 2(x+4) = (x+4)(x+2)$

13. $y^2 + 2y + 3y + 6 = y^2 + 5y + 6 = (y+2)(y+3)$

14. $x^2 + 5x + 6 = (x+2)(x+3)$

15. $m^2 - 7m + 10 = (m-2)(m-5)$

16. $c^2 + 14c + 24 = (c+2)(c+12)$

17. $-6y^2 - 7y + 3 = -1(6y^2 + 7y - 3) = -1(3y-1)(2y+3)$

18. $(x+1)^2 + 5(x+1) + 4 = [(x+1)+4][(x+1)+1] = (x+5)(x+2)$

19. Rewrite as $-1[6(x+5)^2 + 7(x+5) - 3] = -1[3(x+5)-1] \cdot [2(x+5)+3] = -1(3x+14)(2x+13)$

20. $4x^2 - 25 = (2x-5)(2x+5)$

21. $\dfrac{2}{a} + \dfrac{b}{3} = \dfrac{6}{3a} + \dfrac{ab}{3a} = \dfrac{6+ab}{3a}$

22. $\dfrac{2}{u-v} + \dfrac{3}{v-u} = \dfrac{-2}{v-u} + \dfrac{3}{v-u} = \dfrac{1}{v-u}$

23. $\dfrac{7}{c^2-7c+12} - \dfrac{3}{c-4} = \dfrac{7}{(c-4)(c-3)} - \dfrac{3(c-3)}{(c-4)(c-3)} = \dfrac{16-3c}{(c-4)(c-3)}$

24. $(y - \dfrac{y}{3}) \div (y + \dfrac{y}{3}) = \dfrac{2}{3}y \div \dfrac{4}{3}y = (\dfrac{2}{3})(\dfrac{3}{4}) = \dfrac{1}{2}$

25. $(d - \dfrac{20}{d} - 1) \div (d + 2 - \dfrac{8}{d}) = (\dfrac{d^2 - d - 20}{d}) \div (\dfrac{d^2 + 2d - 8}{d}) = [\dfrac{(d-5)(d+4)}{d}] \cdot [\dfrac{d}{(d+4)(d-2)}] = \dfrac{d-5}{d-2}$

TEST 3

DIRECTIONS: Each question or incomplete statement is followed by several suggested answers or completions. Select the one that BEST answers the question or completes the statement. *PRINT THE LETTER OF THE CORRECT ANSWER IN THE SPACE AT THE RIGHT.*

1.____

1. What is the reduced form of $[\frac{(4-y^2)}{3y}] \div [\frac{(y-2)}{2y}]$?

    A. $-3(\frac{4+y}{2})$ B. $-4(\frac{2+y}{3})$ C. $-2(\frac{2+y}{3})$ D. $-3(\frac{2+y}{4})$

2.____

2. What is the reduced form of $\frac{a}{4+a} + \frac{a}{4-a} - \frac{a}{a^2-16}$?

    A. $\frac{a}{[(a+4)(a-4)]}$ B. $\frac{-4a}{[(a+4)(a-4)]}$

    C. $\frac{8a}{[(a+4)(a-4)]}$ D. $\frac{-9a}{[(a+4)(a-4)]}$

3.____

3. What is the reduced form of $2 \div (2 - \frac{2}{2+b})$?

    A. $\frac{2}{(1+b)}$ B. $\frac{(1+b)}{(2+b)}$ C. $\frac{(2+b)}{(1+b)}$ D. $\frac{1}{(2+b)}$

4.____

4. What is the reduced form of the following quotient: $\frac{9x^2-3x}{3x+1} \div \frac{1-3x}{1+3x}$?

    A. $-9x$ B. $-3x$ C. $1-3x$ D. $1-9x$

5.____

5. What is the reduced form of the following product: $\frac{4y^2-10y+4}{10y-5} \cdot \frac{4y+8}{16-4y^2}$?

    A. $-\frac{2}{5}$ B. $-\frac{1}{2}$ C. $-\frac{1}{4}$ D. $-\frac{4}{5}$

6.____

6. What is the reduced form of $(\frac{2}{3}-4) \div (\frac{1}{6}+\frac{4}{24})$?

    A. -4 B. -10 C. -6 D. -12

2 (#3)

7. What is the reduced form of $(\frac{a}{b} - \frac{b}{a}) \div (\frac{a}{b} + \frac{b}{a} + 2)$?

A. $\dfrac{(a+b)}{(a-b)}$ B. $\dfrac{(a+b)}{(a-b+2)}$ C. $\dfrac{(a-b)}{(a+b+2)}$ D. $\dfrac{(a-b)}{(a+b)}$

7.____

8. What is the reduced form of $\dfrac{51}{357}$?

A. $\dfrac{1}{7}$ B. $\dfrac{1}{5}$ C. $\dfrac{1}{9}$ D. $\dfrac{1}{17}$

8.____

9. What is the reduced form of $\dfrac{28x^3y}{91xy^2}$?

A. $\dfrac{4x^2y}{13}$ B. $\dfrac{4y}{13x^2}$ C. $\dfrac{4x^2}{13y}$ D. $\dfrac{4}{13x^2y}$

9.____

10. What is the reduced form of $\dfrac{(ax^2 - 4a)}{[a^2(x+2)]}$?

A. $\dfrac{x+2}{a}$ B. $\dfrac{x+2}{4a}$ C. $\dfrac{x-2}{4a}$ D. $\dfrac{x-2}{a}$

10.____

11. What is the reduced form of $\dfrac{(n^2x + 3n^2)}{(nx^2 - nx - 12n)}$?

A. $\dfrac{3n}{x-4}$ B. $\dfrac{n}{x-12}$ C. $\dfrac{n}{x-4}$ D. $\dfrac{3n}{x-12}$

11.____

12. What is the reduced form of $\dfrac{(d^2 - 8d + 15)}{(9 - 3d)}$?

A. $\dfrac{3-d}{3}$ B. $\dfrac{3-d}{9}$ C. $\dfrac{5-d}{3}$ D. $\dfrac{5-d}{9}$

12.____

13. What is the reduced form of $\dfrac{(y^2 + 8y + 16)}{(y^2 + 6y + 8)}$?

A. $\dfrac{(y+4)}{(y+2)}$ B. $\dfrac{(y+2)}{(y+1)}$ C. $\dfrac{(y+2)}{(y+4)}$ D. $\dfrac{(y+4)}{(y+1)}$

13.____

14. What is the reduced form of $\dfrac{(abx^2 + abx + ab)}{(a^2bx^2 + ab^2)}$?

   A. $\dfrac{(x^2 + x + a)}{(ax^2 + 1)}$ B. $\dfrac{(x^2 + x + a)}{(ax^2 + b)}$ C. $\dfrac{(x^2 + x + 1)}{(ax^2 + 1)}$ D. $\dfrac{(x^2 + x + 1)}{(ax^2 + b)}$

15. What is the simplified form of $\dfrac{2}{\dfrac{1}{3} - \dfrac{2}{\dfrac{3}{4} + \dfrac{1}{1 - \dfrac{1}{2}}}}$?

   A. $-\dfrac{48}{19}$ B. $-\dfrac{66}{13}$ C. $-\dfrac{12}{31}$ D. $-\dfrac{13}{33}$

16. What is the simplified form of $\dfrac{2 + \dfrac{1}{a+1}}{3 - \dfrac{1}{a^2 - 1}}$?

   A. $\dfrac{(2a+3)(a-1)}{(3a^2 - 4)}$ B. $\dfrac{(2a-3)(a+1)}{(3a^2 - 2)}$

   C. $\dfrac{(2a-1)(a+3)}{(3a^2 - 4)}$ D. $\dfrac{(2a+1)(a-3)}{(3a^2 - 2)}$

17. What is the product $4^2 \cdot 4^{18} \cdot 4^{-6}$?

   A. 4^{30} B. 4^{24} C. 4^{14} D. 4^{22}

18. What is the simplified form of $\left[\dfrac{2^2 a^4}{3^3 b^6}\right]^5$?

   A. $\dfrac{(2^{10} a^{20})}{(3^{15} b^{30})}$ B. $\dfrac{(10^{10} a^{20})}{(15^{15} b^{30})}$ C. $\dfrac{(2^7 a^9)}{(3^8 b^{11})}$ D. $\dfrac{(32 a^9)}{(243 b^{11})}$

19. What is the simplified form of $\left[\dfrac{2x^{-1} - y^{-2}}{x^{-2} - 2y^{-1}}\right]^{-2}$?

   A. $\left[\dfrac{x(y - 2x^2)}{y(2y^2 - x)}\right]^2$ B. $\left[\dfrac{x(2y^2 - x)}{y(3y^2 - x)}\right]^2$

   C. $\left[\dfrac{y(y - 2x^2)}{x(3y^2 - x)}\right]^2$ D. $\left[\dfrac{y(y - 2x^2)}{x(2y^2 - x)}\right]^2$

20. What is the reduced form of $\dfrac{(b^{x+2} \cdot b^{x+4})}{[(b^{x+3})^2]}$

   A. b
   B. 1
   C. b^3
   D. b^{x+3}

21. What is the simplified form of $\left[\dfrac{2a^{\frac{1}{2}}b^{\frac{1}{3}}}{3a^{\frac{1}{6}}b^{\frac{1}{2}}}\right]^6$?

   A. $\dfrac{2^6 a^2}{3^6}$
   B. $\dfrac{2^6 a^2}{3^6 b}$
   C. $\dfrac{2^6 a^{\frac{3}{2}}}{3^6}$
   D. $\dfrac{2^6 a^{\frac{3}{2}}}{3^6 b^4}$

22. What is the factored form of $18p^2 + 9p - 14$?

   A. (3p-2)(6p+7)
   B. (3p+2)(6p-7)
   C. (9p-2)(2p+7)
   D. (9p+2)(2p-7)

23. What is the factored form of $y^2 + nxy - 2xy - 2nx^2$?

   A. $(y-n)(y+2x^2)$
   B. (y-nx)(y+2x)
   C. (y+nx)(y-2x)
   D. $(y+n)(y-2x^2)$

24. What is the factored form of $x^2 - 6x + 9 - y^2 - 4y - 4$?

   A. (x-y+5)(x+y+1)
   B. (x-y-5)(x+y-1)
   C. (x-y-1)(x+y+5)
   D. (x-y+1)(x+y-5)

25. What is the factored form of $4x^2 + 8xy + 3y^2 + 4x + 2y$?

   A. (2x+y+2)(2x+y)
   B. (2x+3y+2)(2x+y)
   C. (4x+y+2)(x+y)
   D. (4x+3y+2)(x+y)

KEY (CORRECT ANSWERS)

1. C
2. D
3. C
4. B
5. A

6. B
7. D
8. A
9. C
10. D

11. C
12. C
13. A
14. D
15. B

16. A
17. C
18. A
19. D
20. B

21. B
22. A
23. C
24. B
25. B

SOLUTIONS TO PROBLEMS

1. $\left[\dfrac{(4-y^2)}{3y}\right] \div \left[\dfrac{(y-2)}{2y}\right] = \left[\dfrac{(2-y)(2+y)}{3y}\right]\left[\dfrac{2y}{(y-2)}\right] = -2\dfrac{(2+y)}{3}$

2. $\dfrac{a}{4+a} + \dfrac{a}{4-a} - \dfrac{a}{a^2-16} = \dfrac{a(a-4)-a(a+4)-a}{(a-4)(a+4)} = \dfrac{a^2-4a-a^2-4a-a}{(a-4)(a+4)} = \dfrac{-9a}{(a-4)(a+4)}$

3. $2 \div \left(2 - \dfrac{2}{2+b}\right) = 2 \div \left[\dfrac{2(2+b)-2}{2+b}\right] = 2 \div \left[\dfrac{2+2b}{2+b}\right] = (2)\left[\dfrac{2+b}{2(1+b)}\right] = \dfrac{2+b}{1+b}$

4. $\left[\dfrac{(9x^2-3x)}{(3x+1)}\right] \div \left[\dfrac{(1-3x)}{(1+3x)}\right] = \left[\dfrac{3x(3x-1)}{(3x+1)}\right] \cdot \left[\dfrac{(1+3x)}{(1-3x)}\right] = -3x$

5. $\left[\dfrac{(4y^2-10y+4)}{(10y-5)}\right] \cdot \left[\dfrac{(4y+8)}{(16-4y^2)}\right] = \left[\dfrac{2(2y-1)(y-2)}{(5)(2y-1)}\right] \cdot \left[\dfrac{4(y+2)}{(4)(2-y)(2+y)}\right] = \left[\dfrac{2(y-2)}{5}\right] \cdot \left[\dfrac{1}{(2-y)}\right] = -\dfrac{2}{5}$

6. $\left[\dfrac{2}{3} - 4\right] \div \left[\dfrac{1}{6} + \dfrac{4}{24}\right] = -\dfrac{10}{3} \div \dfrac{1}{3} = -10$

7. $\left[\dfrac{a}{b} - \dfrac{b}{a}\right] \div \left[\dfrac{a}{b} + \dfrac{b}{a} + 2\right] = \left[\dfrac{(a^2-b^2)}{ab}\right] \div \left[\dfrac{(a^2+b^2+2ab)}{ab}\right] = \left[\dfrac{(a-b)(a+b)}{ab}\right] \cdot \left[\dfrac{ab}{(a+b)(a+b)}\right] = \dfrac{(a-b)}{(a+b)}$

8. $\dfrac{51}{357} = \dfrac{1}{7}$

9. $\dfrac{28x^3 y}{91xy^2} = \dfrac{4x^2}{13y}$

10. $\dfrac{(ax^2-4a)}{a^2(x+2)} = \dfrac{a(x-2)(x+2)}{a^2(x+2)} = \dfrac{x-2}{a}$

11. $\dfrac{(n^2 x + 3n^2)}{(nx^2 - nx - 12n)} = \dfrac{n^2(x+3)}{(n)(x-4)(x+3)} = \dfrac{n}{x-4}$

12. $\dfrac{(d^2-8d+15)}{(9+3d)} = \dfrac{(d-3)(d-5)}{(3)(3-d)} = \dfrac{(5-d)}{3}$

13. $\dfrac{(y^2+8y+16)}{(y^2+6y+8)} = \dfrac{(y+4)(y+4)}{(y+4)(y+2)} = \dfrac{(y+4)}{(y+2)}$

14. $\dfrac{(abx^2+abx+ab)}{(a^2bx^2+ab^2)} = \dfrac{(ab)(x^2+x+1)}{(ab)(ax^2+b)} = \dfrac{(x^2+x+1)}{(ax^2+b)}$

15. $2 \div [\dfrac{1}{3} - \dfrac{2}{\dfrac{3}{4}+\dfrac{1}{1-\dfrac{1}{2}}}] = 2 \div [\dfrac{1}{3} - \dfrac{2}{\dfrac{3}{4}+2}] = 2 \div [\dfrac{1}{3} - \dfrac{2}{\dfrac{11}{4}}] = 2 \div [\dfrac{1}{3} - \dfrac{8}{11}] = 2 \div -\dfrac{13}{33} = -\dfrac{66}{13}$

16. $[2+\dfrac{1}{a+1}] \div [3-\dfrac{1}{a^2-1}] = [\dfrac{2a+3}{a+1}] \div [\dfrac{3a^2-4}{a^2-1}] = [\dfrac{2a+3}{a+1}][\dfrac{(a-1)(a+1)}{3a^2-4}] = \dfrac{(2a+3)(a-1)}{(3a^2-4)}$

17. $4^2 \cdot 4^{18} \cdot 4^{-6} = 4^{2+18-6} = 4^{14}$

18. $\dfrac{(2^2 a^4)^5}{(3^3 b^6)^5} = \dfrac{2^{10} a^{20}}{3^{15} b^{30}}$

19. $[\dfrac{(2x^{-1}-y^{-2})}{(x^{-2}-2y^{-1})}]^{-2} = [\dfrac{(\dfrac{2}{x}-\dfrac{1}{y^2})}{(\dfrac{1}{x^2}-\dfrac{2}{y})}]^{-2} = [\dfrac{[\dfrac{(2y^2-x)}{xy^2}]}{[\dfrac{(y-2x^2)}{x^2 y}]}]^{-2} = [\dfrac{x(2y^2-x)}{y(y-2x)}]^{-2} = [\dfrac{y(y-2x^2)}{x(2y^2-x)}]^2$

20. $\dfrac{b^{x+2} \cdot b^{x+4}}{(b^{x+3})^2} = b^{2x+6} \div b^{2x+6} = b^0 = 1$

21. $[\dfrac{2a^{\frac{1}{2}}b^{\frac{1}{3}}}{3a^{\frac{1}{6}}b^{\frac{1}{2}}}]^6 = \dfrac{2^6 a^3 b^2}{3^6 a b^3} = \dfrac{2^6 a^2}{3^6 b}$

22. $18p^2 + 9p - 14 = (3p-2)(6p+7)$

23. $y^2 + nxy - 2xy - 2nx^2 = y(y+nx) - 2x(y+nx) = (y-2x)(y+nx)$

24. $x^2 - 6x + 9 - y^2 - 4y - 4 = (x-3)^2 - (y+2)^2 = [(x-3)-(y+2)][(x-3)+(y+2)] = [x-y-5][x+y-1]$

25. $4x^2 + 8xy + 3y^2 + 4x + 2y = (2x+y)(2x+3y) + 2(2x+y) = (2x+y)(2x+3y+2)$

TEST 4

DIRECTIONS: Each question or incomplete statement is followed by several suggested answers or completions. Select the one that BEST answers the question or completes the statement. *PRINT THE LETTER OF THE CORRECT ANSWER IN THE SPACE AT THE RIGHT.*

1. What is the simplified form of $(\dfrac{2a^4bx^3}{3ab^2y^5})^3$?

    A. $\dfrac{8a^9x^9}{27b^3y^{15}}$ B. $\dfrac{6a^9x^9}{9b^3y^{15}}$ C. $\dfrac{8a^6x^6}{27b^4y^8}$ D. $\dfrac{8a^6x^6b^3}{27y^8}$

    1.___

2. What is the product $(x+a^3)(x^2-ax+a^3)$?

    A. $a^6 + a^4x - a^3x - a^3x^2 + ax^2 - x^3$
    B. $a^6 - a^4x + a^3x + a^3x^2 - ax^2 + x^3$
    C. $a^9 + a^4x + a^3x - a^3x^2 - ax^2 - x^3$
    D. $a^9 - a^4x - a^3x + a^3x^2 + ax^2 + x^3$

    2.___

3. What is the product $(2x-5y)(2x+5y)$?

    A. $4x^2 - 20xy - 25y^2$ B. $4x^2 + 25y^2$
    C. $4x^2 - 20xy + 25y^2$ D. $4x^2 - 25y^2$

    3.___

4. What is the simplified form of $(a+b+c)^2$?

    A. $a^2 + b^2 + c^2 + abc$
    B. $a^2 + b^2 + c^2 + ab + bc + ac$
    C. $a^2 + b^2 + c^2 + a^2b + b^2c + c^2a$
    D. $a^2 + b^2 + c^2 + 2ab + 2bc + 2ac$

    4.___

5. What is the product $(a^2-b^2) \cdot [\dfrac{x^2}{(xb-xa)}]$?

    A. $-x(a+b)$ B. $-x(a-b)$ C. $-x(a+2b)$ D. $-x(a-2b)$

    5.___

6. What is the sum $\sqrt{2}+\sqrt{8}$?

    A. $5\sqrt{2}$ B. $3\sqrt{2}$ C. $\sqrt{10}$ D. $2\sqrt{2}$

    6.___

7. What is the product $(2+3i)(5-4i)$?

    A. $22+7i$ B. $-2-7i$ C. $22-7i$ D. $-2+7i$

    7.___

8. What is the simplified form of $(3-7i)-(3+2i)$?

    A. $6-5i$ B. $-5i$ C. $-9i$ D. $6-9i$

    8.___

9. What is the reduced form of $\dfrac{3x}{v} - \dfrac{x}{2v}$?

   A. $\dfrac{x}{v}$ B. $\dfrac{2x}{v}$ C. $\dfrac{5x}{2v}$ D. $\dfrac{7x}{2v}$

10. What is the reduced form of $\dfrac{(y^2 - 4y - 5)}{(y^2 - 25)}$?

    A. $\dfrac{(y-4)}{(y+5)}$ B. $\dfrac{(y-4)}{(y-5)}$ C. $\dfrac{(y+1)}{(y-5)}$ D. $\dfrac{(y+1)}{(y+5)}$

11. What is the reduced form of $\dfrac{x(x-3)}{(6-2x)}$?

    A. $-x(3-x)$ B. $-\dfrac{x}{6}$ C. $-\dfrac{x}{2}$ D. $-x(6-x)$

12. Which of the following is the simplification of $\sqrt[3]{\dfrac{27x^3}{8y^2}}$?

    A. $\dfrac{9x}{[2 \cdot \sqrt[3]{y}]}$ B. $\dfrac{3x}{[2 \cdot \sqrt[3]{y^2}]}$ C. $\dfrac{9x}{[2 \cdot \sqrt[3]{y^2}]}$ D. $\dfrac{3x}{[2 \cdot \sqrt[3]{y}]}$

13. What is the reduced form of $\dfrac{(1+\frac{1}{n})}{(2+\frac{1}{n})}$?

    A. $\dfrac{1}{n}$ B. $\dfrac{(n+1)}{(2n+1)}$ C. $\dfrac{1}{2}n$ D. $\dfrac{(2n+1)}{(n+1)}$

14. What is the smallest natural number?

    A. -1   B. 0   C. 2   D. 1

15. Let x be a natural number.
    For which of the following equations must a-b be negative?

    A. $ab = x$ B. $\dfrac{a}{x} = b$ C. $b = a + x$ D. $a = b + x$

16. Which of the following is an integer which is neither positive nor negative?

    A. 0   B. 1   C. $\frac{1}{2}$ D. -1

17. If (5, 3) means 5-3, what is the value of $(\frac{1}{2}, -\frac{1}{2})$?

    A. 1   B. $\frac{1}{2}$ C. 0   D. $\frac{1}{4}$

18. If b·x = b, then which of the following MUST be true?

    A. b = x   B. x = 1   C. b = 1   D. x<b

KEY (CORRECT ANSWERS)

1. A   11. C
2. B   12. B
3. D   13. B
4. D   14. D
5. A   15. C

6. B   16. A
7. A   17. A
8. C   18. B
9. C
10. D

SOLUTIONS TO PROBLEMS

1. $\left[\dfrac{2a^4bx^3}{3ab^2y^5}\right]^3 = \dfrac{8a^{12}b^3x^9}{27a^3b^6y^{15}} = \dfrac{8a^9x^9}{27b^3y^{15}}$

2. $(x+a^3)(x^2-ax+a^3) = x^3 + a^3x^2 - ax^2 - a^4x + a^3x + a^6$

3. $(2x-5y)(2x+5y) = 4x^2 + 10xy - 10xy - 25y^2 = 4x^2 - 25y^2$

4. $(a+b+c)^2 = a^2 + ab + ac + ab + b^2 + bc + ac + bc + c^2 = a^2 + b^2 + c^2 + 2ab + 2ac + 2bc$

5. $(a^2-b^2)\cdot\dfrac{x^2}{xb-xa} = (a-b)(a+b)\cdot\dfrac{x^2}{x(b-a)} = -x(a+b)$

6. $\sqrt{2}+\sqrt{8} = \sqrt{2}+2\sqrt{2} = 3\sqrt{2}$

7. $(2+3i)(5-4i) = 10-8i+15i-12i^2 = 22+7i$

8. $(3-7i)-(3+2i) = -9i$

9. $\dfrac{3x}{v}-\dfrac{x}{2v} = \dfrac{6x}{2v}-\dfrac{x}{2v} = \dfrac{5x}{2v}$

10. $(y^2-4y-5)\div(y^2-25) = \left[\dfrac{(y-5)(y+1)}{(y-5)(y+5)}\right] = \dfrac{(y+1)}{(y+5)}$

11. $\dfrac{x(x-3)}{(6-2x)} = \dfrac{x(x-3)}{2(3-x)} = -\dfrac{x}{2}$

12. $\sqrt[3]{\dfrac{27x^3}{8y^2}} = \dfrac{3}{2}\cdot\dfrac{x}{\sqrt[3]{y^2}} = \dfrac{3x}{2\cdot\sqrt[3]{y^2}}$

13. $\dfrac{(1+\frac{1}{n})}{(2+\frac{1}{n})} = \dfrac{n+1}{n}\div\dfrac{2n+1}{n} = \dfrac{n+1}{2n+1}$

14. If a is any natural number, the next natural number is a+1. The smallest natural number is 1.

15. Let a-b mean (a, b). Then (a, b) is negative if b = a+x where b = a+x for some natural number x. For example, (5, 8) = 5-8 is negative since 8 = 5+3.

16. Zero is neither negative nor positive.

17. The pair (5, 3) = 5-3 = 2. Thus, $(\frac{1}{2}, -\frac{1}{2}) = \frac{1}{2} - (-\frac{1}{2}) = \frac{1}{2} + \frac{1}{2} = 1$

18. b·1 = b for all reals, including zero and negative numbers. Thus, 2 = 2·1, 0 = 0·1, -5 = (-5)(1), for example.

18.___

EXAMINATION SECTION
TEST 1

DIRECTIONS: Each question or incomplete statement is followed by several suggested answers or completions. Select the one that BEST answers the question or completes the statement. *PRINT THE LETTER OF THE CORRECT ANSWER IN THE SPACE AT THE RIGHT.*

1. If $\dfrac{3x}{2y} = \dfrac{4z}{3}$ = and $\dfrac{3z}{2x} = w$, then y equals to

   A. $\dfrac{27W}{32}$ B. $\dfrac{27X}{8}$ C. $\dfrac{8XW}{27}$ D. $\dfrac{27}{16w}$

2. The factors of $2x^2 - 11x - 21$ are

   A. $(2x+7)(x-3)$ B. $(x-7)(2x+3)$
   C. $(x+7)(2x-3)$ D. $(2x-7)(x+3)$

3. In the equation $x = ry$, r is a constant.
   If, when $x = 8$, $y = 3$, the value of y when $x = 2/3$ is

   A. 1/12 B. 1/4 C. 16/9 D. 9/16

4. To complete the square in the terms $x^2 + 10x$, we would have to ADD

   A. 20 B. 25 C. 30 D. 100

5. If $y = x^3$, $\dfrac{d^2y}{dx^2}$ is equal to

   A. $6x$ B. $3x^2$ C. $\dfrac{x^5}{20}$ D. $2x^3$

6. The expression $\dfrac{x^{-2}y^2}{y} \cdot \dfrac{x^2}{x^4} + y^0$ reduces to

   A. $\dfrac{xy}{x^4}$ B. $\dfrac{y^2}{y-x^4}$ C. $\dfrac{y-1}{x^2}+1$ D. $\dfrac{y-1}{x^2+y}$

7. The THIRD term in the expansion $(a+b)^6$ is

   A. $15a^4b^2$ B. $20a^4b^2$ C. $30a^4b^4$ D. $10a^4b^2$

8. If $x = 1$ and $x^3 + x^2 + x^1 + x^0 + x^{-1} = y$, y equals

   A. 2 B. 3 C. 4 D. 5

9. The expression $\sqrt{28} - \sqrt{7}$ reduces to

   A. $\sqrt{7}$ B. $3\sqrt{7}$ C. $\sqrt{21}$ D. $-\sqrt{35}$

10. The product $\dfrac{6xy}{x^2-4} \cdot \dfrac{5x-10}{3xy}$ is equal to

    A. $\dfrac{2xy}{x^2-40}$ B. $\dfrac{30x^2}{x^2 y}$ C. $\dfrac{10}{x+2}$ D. $\dfrac{18x^3 y}{x+10}$

11. y varies inversely with x^2. If y = 12 when x = 2, then when x = 4, y is equal to

    A. 2   B. 3   C. 4   D. 6

12. The numerical value of $9^{\frac{3}{2}}$ is

    A. 18   B. 27   C. 36   D. 81

13. The numerical value of $\sqrt{640}$ is MOST NEARLY

    A. 80   B. 25.3   C. 24.3   D. 20

14. The value of $5\sqrt{12} - 2\sqrt{27}$ is equal to

    A. $4\sqrt{3}$ B. $3\sqrt{5}$ C. $5\sqrt{2}$ D. $3\sqrt{15}$

15. The number 8^6 is the SAME as the number

    A. 2^{48} B. 2^{15} C. 2^{18} D. 4^{16}

16. When $\dfrac{x}{3} - 2$ is subtracted from $\dfrac{x+6}{3}$, the answer is

    A. 0   B. 2   C. -2   D. 4

17. The length of a rectangle is 4 times the width. If the area of the rectangle is 324 square feet, the dimensions of the rectangle, in feet, are

    A. 4 x 81   B. 8 x 41   C. 9 x 36   D. 12 x 27

18. The reciprocal of $\dfrac{25x^2}{y}$ is

    A. $-\dfrac{y}{25x^2}$ B. $-\dfrac{25x^2}{y}$ C. $\dfrac{y}{25x^2}$ D. $\dfrac{25y}{x^2}$

19. If $\frac{3a-1}{4} = 2$, then a equals

   A. 2	B. 3	C. 4	D. 9

20. The angles of a triangle are in the ratio of 3:5:7. The number of degrees in the SMALLEST angle of the triangle is

   A. 24	B. 30	C. 36	D. 45

KEY (CORRECT ANSWERS)

1. D	6. C	11. B	16. D
2. B	7. A	12. B	17. C
3. B	8. D	13. B	18. C
4. B	9. A	14. A	19. B
5. A	10. C	15. C	20. C

SOLUTIONS TO PROBLEMS

1. From $\dfrac{3x}{2y} = \dfrac{4z}{3}$ we get 8YZ = 9x. Then, $y = \dfrac{9x}{8z}$.

   Since 3z/2x = w, we can write 3z = 2xw or z = 2xw/3. Return to y = 9x/8z and substitute z = 2xw/3 to get y = 9x ÷ (8[2xw]/3) = (9x)(3/16xw) = 27/16w

2. $2x^2 - 11x - 21 = (2x+3)(x-7)$

3. x = ry, so 8 = (r)(3) and r = 8/3. Now, $\dfrac{2}{3} = \dfrac{8}{3}y$

   Solving, $y = \dfrac{2}{3} \div \dfrac{8}{3} = \dfrac{1}{4}$

4. Add 25 to get $x^2 + 10x + 25$, which is $(x+5)^2$

5. $y = x^3$, $\dfrac{dy}{dx} = 3x^2$, and $\dfrac{d^2y}{dx^2} = 6x$

6. $x^{-2}y^2/y - x^2/x^4 + y^0 = y/x^2 - 1/x^2 + 1 = \dfrac{y-1}{x^2} + 1$

7. For $(a+b)^6$, the 3rd term is $\dfrac{(6)(5)}{(1)(2)}a^4b^4 = 154a^4b^2$

8. $y = 1^3 + 1^2 + 1^1 + 1^0 + 1^{-1} = 1+1+1+1+1 = 5$

9. $\sqrt{28} - \sqrt{7} = \sqrt{4}\sqrt{7} - \sqrt{7} = 2\sqrt{7} - \sqrt{7} = \sqrt{7}$

10. $[6xy/(x^2-4)][(5x-10)/3xy] = [6xy/(x-2)(x+2)][5(x-2)/3xy] = 10/(x+2)$

11. If y varies inversely as x^2, then $y_1/y_2 = x_2^2 / x_1^2$
    Then, 12/y = 16/4. 12/y = 4, so y = 3

12. $9^{\frac{3}{2}} = (\sqrt{9})^3 = 3^3 = 27$

13. $\sqrt{640} \approx 25.298 \approx 25.3$

14. $5\sqrt{12} - 2\sqrt{27} = 5\sqrt{4}\sqrt{3} - 2\sqrt{9}\sqrt{3} = 10\sqrt{3} - 6\sqrt{3} = 4\sqrt{3}$

15. $8^6 = (2^3)^6 = 2^{18}$

16. $\dfrac{x+3}{3} - (\dfrac{x}{3} - 2) = \dfrac{x+6}{3} - \dfrac{x-6}{3} = \dfrac{12}{3} = 4$

17. Let x = width, 4x = length. Then, $4x^2 = 324$, $x^2 = 81$, and x = 9. The dimensions are 9x36

18. The reciprocal of $\dfrac{25x^2}{y}$ is $\dfrac{y}{25x^2}$

19. $\dfrac{3a-1}{4} = 2$ Then, 3a - 1 = 8, 3a=9, so a = 3

20. Let 3x, 5x, 7x represent the 3 angles. Then, 3x + 5x + 7x = 180. 15x = 180, so x = 12. The smallest angle, in degrees, is (12)(3) = 36

TEST 2

DIRECTIONS: Each question or incomplete statement is followed by several suggested answers or completions. Select the one that BEST answers the question or completes the statement. *PRINT THE LETTER OF THE CORRECT ANSWER IN THE SPACE AT THE RIGHT.*

1. The line $2y = 6x+4$ intersects the x axis at

    A. 2   B. 2/3   C. -1/2   D. -2/3

    1.___

2. If $x = 3$ and $3x^4 - x + 4x^0 - 3x^{-1} = y$, then y equals

    A. 81   B. 235   C. 240   D. 243

    2.___

3. If $\sqrt{x^2 + 9} - x = 1$, then x is

    A. 9   B. 5   C. 4   D. 2

    3.___

4. If $\frac{1}{x} = y + \frac{1}{2}$, then x is equal to

    A. $\frac{2+1}{2y+1}$ B. $\frac{y^2}{2}$ C. Y^2 D. $\frac{2}{2y+1}$

    4.___

5. If $\sqrt{x} = \frac{y^2}{z}$ then y is equal to

    A. x^2z^3 B. $xz^{\frac{3}{2}}$ C. $(x^2z)^{\frac{1}{3}}$ D. $(xz^2)^{\frac{1}{4}}$

    5.___

6. The square root of $4x^2 - 12xy + 9y^2$ is

    A. $(2x-9y)(2x-y)$ B. $(2x-3y)$
    C. $(2x-3y)(2x+3y)$ D. $(2x-3y)(2x-3y)$

    6.___

7. In the simultaneous equations: $(2x^2-3y^2 = 50)$, one value of x is
   $(3x^2-2y^2 = 115)$

    A. 4   B. 5   C. 6   D. 7

    7.___

8. The expression $(-\frac{T^6}{27})^{\frac{1}{3}}$ is equivalent to

    A. $\frac{-T^2}{3}$ B. $\frac{T^{\frac{2}{3}}}{9}$ C. $\frac{T^{18}}{3}$ D. $\frac{T^{\frac{1}{2}}}{9}$

    8.___

9. The fraction $\dfrac{R - \frac{R}{t}}{\frac{1}{t} - 1}$ is equal to

   A. R B. 1/R C. -R D. -Rt

10. If the product of 0.02 and 0.0003 is written in the form 6×10^n, the value of n is

    A. -3 B. -4 C. -5 D. -6

11. The value of $\sqrt{275.56}$ is

    A. 15.8 B. 16.2 C. 16.6 D. 16.9

12. Function y varies inversely as x. If y = 1 when x = 9, then when x = 3, y is equal to

    A. 2 B. 3 C. 12 D. 18

13. The expression $(10a^2 - 3a - 18)$ divided by $(5a+6)$ is equal to

    A. (2a+3) B. (3a-2) C. (3a+2) D. (2a-3)

14. The roots of the equation $2x^2 - x - 15 = 0$ are

    A. -3.0 + 2.5
    B. +3.0, -5.0
    C. +1.5, -5.0
    D. +3.0, -2.5

15. The equation $\dfrac{x^2}{a^2} - \dfrac{y^2}{b^2} = 1$ is the formula for a(n)

    A. catenary B. ellipse C. hyperbola D. cycloid

16. The value of x that will satisfy the equation $x^3 - x^2 - 4 = 0$ is

    A. 3 B. 2 C. 1 D. -1

17. In the two simultaneous equations (3x+y=17), (2x-y=8), the value of y is

    A. 1 B. 2 C. 3 D. 4

18. The value of $\dfrac{3+\sqrt{y}}{3-\sqrt{y}} - \dfrac{3-\sqrt{y}}{3+\sqrt{y}}$ is equal to

    A. 9 B. $\dfrac{\sqrt{y}}{3}$ C. $\dfrac{12\sqrt{y}}{9-y}$ D. $\dfrac{12y}{24-y^2}$

19. (x+3y)(x-y) is equal to

    A. $x^2 + 2xy - 3y^2$ B. $x^2 + 4xy - 3y^2$
    C. $x^2 - 3y^2$ D. $x^2 + 4xy + 3y^2$

20. If $f = k(\frac{1}{r})^2$, then 1 is equal to

    A. $r\dfrac{\sqrt{f}}{k}$ B. $\dfrac{\sqrt{rf}}{k}$ C. $\dfrac{\sqrt{k}}{rf}$ D. $\dfrac{\sqrt{fk}}{r}$

KEY (CORRECT ANSWERS)

1. D	6. B	11. C	16. B
2. D	7. D	12. B	17. B
3. C	8. A	13. D	18. C
4. D	9. C	14. D	19. A
5. D	10. D	15. C	20. A

4 (#2)

SOLUTIONS TO PROBLEMS

1. When a line intersects the x-axis, the y value is zero. Thus, $2(0) = 6x + 4$. $6x = $, so $x = -\frac{4}{6} = -\frac{2}{3}$

2. $y = 3(3^4) - 3 + 4(3^0) - 3(3^{-1}) = 243 - 3 + 4 - 1 = 243$

3. $\sqrt{x^2+9} - x = 1$. Then $\sqrt{x^2+9} = x+1$ Squaring both sides, $x^2 + 9 = x^2 + 2x + 1$. Simplifying, $9 = 2x + 1$. Thus, $x = 4$.

4. $\frac{1}{x} = y + \frac{1}{2}$. Then, $\frac{1}{x} = \frac{1}{y+\frac{1}{2}} = \frac{1}{(2x+1)/2} = \frac{2}{2y+1}$

5. $\sqrt{x} = \frac{y^2}{z}$. Then, $y^2 = z\sqrt{x}$. Thus, $y = (z\sqrt{x})^{\frac{1}{2}} = (zx^{\frac{1}{2}})^{\frac{1}{2}} = x^{\frac{1}{4}} z^{\frac{1}{2}} = (xz^2)^{\frac{1}{4}}$

6. $\sqrt{4x^2 - 12xy + 9y^2} = \sqrt{(2x-3y)^2} = 2x - 3y$

7. Multiply the 1st equation by 2 and the 2nd equation by 3 to get $4x^2 - 6y^2 = 100$ and $9x^2 - 6y^2 = 345$. Subtracting, we get $5x^2 = 245$. So, $x^2 = 49$ and $x = 7$

8. $(-\frac{T^6}{27})^{\frac{1}{3}} = -\frac{T^2}{3}$ Then 1/3 power means cube root.

9. $(R - \frac{R}{t}) \div (\frac{1}{t} - 1) = \frac{Rt-R}{t} \div \frac{1-t}{t} = \frac{R(t-1)}{t} \cdot \frac{t}{1-t} = -R$ ·
    Note: t-1 is the additive inverse of 1-t

10. $(.02)(.0003) = .000006 = 6 \times 10^{-6}$. Thus, $n = -6$

11. $\sqrt{275.56} = 16.6$

12. $\frac{1}{y} = \frac{3}{9}$. $3y = 9$, so $y = 3$

13. $(10a^2 - 3a - 18) \div (5a+6) = 2a - 3$

```
            2a - 3
  5a+6 )10a² - 3a - 18
        10a² + 12a
        ─────────
             -15a - 18
             -15a - 18
             ─────────
                     0
```

14. $2x^2 - x - 15 = 0$. Factoring, $(2x+5)(x-3) = 0$.
    Solving, $x = -5/2$ = and $x = 3$

15. $\dfrac{x^2}{a^2} - \dfrac{y^2}{b^2} = 1$ represents a hyperbola

16. 2 is a root since $2^3 - 2^2 - 4 = 8 - 4 - 4 = 0$

17. Adding the equations yields $5x = 25$, so $x = 5$. Substituting into the 1st equation, $(3)(5) + y = 17$. $15 + y = 17$, so $y = 2$

18. $(3 + \sqrt{y}) \div (3 - \sqrt{y}) = [(3 + \sqrt{y})(3 + \sqrt{y})] \div [(3 - \sqrt{y})(3 + \sqrt{y})] =$

    $(9 + 6\sqrt{y} + y) \div (9 - y)$. Thus, the 2nd given fraction must be equivalent to

    $(9 - 6\sqrt{y} + y) \div (9 - y)$. Subtracting, we get

    $[(9 + 6\sqrt{y} + y) - (9 - 6\sqrt{y} + y)] \div (9 - y) = 12\sqrt{y} / (9 - y)$

19. $(x + 3y)(x - y) = x^2 - xy + 3xy - 3y^2 = x^2 + 2xy - 3y^2$

20. $f = k(\tfrac{1}{r})^2 \cdot \dfrac{f}{k} = (\tfrac{1}{r})^2$. Taking square roots, $\sqrt{\dfrac{f}{k}} = \dfrac{1}{r}$

    Then, $1 = r\sqrt{\dfrac{f}{k}} = \dfrac{r}{k}\sqrt{fk}$

TEST 3

DIRECTIONS: Each question or incomplete statement is followed by several suggested answers or completions. Select the one that BEST answers the question or completes the statement. *PRINT THE LETTER OF THE CORRECT ANSWER IN THE SPACE AT THE RIGHT.*

1. If $x = \sqrt{.64y^2}$, then $x^2 =$

   A. $.8y$ B. $.64y^2$ C. $\sqrt{.8y}$ D. $.8\sqrt{y}$

2. If $x = \sqrt{p-r}$, then $x =$

   A. $\dfrac{1}{(p-r)^2}$ B. $\dfrac{1}{(p-r)}$ C. $(p-r)^{\frac{1}{2}}$ D. $\sqrt{p}-\sqrt{r}$

3. The reciprocal of $2p/5r$ is

   A. $-\dfrac{2p}{5r}$ B. $\dfrac{\sqrt{2p}}{5r}$ C. $\dfrac{5r}{2p}$ D. $10pr$

4. $(7x-2y)(3x+9y) =$

   A. $21x^2 + 57xy - 18y^2$
   B. $21x^2 + 11xy - 18y^2$
   C. $10x^2 + 11xy + 7y^2$
   D. $7x^2 + 19xy - 6y^2$

5. The $\sqrt{543}$ is MOST NEARLY equal to

   A. 23.20   B. 23.25   C. 23.30   D. 23.35

6. $\dfrac{x-2}{x^2-6x+8}$ can be reduced to

   A. $\dfrac{1}{x-2}$ B. $\dfrac{x-2}{x-4}$ C. $\dfrac{1}{x-4}$ D. $\dfrac{1}{x+4}$

7. The expression $\sqrt{7} + \sqrt{28}$ reduces to

   A. $3\sqrt{7}$ B. $\sqrt{35}$ C. $\sqrt{196}$ D. $7^{\frac{3}{2}}$

8. $(1+r)^4$ is equal to

   A. $1+3r+6r^2+3r^3+r^4$
   B. $1+2r+3r^2+2r^3+r^4$
   C. $1+4r+6r^2+4r^3+r^4$
   D. $1+6r+12r^2+6r^3+r^4$

9. Which of the following is a root in the equation $3x^3 + 8x^2 + 9x + 10 = 0$?

   A. -5   B. -4   C. -3   D. -2

10. If $r = \dfrac{\sqrt{I}}{A}$ then I equals

    A. r^2-A B. $\sqrt{rA}$ C. r^2A^2 D. r^2A

11. If $y = x^{2x}$, the value of y for $x = 3$ is

    A. 27   B. 81   C. 243   D. 729

12. The factors of $x^{2n}-1$ are

    A. $(x^n+1),(x^n-1)$ B. $(x^2+1),(x^{n-1})$
    C. $(x^{2n}+1),(x-1)$ D. $(x^2-1),(x^n)$

13. If $4\sqrt{2} = \sqrt{n}$, the value of n is

    A. 8   B. 36   C. 32   D. 16

14. If it costs <u>a</u> cents for the first 10 words and <u>b</u> cents for each additional word, a formula for finding the cost <u>c</u> of sending a telegram is for n words

    A. $c = a + b(n-10)$ B. $c = a + 10 + bn$
    C. $c = a + b(10-n)$ D. $c = 2 + 10(b-n)$

15. If n is b greater than r, the one of the following that is NOT true is

    A. $n - b = r$ B. $n = b + r$ C. $n - r = b$ D. $n + b = r$

16. $2^3 \times 2^{-1} + 2^0$ is equal to

    A. 5   B. 6   C. -16   D. 8

17. 32 x 72 is equal to

    A. $3^8 \times 2^3$ B. $3^2 \times 2^8$ C. $3^2 \times 2^6$ D. $3^3 \times 2^8$

18. $A = \{a,b,c,d,e\}$
    $B = \{a,d,e,g\}$
    A U B is

    A. $\{d,e\}$ B. $\{2a,b,c,2d,2e,g\}$
    C. $\{a,b,c,d,e,g\}$ D. $\{b,c,g\}$

19. The positive root of $x^2 + 5x - 36 = 0$ is

    A. 4   B. 9   C. 12   D. 3

20. The SMALLEST of 3 consecutive numbers is n.   20.____
    The average of these 3 integers is

    A. $\dfrac{n+2}{3}$ B. $(n+1)$ C. $\dfrac{3(n+1)}{2}$ D. $\dfrac{3n}{3}$

KEY (CORRECT ANSWERS)

1. B	6. C	11. D	16. A
2. C	7. A	12. A	17. B
3. C	8. C	13. C	18. C
4. A	9. D	14. A	19. A
5. C	10. C	15. D	20. B

SOLUTIONS TO PROBLEMS

1. $x^2 = (\sqrt{.64y^2})^2 = .64y^2$

2. $\sqrt{p-r}$ is equivalent to $(p-r)^{\frac{1}{2}}$

3. The reciprocal of $\frac{2p}{5r}$ is $\frac{5r}{2p}$

4. $(7x-2y)(3x+9y) = 21x^2 + 63xy - 6xy - 18y^2 = 21x^2 + 57xy - 18y^2$

5. $\sqrt{543} \approx 23.30$

6. $(x-2)/(x^2-6x+8) = (x-2)/[(x-2)(x-4)] = \frac{1}{x-4}$

7. $\sqrt{7} + \sqrt{28} = \sqrt{7} + \sqrt{4}\sqrt{7} = \sqrt{7} + 2\sqrt{7} = 3\sqrt{7}$

8. $(1+r)^4 = 1^4 + (4)(1^3)(r) + (6)(1^2)(r^2) + (4)(1)(r^3) + r^4 = 1 + 4r + 6r^2 + 4r^3 + r^4$

9. By substitution, -2 is a root since $3(-2)^3 + 8(-2)^2 + 9(-2) + 10 = -24 + 32 - 18 + 10 = 0$

10. $r = \frac{\sqrt{I}}{A}$. Then, $rA = \sqrt{I}$, so $I = r^2A^2$

11. $y = 3^{2(3)} = 3^6 = 729$

12. $x^{2n} - 1 = (x^n - 1)(x^n + 1)$

13. $4\sqrt{2} = \sqrt{n}$. Then, $n = (4\sqrt{2})^2 = (16)(2) = 32$

14. Suppose n = 25 words. The cost would be a cents for the first 10 words and b cents for each additional word of the remaining 15 words. In general, c = a + b(n-10)

15. If n is b greater than r, then we could write n = b + r. The statement which is false is n + b = r

16. $2^3 \times 2^{-1} + 2^0 = 8 \times \frac{1}{2} + 1 = 4 + 1 = 5$

17. $32 = 2^5$, $72 = 2^3 \times 3^2$. Then, 32 x 72 could be written as $2^5 \times 2^3 \times 3^2 = 3^2 \times 2^8$

18. A∪B means all elements in A or B or both A and B = {a,b,c,d,e,g}

19. $x^2 + 5x - 36 = 0$ can be factored as $(x+9)(x-4) = 0$. The positive root is $x = 4$

20. The 3 consecutive numbers are n, n+1, and n+2. Their average is n+1

TEST 4

DIRECTIONS: Each question is followed by several suggested answers. Select the one that BEST answers the question and write the letter of your answer in the space at right.

1. If the number 32,71x,357,86y (x and y representing digits in the decimal system) is divisible by 9, then

    A. x + y must equal 3
    B. y cannot equal 0
    C. x + y must equal 3 or 12
    D. x cannot equal 0

    1.___

2. An auto leaves point A at 8:00 A.M. traveling at the uniform rate of 40 miles per hour. If a second auto leaves point A at 8:30 A.M. traveling at the uniform rate of 50 miles per hour, the second auto will overtake the first auto at

    A. 10:00 A.M.
    B. 10:30 A.M.
    C. 11:00 A.M.
    D. 11:30 A.M.

    2.___

3. $\underline{A}$ can do a piece of work in 9 days. $\underline{B}$ is 50% more efficient than A. The number of days it takes $\underline{B}$ to do the same piece of work is

    A. 13 1/2
    B. 4 1/2
    C. 6
    D. 3

    3.___

4. If $2x^2 - kx = -18$, the two roots of the equation are equal when k equals

    A. 12
    B. -6
    C. 6
    D. ±12

    4.___

5. If x and y are positive integers greater than 1, the arrangement of the expressions,

    $a = \dfrac{x-1}{y+1}$ $b = \dfrac{x}{y-1}$ $c = \dfrac{x-1}{y}$ $d = \dfrac{x}{y}$ in ascending order of value, is

    A. d, b, c, a
    B. a, b, c, d
    C. b, d, a, c
    D. a, c, d, b

    5.___

6. The number of quarts of a 60% strength solution that should be added to 12 quarts of a 30% strength solution to make a 50% strength solution is

    A. 6 B. 12 C. 24 D. 36

    6.___

7. If 64 is divided into three parts proportional to 2, 4 and 6, the smallest part is   7.____

   A. 5 1/3
   B. 11
   C. 10 2/3
   D. 5

8. A tree casts a shadow 3 yards 1 foot long at the same time that a pole 7 feet 6 inches   8.____
   high casts a shadow 2 feet long (the tree and the pole are perpendicular to the ground).
   The height of the tree in yards is

   A. 11 1/2
   B. 12
   C. 12 1/2
   D. 13

9. The graph of y = x is a   9.____

   A. straight line
   B. broken line
   C. curved line
   D. single point

10. If the digit 1 is placed after a two digit number whose tens' digit is t, and whose units' digit   10.____
    is u, the new number is

    A. 10t + u + 1
    B. 100t + 10u + 1
    C. 1000t + 10u + 1
    D. t + u + 1

11. A number is represented by 321 written in the base 4. Rewritten in the base 10, the num-   11.____
    ber is

    A. 40
    B. 46
    C. 57
    D. 214

12. If d is a member of the set of odd numbers and e is a member of the set of even num-   12.____
    bers, an INCORRECT statement is

    A. d x d = an odd number
    B. e x d = an even number
    C. d + d = an odd number
    D. e + d = an odd number

13. When a student states that $\frac{5y-8}{4} = 5y - 2$, he is failing to make proper use of the

    A. associative principle
    B. distributive principle
    C. commutative principle
    D. additive inverse

13.___

KEY (CORRECT ANSWERS)

1. **C**
   In order for a number to be divisible by 9, the sum of its digits must be divisible by 9. Thus, $3 + 2 + 7 + 1 + x + 3 + 5 + 7 + 8 + 6 + y = 42 + x + y$ must be divisible by 9. Since 45 is one such number, $x + y = 3$ is a possibility. Also 54 is divisible by 9, so $x + y = 12$ is another option. NOTE: Although 63 also is divisible by 9, this would force $x + y = 21$; this is impossible because x and y are only single digits.

2. **B**
   Let x = time traveled by the 2nd auto and x + 1/2 = time traveled by the 1st auto. These times represent hours. Using (rate) x (time) = distance and noting that the distances are equal for the two autos, $40 (x + 1/2) = 50x$. This becomes $40x + 20 = 50x$. Solving, x = 2 hours. Add the 2 hours to 8:30 A.M. to get 10:30 A.M.

3. **C**
   Since B is 50% more efficient, B can accomplish 1.5 times as much as A in the same time. Thus, if the same work needs to be done by both A and B, just divide A's time by 1.5 to get B's time. So, $9 \div 1.5 = 6$.

4. **D**
   Rewrite the equation as $2x^2 - kx + 18 = 0$. By the Quadratic Formula, the roots are:

   $$\frac{k + k^2 - (4)(2)(18)}{(2)(2)} \text{ and } \frac{k - k^2 - (4)(2)(18)}{(2)(2)}$$

   For these roots to be equal, $k^2 - 144$ must equal 0.
   Then, $k^2 - 144 = (k-12)(k+12) = 0$, which leads to k = 12 and -12.
   As a check, if k = 12, the roots are 3. If k = -12, the roots are -3.

4 (#4)

5. **D**

   A fraction is made bigger by increasing the numerator and/or decreasing the denominator. $\frac{x-y}{y}$ must be less than $\frac{x}{y}$. $\frac{x}{y}$ must be less than $\frac{x}{y-1}$. Finally, $\frac{x-1}{y+1}$ must be less than $\frac{x-1}{y}$. The correct order: $\frac{x-1}{y+1}, \frac{x-y}{y}, \frac{x}{y}, \frac{x}{y-1}$

6. **C**

   Let x = number of required quarts. Then .60x + (.30)(12) = (.50)(x +12). Simplifying, .60x + 3.6 = .50x + 6. This becomes .10x = 2.4. Solving, x = 24.

7. **C**

   Let 2x = smallest part, and 4x, 6x = other two parts. Then 2x + 4x + 6x = 64. 12x = 64. x = 51/3. So the smallest part, 2x, is 10 2/3.

8. **C**

   The ratio of the tree's height to its shadow must equal the ratio of the pole's height to its shadow. Let x = height of the tree in feet. Then $\frac{x}{10} = \frac{7.5}{2}$.

   Solving, $x = 37.5 \text{ feet} = \frac{37.5}{3}$ yards or 12 1/2 yards.

9. **A**

   Any equation of the form y = mx + b, m,b constants, must be a straight line. y = x can be written as y = 1 x + 0, and so must be a straight line.

10. **B**

    The t gets shifted to the hundreds place and the u gets shifted to the tens place. The number appears as "tu1" and has a value of 100t + 10u + 1.

11. **C**

    321 in base 4 means (in base 10), $3 \times 4^2 + 2 \times 4^1 + 1 = 48 + 8 + 1 = 57$.

12. **C**

    Since the sum of two odd numbers is always an even number, d + d = odd number is wrong.

13. **B**

    $\frac{5y-8}{4} = \frac{5}{4}y - \frac{8}{4}$ or $\frac{5}{4}y - 2$ By incorrectly writing 5y-2, the Distributive Principle has not been used properly.

EXAMINATION SECTION
TEST 1

DIRECTIONS: Each question or incomplete statement is followed by several suggested answers or completions. Select the one that BEST answers the question or completes the statement. *PRINT THE LETTER OF THE CORRECT ANSWER IN THE SPACE AT THE RIGHT.*

1. What is the equation of the locus of points P such that the sum of the distances from P to the two points (5,0) and (-5,0) is always 14 units? 1._____

    A. $24x^2 + 49y^2 = 1176$
    B. $24x^2 + 25y^2 = 600$
    C. $49x^2 + 24y^2 = 1176$
    D. $25x^2 + 24y^2 = 600$

2. If f = {(0,3), (1,5), (2,7)} and g = {(0,-1), (1,0), (2,3)}, then f - 2g is equal to 2._____

    A. {(0,8), (1,5), (2,1)}
    B. {(0,4), (1,5), (2,4)}
    C. {(0,8), (1,5), (2,4)}
    D. {(0,5), (-1,5), (-2,1)}

3. The line segment joining A(1,-4,3) to B(5,6,-1) in space is extended its own length through B to D. 3._____
   If the coordinates of D are (x_1, y_1, z_1), then z_1 =

    A. 5   B. -5   C. 1   D. -5/2

4. The center and radius of the sphere whose equation is $x^2 + 4x + y^2 - 2y + z^2 = 59$ are, respectively, 4._____

    A. (2, -1, 0) and 4
    B. (2, -1, 0) and 8
    C. (-2, 1, 0) and 4
    D. (-2, 1, 0) and 8

5. Given the following sets: the set of 5._____
    I. positive integers under addition
    II. integers under multiplication
    III. non-zero rational numbers under addition
    IV. non-zero rational numbers under multiplication
   Which one of the above sets forms a group?

    A. I   B. II   C. III   D. IV

6. If the roots of a quadratic equation, $ax^2 + bx + c = 0$, are x_1 and x_2, then 6._____

    A. $x_1 + x_2 = -\dfrac{b}{a}$ and $x_1 \cdot x_2 = \dfrac{c}{a}$

    B. $x_1 + x_2 = \dfrac{a}{b}$ and $x_1 \cdot x_2 = \dfrac{a}{c}$

    C. $x_1 + x_2 = \dfrac{b}{a}$ and $x_1 \cdot x_2 = -\dfrac{c}{a}$

    D. $x_1 + x_2 = -\dfrac{c}{a}$ and $x_1 \cdot x_2 = \dfrac{b}{a}$

7. $\dfrac{a^{-1}b^{-1}}{a^{-3}-b^{-3}}$ where $a \neq b$, equals which one of the following expressions?

   A. $\dfrac{a^2b^2}{a^3-b^3}$ B. $\dfrac{a^3-b^3}{a^2b^2}$ C. $\dfrac{b^3-a^3}{a^2b^2}$ D. $\dfrac{a^2b^2}{b^3-a^3}$

8. If an automobile travels at the rate of m miles per hour for p hours, and n miles per hour for q hours, then its average rate, in miles per hour, for the entire distance is which one of the following?

   A. $\dfrac{m+n}{2}$ B. $\dfrac{m}{p}+\dfrac{n}{q}$ C. $\dfrac{mp+nq}{2}$ D. $\dfrac{mp+nq}{p+q}$

9. If log 2 = .30 and log 3 = .48, then log 72 equals which one of the following?

   A. 1.38 B. 1.56 C. 1.86 D. 2.34

10. If the determinant $\begin{vmatrix} 2 & -x & 1 \\ 2 & -3 & 1 \\ -4 & 3 & 1 \end{vmatrix}$ is equal to zero, then x equals

    A. 1 B. 2 C. 3 D. -3

11. If $(x+iy)(2x-iy) = 4$, where x and y are real numbers and $i = \sqrt{-1}$ then which one of the following is always TRUE?

    A. $2x^2-y^2=4$
    B. $xy = 4$
    C. $xy = 0$
    D. $2x^2 + y^2 = 0$

12. If $x^3 + kx + 48$ is divisible by $(x-2)$, then it is also divisible by which one of the following binomials?

    A. x-1 B. x-3 C. x-4 D. x-6

13. If the sum of two of the roots of $9x^3 - 45x^2 - 4x + k = 0$ is 0, then the value of k is

    A. 0 B. 5 C. 10 D. 20

14. The real values of x such that $x^2 - x - 2 > 0$ can be described in which of the following ways?

    A. Either x < -1 or x > 2
    B. -1 < x < 2
    C. Either x < -2 or x > 1
    D. -2 < x < 1

15. The non-terminating, repeating decimal 2.525252... can be written as a rational fraction. When reduced to lowest terms, the sum of the numerator and denominator of this fraction equals

    A. 141 B. 299 C. 349 D. 399

16. If x is a real number, then $\sqrt{x^2}$ equals which one of the following?

    A. x B. -x C. ±x D. $|x|$

17. If U is the set of real numbers, which one of the following is NOT in the domain of the function defined by xy + 2x - 4 - 3y = 0?

    A. 2 B. -3 C. 3 D. -2

18. If $f(X) = X + \dfrac{1}{X}, X \neq 0$ then $f(1+\dfrac{1}{y})$, $y \neq 0$, $y \neq -1$ equals

    A. $y + \dfrac{1}{y} + 1$
    B. $\dfrac{2y^2 + 2y + 1}{y(y+1)}$
    C. $y^2 + \dfrac{2}{y} + 1$
    D. $\dfrac{y^2 + 2y + 1}{y^2 + 1}$

19. The value of x which satisfies the equation is

    A. $\dfrac{1+\sqrt{3201}}{20}$ B. $2\dfrac{1}{3}$ C. 3 D. 1000

20. If U is the set of real numbers, then the graph of {(x,y) | (2x+3y < 12} is the half-plane

    A. above the line 2x + 3y = 12
    B. to the right of the line 2x + 3y = 12
    C. below the x-axis
    D. below the line 2x + 3y = 12

KEY (CORRECT ANSWERS)

1. A	6. A	11. C	16. D
2. D	7. D	12. C	17. C
3. B	8. D	13. D	18. C
4. D	9. C	14. A	19. D
5. D	10. C	15. C	20. D

SOLUTIONS TO PROBLEMS

1. Let P be located at (x,y). Then, $\sqrt{(x-5)^2 + (y-0)^2} + \sqrt{(x+5)^2 + (y-0)^2} = 14$

   Simplified, this equation becomes $24x^2 + 49y^2 = 1176$, which represents an ellipse. (Ans. A)

2. $2g = \{(0,-2), (2,0), (4,6)\}$. Thus, $f - 2g = \{(0,5), (-1,5), (-2,1)\}$, (Ans. D)

3. Since B is the midpoint of $\overline{AD}$, $-1 = \dfrac{3+z_1}{2}$, $z_1 = -5$. (Ans. B)

4. Rewrite $x^2 + 4x + y^2 - 2y + z^2 = 59$ as $(x+2)^2 + (y-1)^2 + (z-0)^2 = 64$. The center of the sphere is $(-2,1,0)$ and the radius = 8. (Ans. D)

5. A group must have associativity, closure, identity element, and inverses. The non-zero rational numbers under multiplication would satisfy each requirement. The identity element = 1 and for each x, the number $\dfrac{1}{x}$ = inverse (Ans. D)

6. The sum of roots = $-\dfrac{b}{a}$, and the product of roots = $\dfrac{c}{a}$. (Ans. A)

7. $a^{-1} \cdot b^{-1} = \dfrac{1}{ab}$. $a^{-3} - b^{-3} = \dfrac{1}{a^3} - \dfrac{1}{b^3} = (b^3 - a^3)/a^3b^3$

   Thus, the original fraction can be written as:

   $\dfrac{1}{ab} \div [(b^3 - a^3)/a^3b^3] = a^2b^2 / (b^3 - a^3)$. (Ans. D)

8. Total distance = mp + nq. Total time = p + q.
   Average rate = (mp+nq)/(p+q). (Ans. D)

9. Log 72 = Log (9·8) = Log 9 + Log 8 = 2 Log 3 + 3 Log 2 = 1.86 (Ans. C)

10. $-6 + 4x + 6 - (12 - 2x + 6) = 0$. Solving, x = 3. (Ans. C)

11. $(x+iy)(2x-iy) = 2x^2 + ixy + y^2 = 4$. This implies that xy = 0. (Ans. C)

12. 2 must be a solution of $x^3 + kx + 48 = 0$. Thus, $2^3 + (k)(2) + 48 = 0$, and so k = -28. The original polynomial equation is $x^3 - 28x + 48 = 0$. Since 4 is also a solution to this equation, x-4 is a factor. (Ans. C)

13. If k = 20, $9x^3 - 45x^2 - 4x + 20 = 0$ becomes $9x^2(x-5) - 4(x-5) = 0$. This equation further simplifies to $(3x-2)(3x+2)(x-5) = 0$, and two of the roots are $\dfrac{2}{3}$ and $-\dfrac{2}{3}$. (Ans. D)

14. $x^2 - x - 2 > 0$ means $(x-2)(x+1) > 0$, which implies both $x - 2 > 0$ and $x + 1 > 0$ or both $x - 2 < 0$ and $x + 1 < 0$. The solution is $x > 2$ or $x < -1$. (Ans. A)

15. Let $N = 2.\overline{52}$. Then, $100N = 252.\overline{52}$. By subtraction, $99N = 250$ and $N = \dfrac{250}{99}$. The sum of the numerator and denominator is 349. (Ans. C)

16. $\sqrt{x^2}$ always $= |x|$ whether $x \geq 0$ or $x < 0$. (Ans. D)

17. If x were 3, we would have 3y+6-4-3y=0, which leads to the contradiction 2=0. (Ans. C)

18. $f(1+\dfrac{1}{y}) = 1+\dfrac{1}{y}+[1\div(1+\dfrac{1}{y})] = 1+\dfrac{1}{y}+\dfrac{y}{y+1} = \dfrac{2y^2+2y+1}{y(y+1)}$

19. $\text{Log } x^2 = 2 \text{ Log } x$ and $\text{Log}\dfrac{x}{10} = \text{Log} x - \text{Log} 10 = \text{Log } x - 1$.
    Rewrite the original equation as $2 \text{ Log } x + \text{Log } x - 1 = 8$. This becomes $3 \text{ Log } x = 9$, which has the solution $x = 1000$. (Ans. D)

20. Since $2x + 3y < 12$ becomes $y < -\dfrac{2}{3}x + 4$, its graph lies below $2x + 3y = 12$. (Ans. D)

TEST 2

DIRECTIONS: Each question or incomplete statement is followed by several suggested answers or completions. Select the one that BEST answers the question or completes the statement. *PRINT THE LETTER OF THE CORRECT ANSWER IN THE SPACE AT THE RIGHT.*

1. Of the following sets of ordered pairs, the one set that is NOT a function is 1.___

    A. $\{(0,1), (1,1), (2,1), (3,1), (4,1)\}$
    B. $\{(0,0), (1,1), (2,2), (3,3), (4,4)\}$
    C. $\{(-1,-2), (0,-1), (1,0), (2,1), (3,3)\}$
    D. $\{(-1,1), (-1,-1), (0,0), (1,1), (1,-1)\}$

2. The set of real numbers which satisfies $|2x-3| = 5$ is 2.___

    A. $\{4\}$ B. $\{-1\}$ C. $\{-1,4\}$ D. the empty set

3. The equation of the line parallel to the line $2y = 3x - 5$ and passing through the midpoint of the line segment whose end points are at (-5,6) and (1,4) is which one of the following? 3.___

    A. $2x - 3y + 19 = 0$ B. $3x - 2y + 4 = 0$
    C. $2y - 3x + 16 = 0$ D. $3x - 2y + 16 = 0$

4. The radius of the circle $x^2 + 8x + y^2 - 10y - 8 = 0$ is 4.___

    A. $\sqrt{8}$ B. $\sqrt{41}$ C. 7 D. 8

5. Which one of the following is the equation of the parabola with vertex at (3, 2) and focus at (3, 4)? 5.___

    A. $y^2 - 6y - 4x + 17 = 0$ B. $x^2 - 6x - 4y + 17 = 0$
    C. $x^2 - 6x - 8y + 25 = 0$ D. $y^2 - 6y - 8x + 25 = 0$

6. The number of negative real roots of the equation $x^3 + 3x = 5$ is 6.___

    A. 0 B. 1 C. 2 D. 3

7. All of the following are correct EXCEPT 7.___

    A. $\log(x^{-a}) = -a \log x$ B. $\log \sqrt[a]{x} = \frac{1}{a} \log x$
    C. $\log(x^{-a}) = -a \log x^a$ D. $\log \frac{x}{a} = \log x - \log a$

8. The MAXIMUM number of subsets which a set of eight different elements has is 8.___

    A. 8 B. 8^2 C. 256 D. 512

9. The ordered pairs of numbers which make both inequalities $x + y > 2$ and $x - y < 1$ true lie in quadrants 9.___

    A. 2 and 3 B. 1 and 4 C. 1 and 2 D. 3 and 4

90

10. In the universe of real numbers, the one of the following in which the relation is a function is

   A. $\{(x,y) \mid y = |x-5|\}$
   B. $\{(x,y) \mid x = |2-y|\}$
   C. $\{(x,y) \mid y > x + 2\}$
   D. $\{(x,y) \mid x = -5\}$

11. $\{x \mid x < 4\} \cap \{x \mid x > -3\}$ equals

   A. $\{-3 < x < 4\}$
   B. $\{4 < x < -3\}$
   C. $\{x > -3\}$
   D. $\{x < 4\}$

12. If $\log_{10} 2 = .30$, $\log_{10} 3 = .48$, and $\log_{10} 5 = .70$, the value of $\log_{10} \dfrac{(675)^3}{\sqrt[5]{576}}$ is

   A. 2.29
   B. 5.76
   C. 7.97
   D. 9.07

13. If a, b, and c are in arithmetic progression, and b, c, and d are in geometric progression, a equals

   A. $b(2-d)$
   B. $\dfrac{c(2c-d)}{d}$
   C. $\dfrac{c^2}{d} - c$
   D. $c(2c-1)$

14. The number of terms in the expansion of $(a+b+c)^4$ is

   A. 7
   B. 12
   C. 15
   D. 16

15. If $x + 2y + (2x-y)i = 5 - 2i$, then

   A. $x = 5$ and $y = -2$
   B. $x = 3$ and $y = 1$
   C. $x = \dfrac{4}{5}$ and $y = \dfrac{16}{5}$
   D. $x = \dfrac{1}{5}$ and $y = \dfrac{12}{5}$

16. The solution of the inequalities $6y < 7y + 4$ and $2 - 3y \geq -1$ is

   A. $-4 < y \leq 1$
   B. $-3 < y \, 2$
   C. $-5 < y \leq 4$
   D. none of these

17. The third term of the expansion of $(3+2x)^{\frac{1}{2}}$ is

   A. $-\dfrac{\sqrt{3}}{18} x^2$
   B. $-\dfrac{x}{\sqrt{3}}$
   C. $\dfrac{\sqrt{3}}{54} x^3$
   D. $\sqrt[2]{3x}$

18. If $p = \dfrac{A[1-(1+i)^{-n}]}{i}$, n equals

   A. $\dfrac{\log A - \log ip}{\log(1+i)}$

   B. $\dfrac{\log(1+i)}{\log A - \log(A-ip)}$

   C. $\dfrac{\log A \log(A-ip)}{\log(1+i)}$

   D. $\dfrac{\log A - \log(A-ip)}{\log(1+i)}$

19. When a and b are positive integers, a - b can be factored for all values of a and b, if the domain of the factors is the

   A. integers
   B. rational numbers
   C. numbers with bases other than 10
   D. real numbers

20. If one root of the equation $x^3 - kx^2 + 17x - 13 = 0$ is $2 + 3i$, another root is

   A. -1   B. +1   C. -13   D. +13

KEY (CORRECT ANSWERS)

1. D	6. A	11. A	16. A
2. C	7. B	12. C	17. A
3. D	8. C	13. B	18. D
4. C	9. C	14. C	19. B
5. C	10. A	15. D	20. B

SOLUTIONS TO PROBLEMS

1. $\{(-1,1), (-1,-1), (0,0), (1,1), (1,-1)\}$ is NOT a function since it can be shown that for at least one given x, there corresponds more than one y-value. For example, when $x = -1$, y can equal either 1 or -1. (Ans. D)

2. $|2x-3| = 5$ means $2x-3 = 5$ or $2x-3 = -5$. Solving these equations, we get 4, -1. (Ans. C)

3. The midpoint of the segment connecting (-5, 6) and (1, 4) is (-2, 5). The line's slope = which is the same as the of the line $2y = 3x-5$. Equation of the required line is

    $y - 5 = \frac{3}{2}(x + 2)$, which can be written as $3x - 2y + 16 = 0$. (Ans. D)

4. Rewrite as $(x^2+8x+16) + (y^2-10y+25) - 8 - 16 - 25 = 0$, which simplifies to $(x+4)^2 + (y-5)^2 = 49$. Thus, the radius = 7. (Ans. C)

5. The directrix is the x-axis. Any point (x, y) on the parabola must be the same distance to the x-axis as (x, y) is to (3, 4). Thus, $\sqrt{(x-3)^2 + (y-4)^2} = y$. This simplifies to $x^2 - 6x - 8y + 25 = 0$. (Ans. C)

6. The only possible rational roots of $x^3 + 3x - 5 = 0$ are 1, -1, 5, and -5; however, none of these numbers check the equation. By graphing, it can be seen that the one irrational root is +. (Ans. A)

7. $-\text{Log} x^a = \text{Log} x^{-a} = \text{Log} \frac{1}{x^a}$. However, $\text{Log}(-x^a)$ is not defined if $-x^a$ is a negative quantity. (Ans. B)

8. The maximum number of subsets associated with a set of n elements is 2^n. Thus, for a set of 8 elements, $2^8 = 256$ is the maximum number of subsets. (Ans. C)

9. 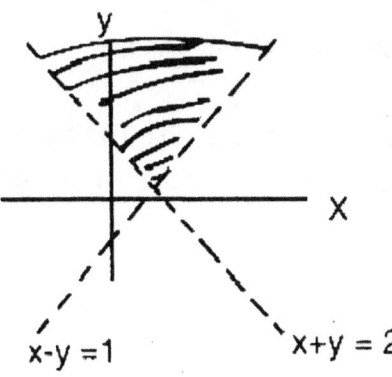 The shaded area represents the intersection of $x + y > 2$ and $x - y < 1$. (Ans. C)

10. $\{(x,y): y = |x-5|\}$ is a function since for each value of x, only one value of y is obtained. (Ans. A)

11. The intersection refers to the set of numbers common to both conditions, which is $-3 < x < 4$. (Ans. A)

5 (#2)

12. $\text{Log}\dfrac{(675)^3}{\sqrt[5]{576}} = 3\text{Log}\,675 - \dfrac{1}{5}\text{Log}\,576$. But, $675 = 5^2 \cdot 3^3$ and $576 = 2^6 \cdot 3^2$. Log 675 = 2 Log 5+3 Log 3 = 2.84. Log 576 = 6 Log 2+2 Log 3 = 2.76

    Thus, $3\text{Log}\,675 - \dfrac{1}{5}\text{Log}\,576 = 3(2.84) - \dfrac{1}{5}(2.76) = 7.97$. (Ans. C)

13. c - b = b - a if a, b, c are in arithmetic progression. b:c = c:d if b, c, d are in geometric progression.
    Thus, a = 2b - c, and since $b = c^2/d$, $a = 2c^2/d - c$ or $c(2c-d)/d$. (Ans. B)

14. $(a+b+c)^4 = [(a+b)+c]^4 = (a+b)^4 + 4(a+b)^3 c + 6(a+b)^2 c^2 + 4(a+b)c + c^4$, for which the number of terms = 5+4+3+2+1 = 15. (Ans. C)

15. Equating the real parts, x + 2y = 5. Equating the imaginary parts, 2x - y = -2. Solving,
    $x = \dfrac{1}{5}$ and $y = \dfrac{12}{5}$. (Ans. D)

16. 6y < 7y + 4 becomes y > -4 and 2 - 3y -1 becomes y ≤ 1.
    The solution of the intersection is - 4 < y ≤ 1. (Ans. A)

17. The third term $= \dfrac{(\frac{1}{2})(-\frac{1}{2})(3)^{-\frac{3}{2}}(2x)^2}{2} = \dfrac{-\sqrt{3}x^2}{18}$. (Ans. A)

18. $Pi = A - A(1+i)^{-n}$. Then, $(A-Pi)/A = (1+i)^{-n}$.
    Log (A-Pi) - Log A = -n Log (1+i). Finally,
    n = [Log A - Log (A-iP)]/Log (1+i) (Ans. D)

19. If we allow n = 1.n to be considered a factoring for an integer n, then either choice A or B is correct. However, if 1.n is disallowed, then choice B is the only correct answer. For example, if a = 7 and b = 2, a-b = 5 and (to illustrate) $5 = (4)(\dfrac{5}{4})$. (Ans. B)

20. A second root must be 2 - 3i and so x - 2 - 3i and x - 2 + 3i must both be factors of $x^3 - kx^2 + 17x - 13 = 0$. Now, the product of these two factors is $x^2 - 4x + 13$, so that the third factor must be x-1. The last root is therefore 1.
    (The value of k is 5.) (Ans. B)

TEST 3

DIRECTIONS: Each question or incomplete statement is followed by several suggested answers or completions. Select the one that BEST answers the question or completes the statement. *PRINT THE LETTER OF THE CORRECT ANSWER IN THE SPACE AT THE RIGHT.*

1. Two numbers have an arithmetic mean of 17 and a geometric mean of 15. Hence, the quadratic equation of which the numbers are roots is

    A. $x^2 + 15x + 17 = 0$
    B. $x^2 + 34x + 225 = 0$
    C. $x^2 - 34x + 225 = 0$
    D. $x^2 - 17x + 255 = 0$

    1._____

2. Assume three consecutive integers represented by (x-1), x, and (x+1). Which one of the following represents an equation which will determine these integers, provided it is known that the sum of the reciprocals of the integers is 47/60?

    A. $47x^3 + 180x^2 + 47x - 60 = 0$
    B. $47x^3 + 39x^2 - 266x - 120 = 0$
    C. $47x^3 - 180x^2 - 47x + 60 = 0$
    D. $47x^3 - 39x^2 + 266x - 120 = 0$

    2._____

3. The equation of a line perpendicular to the line $3x + 2y = 5$ and having an x intercept of -3 is

    A. $3x + 2y + 9 = 0$
    B. $2x - 3y + 6 = 0$
    C. $2x - 3y = 9$
    D. $3x + 2y + 6 = 0$

    3._____

4. By Kepler's Law, the square of the time for a complete revolution of a planet is proportioned to the cube of its mean distance from the sun.
If Planet X were 9 times as far from the sun as Earth, its time, in years, for one complete revolution would be

    A. 9   B. 15   C. 21   D. 27

    4._____

5. Of the following, the illustration of a denumerable set is the set of _____ numbers.

    A. rational   B. irrational   C. real   D. transcendental

    5._____

6. In the universe of real numbers, the one of the following in which the relation is a function is

    A. $\{(x,y) | x = y^2 - 1\}$
    B. $\{(x,y)\ y = x^2 + 1\}$
    C. $\{(x,y) | y = \pm\sqrt{16 - x^2}\}$
    D. $\{(x,y)\ y < x - 2\}$

    6._____

7. If A = ( ) and B = ( ), then A Ω B, the
       (a, b, c)   (b, c, d)
   intersection of A and B, equals

    A. ( )
        (a,b,c,d)
    B. ( )
        (b,c)
    C.
    D. ( )
        (d)

    7._____

8. In a Venn diagram, shown at the right, in which the circle A represents the set of rhombi and B the set of rectangles, the section C represents the set of

   A. squares
   B. trapezoids
   C. parallelograms
   D. quadrilaterals

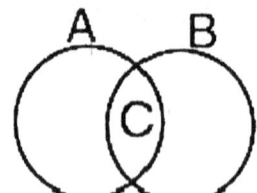

9. Of the following, the length of the vector that could CORRECTLY be used to represent the number $3 - i\sqrt{2}$ in the complex plane is _____.

   A. 11   B. $\sqrt{11}$ C. $3 - \sqrt{2}$ D. $\sqrt{5}$

10. Of the following, the statement which is FALSE is

    A. $\sqrt[b]{x^a} = x^{\frac{a}{b}}$
    B. $\sqrt[b]{x} \div \sqrt[b]{y} = \sqrt[b]{\frac{x}{y}}$
    C. $\sqrt[b]{x} + \sqrt[b]{y} = \sqrt[b]{x+y}$
    D. $\sqrt[b]{x} \cdot \sqrt[b]{y} = \sqrt[b]{xy}$

11. If $\dfrac{1}{x} - \dfrac{1}{y} = \dfrac{1}{z}$ then z equals

    A. $\dfrac{xy}{y-x}$ B. $\dfrac{xy}{y-x}$ C. $\dfrac{y-x}{xy}$ D. $\dfrac{x-y}{xy}$

12. The sum of the first n odd integers is

    A. $2n^2$ B. $2n^2 + 1$ C. n^2 D. $n^2 + 1$

13. The value of $5x^0 + 3x^{\frac{3}{4}} 4x^{-\frac{1}{2}}$ when x = 16, is

    A. 30   B. 33   C. 75   D. 105

14. Which one of the following characteristics is applicable to the equation $x + \dfrac{1}{x-1} = 1 + \dfrac{1}{x-1}$?

    A. It is equivalent to x = 1.
    B. It is equivalent to $x^2 - 2x + 1 = 0$.
    C. It has no roots.
    D. It has complex roots.

15. Since the period of a pendulum is proportional to the square root of its length, when the length of a pendulum is doubled, its period is

    A. doubled
    B. decreased between 50% and 60%
    C. increased between 40% and 50%
    D. quadrupled

16. The second term of the expansion of $(x+\frac{1}{x^3})^5$ is

    A. $5x^5$ B. $10x^5$ C. $5x^7$ D. $10x^7$

17. Which one of the following expresses the geometric mean (GM) CORRECTLY in terms of the arithmetic mean (AM) and the harmonic mean (HM)?

    A. $GM = \sqrt{AM \cdot HM}^1$
    B. $GM = \sqrt{AM \cdot HM}$
    C. $GM = AM \cdot HM$
    D. $GM = \overline{AM}^2 \, \overline{HM}^2$

18. If $\log_8 a = 2.5$ and $\log_2 b = 5$, then a, expressed in terms of b is

    A. $a = b^2$ B. $a = b^8$ C. $a = b^{\frac{3}{2}}$ D. $a = b^{\frac{5}{2}}$

19. Which one of the following statements concerning the method of interpolation by proportional parts is TRUE? It

    A. gives the exact value of the function
    B. assumes that the value of the function lies halfway between the two known values
    C. assumes that the curve between the two known points approximates closely the chord between these points
    D. is the process of estimating values of a function beyond the range of values of the variables actually plotted or calculated

20. Of the following, a representation of the product of three consecutive odd numbers where n is any positive integer is

    A. $n^3 - 4n$
    B. $n^3 - n$
    C. $n^3 + 6n^2 + 8n$
    D. $8n^3 + 3(4n^2 - 1) - 2n$

KEY (CORRECT ANSWERS)

1. C	6. B	11. A	16. A
2. C	7. B	12. C	17. B
3. B	8. A	13. A	18. C
4. D	9. B	14. C	19. C
5. A	10. C	15. C	20. C

SOLUTIONS TO PROBLEMS

1. Let x and 34-x be the two numbers whose mean is 17. Also, x:15 = 15:(34-x), which becomes $x^2 - 34x + 225 = 0$. (Ans. C)

2. $\dfrac{1}{x-1} + \dfrac{1}{x} + \dfrac{1}{x+1} = \dfrac{47}{60}$. $60x^2 + 60x + 60x^2 - 60 = 47x^3 - 47x$.
   This equation will simplify to $47x^3 - 180x^2 - 47x + 60 = 0$. (Ans. C)

3. A line perpendicular to $3x + 2y = 5$ has the general form of $2x - 3y = k$. Since this new line passes through (-3,0), k = -6. The desired equation is $2x - 3y + 6 = 0$. (Ans. B)

4. $\dfrac{t_1^2}{t_2^2} = \dfrac{d_1^3}{d_2^3}$. If $d_2 = 9 d_1$, then $d_1^3/d_1^3 = \dfrac{1}{729}$; since $t_1^2/t_2^2 = \dfrac{1}{729}$, $t_1/t_2 = \dfrac{1}{27}$. Thus, $t_2 = 27\,t$. (Ans. D)

5. The set of rational numbers is denumerable, since each rational number can be placed in a one-to-one correspondence with the positive integers. The method is:

$$\dfrac{1}{1}\ \dfrac{2}{1}\ \dfrac{3}{1}\ \dfrac{4}{1}\ ...$$

$$\dfrac{1}{2}\ \dfrac{2}{2}\ \dfrac{3}{2}\ \dfrac{4}{2}\ ...$$

$$\dfrac{1}{3}\ \dfrac{2}{3}\ \dfrac{3}{3}\ \dfrac{4}{3}\ ...$$

$$\dfrac{1}{4}\ \dfrac{2}{4}\ \dfrac{3}{4}\ \dfrac{4}{4}\ ...$$

By counting in a diagonal fashion, each rational number will be accounted for. (Ans. A)

6. $y = x^2 + 1$ represents a function, since for each value of x, there is only one value of y. (Ans. B)

7. The intersection of (a, b, c) and (b, c, d) = (b, c), since the intersection consists only of elements common to both sets. (Ans. B)

8. C must contain the properties of both rhombi and rectangles, i.e., figures with four equal sides and four right angles. Only squares fulfill these conditions. (Ans. A)

9. The vector's length for $3 - \sqrt{2}i = \sqrt{3^2 + (\sqrt{2})^2} = \sqrt{11}$. (Ans. B)

10. $\sqrt[b]{x}+\sqrt[b]{y} \neq \sqrt[b]{x+y}$. This can be shown letting b = 2, x = 4, and y = 9.

    $\sqrt{4}+\sqrt{9} = 2+3 = 5 \neq \sqrt{13}$. (Ans. C)

11. $\frac{1}{x}-\frac{1}{y}=\frac{1}{z}$. Then, yz - xz = xy. Thus, z(y-x) = xy, and finally, z = xy/(y-x). (Ans. A)

12. $\sum_{x=1}^{n} 2x-1 = 1+3+5+...+(2n-1)$. Using the formula for an arithmetic progression,

    sum $=\frac{n}{2}(a+L)$ where a = 1st term, L = last term, sum $=\frac{n}{2}(1+2n-1) = n^2$. (Ans. C)

13. $5 \cdot 16^0 + 3 \cdot 16^{\frac{3}{4}} + 4 \cdot 16^{-\frac{1}{2}} = (5)(1)+(3)(8)+4(\frac{1}{4}) = 30$. (Ans. A)

14. Multiplying all terms by x-1, we get x(x-1) + 1 = x-1 + 1, which becomes $x^2 - 2x + 1 = 0$. The solution would be x = 1, but this value would make undefined. Thus, there exists no roots for the original equation. (Ans. C)

15. $P = K\sqrt{L}$ where P = period, K = constant, L = length. When L is doubled, This means that the period has been multiplied by $\sqrt{2}$ which represents an increase of about 41.4%. (Ans. C)

16. The second term $(5)(x^2)^4(\frac{1}{x^3}) = 5x^5$. (Ans. A)

17. Let $x_1, x_2, ..., x_n$ be the original n numbers. Then

    $AM = \frac{x_1+...+x_n}{n}$ $HM = n/(\frac{1}{x_1}+...+\frac{1}{x_n})$. Now, $\sqrt{AM \cdot HM} = \sqrt{(x_1)(x_2)(...)(x_n)} = GM$

    (Ans. B)

18. $Log_8 a = 2.5$ means $a = 8^{2.5} = 2^{7.5} = 2^7\sqrt{2}$ or $128\sqrt{2}$ $Log_2 b = 5$ means $b = 2^5 =$ 32. Since $a = 2^{7.5}$ and $b = 2^5$, $a = b^{\frac{3}{2}}$. (Ans. C)

19. Interpolation by proportional parts assumes the curve between two points can be approximated by the line segment joining these points. (Ans. C)

20. The three consecutive odd numbers are n, n+2, n+4. Then, $n(n+2)(n+4) = n^3 + 6n^2 + 8n$. (Ans. C)

TEST 4

DIRECTIONS: Each question or incomplete statement is followed by several suggested answers or completions. Select the one that BEST answers the question or completes the statement. PRINT THE LETTER OF THE CORRECT ANSWER IN THE SPACE AT THE RIGHT.

1. The fraction $\dfrac{a^2+b^2-c^2+2ab}{a^2+c^2-b^2+2ac}$ is (with suitable restrictions on the value of a, b, and c) reducible to which one of the following?

    A. $\dfrac{a+b+c}{a+b-c}$ B. 1   C. $\dfrac{a+b-c}{a-b+c}$ D. None of these

2. Which one of the following choices represents the center and radius of the circle $x^2 + y^2 - 6x + 4y - 12 = 0$? Center

    A. (9, 4) radius 25   B. (-3, 2) radius 5
    C. (3, -2) radius 5   D. (-6, 4) radius 25

3. Which one of the following statements is TRUE concerning the graphs of the lines $5x + 4y = 3$ and $4x = 5y + 3$? They

    A. are parallel
    B. are identical
    C. intersect at right angles
    D. intersect at angles other than right angles

4. The number of distinct points common to the graphs of $x^2 + y^2 = 9$ and $y^2 = 9$ is

    A. zero   B. one   C. two   D. four

5. Which one of the following choices gives the two asymptotes of $\dfrac{x^2}{25} - \dfrac{y^2}{9} = 1$?

    A. $-5x = 3y, 5x = -3y$ B. $5x = 3y, 5x = -3y$
    C. $-3x = 5y, 3x = -5y$ D. $3x = 5y, 3x = -5y$

6. Of the following, the quadratic equation whose roots are (2+i) and (2-i) is

    A. $x^2 - 4x + 5 = 0$ B. $x^2 + 4x - 5 = 0$
    C. $2x^2 + 2x - 1 = 0$ D. $2x^2 - 2x + 1 = 0$

7. Of the following, which one is a factor of $(x^{99} + 1)$?

    A. (x+1)   B. (x-1)   C. (x+3)   D. (x-3)

8. Assume that an investment depreciates 20% of the original value during the first year, and then during the second year depreciates 80% of the value it had at the beginning of the second year.
   The uniform yearly rate of decrease that would have yielded the same resulting value at the end of two years is

   A. 40%   B. 47%   C. 50%   D. 60%

9. U represents the operation of the union of two sets. If A is the set of all numbers of the form 2n and B the set of all numbers of the form 2n+1, n being any integer, then A ∪ B is the set of all

   A. odd integers
   B. even integers
   C. rational numbers
   D. integers

10. Using a Venn diagram in which the circle A represents the set of rational numbers and B the set of non-terminating decimals, the section C represents the set of all

    A. transcendental numbers
    B. irrational numbers
    C. real numbers
    D. repeating decimals

11. The following *proof* was offered to show that 2=1. Suppose a and b are two names for the same number, then
    $a = b$
    $a^2 - b^2 = ab - b^2$
    $(a+b)(a-b) = b(a-b)$
    $a + b = b$
    $2b = b$
    $2 = 1$
    This *proof* is invalid because

    A. the commutative law does not hold for subtraction
    B. zero has no multiplicative inverse
    C. the commutative law does not hold for division
    D. the associative law does not hold for subtraction

12. Assume that for the first 90 miles of a 156 mile trip, a man averages 36 miles per hour. To achieve an average rate of 39 miles per hour for the entire trip, his average rate for the remainder of the trip, in miles per hour, must be

    A. 40   B. 42   C. 44   D. 48

13. A varies directly as the square of b and inversely as the cube of c. If b is tripled and c is doubled, the value of A is multiplied by

    A. 3/2   B. 6   C. 9/8   D. 2

14. $\dfrac{10}{\sqrt{3}} \times \dfrac{3\sqrt{2}}{\sqrt{5}}$ equals which one of the following?

   A. $2\sqrt{2}$ B. $10\sqrt{6}$ C. $6\sqrt{10}$ D. $2\sqrt{30}$

15. The root(s) of the equation $2\sqrt{x} = x - 3$ is (are)

   A. 9, 1   B. 9   C. -3, 1   D. 3, -1

16. Of the following, an equivalent sentence to
    $5(x+3) - 7 = 3x - 4(1+x)$ is

   A. $5x + 15 = 3x + 7 - 4 - 4x$
   B. $7x - 5x = 8 + 4$
   C. $5x + 3x - 4x = 7 - 15 - 4$
   D. $15 - 7 - 4 = 7x - 5x$

17. Of the following, the equation that expresses the relationship between the variables in the given table is

X	-1	2	3	-2
Y	-2	1	6	1

    is

    A. $y = 2x$
    B. $y - x^2 = -3$
    C. $y = x + 3$
    D. $y = x - 1$

18. If a certain wheel makes 100 revolutions in going a certain distance and a wheel foot less in diameter makes 25 more revolutions in going the same distance, then the diameter of the larger wheel is _____ feet.

   A. 2   B. 2.5   C. 4   D. 5

19. If 4 quarts of a certain mixture of alcohol and water is at 50% strength, the number of quarts of water that must be added to make the alcohol strength of the new mixture 40% is

   A. 1   B. 2   C. 3   D. 10

20. When the price of a certain article increases from 20¢ to 25¢, the number of articles that can be purchased for d dollars decreases by

   A. $\dfrac{d}{100}$ B. $\dfrac{d}{20}$ C. $5b$ D. d

KEY (CORRECT ANSWERS)

1. C	6. A	11. B	16. A
2. C	7. A	12. C	17. B
3. C	8. D	13. C	18. B
4. C	9. D	14. D	19. A
5. D	10. D	15. B	20. D

SOLUTIONS TO PROBLEMS

1. Rewrite the fraction as $\dfrac{(a+b)^2-c^2}{(a+c)^2-b^2} = \dfrac{(a+b-c)(a+b+c)}{(a+c-b)(a+c+b)} = (a+b-c)/(a+c-b)$. (Ans. C)

2. Rewrite as $(x^2 - 6x + 9) + (y^2 + 4y + 4) - 9 - 4 - 12 = 0$, which becomes $(x-3)^2 + (y+2)^2 = 25$. The center is located at $(3,-2)$ and the radius is 5. (Ans. C)

3. The slopes of $5x+4y = 3$ and $4x = 5y+3$ are $-\dfrac{5}{4}$ and $\dfrac{4}{5}$. Since their slopes are negative reciprocals of each other, they intersect at right angles. (Ans. C)

4. The graphs of $x^2 + y^2 = 9$ and $y^2 = 9$ intersect at the two points $(0,3)$ and $(0,-3)$. (Ans. C)

5. Rewrite as $y = \pm\dfrac{3}{5}\sqrt{x^2 - 25}$. Then, the equations of the asymptotes are $y = \dfrac{3}{5}x$ and $y = -\dfrac{3}{5}x$. These can also be written as $3x = 5y$ and $3x = -5y$. (Ans. D)

6. The equation with roots $2 \pm i$ can be written as $[x-(2+i)][x-(2-i)] = 0$. This reduces to $x^2 - 4x + 5 = 0$. (Ans. A)

7. $x+1$ is a factor of $x^{99}+1$, since -1 is a root of $x^{99} + 1 = 0$. (Ans. A)

8. Let x = uniform yearly rate of decrease, expressed as a percent. Then,
$(1-\dfrac{x}{100})(1-\dfrac{x}{100}) = (.80)(.20) = .16$. Solving, we get $x = 60$. (Ans. D)

9. All integers can be represented by either $2n$ or $2n+1$, depending on whether the integer is even or odd. (Ans. D)

10. A repeating decimal is both non-terminating and rational. For example, $.\overline{6} = \dfrac{2}{3}$, which is rational. (Ans. D)

11. The fallacy of the argument occurs when one proceeds from line 3 to line 4. Dividing by $a-b$ means dividing by zero, but zero has no multiplicative inverse. (Ans. B)

12. Let x = average rate for the remaining 66 miles. Since total distance ÷ total time = average rate for entire trip, $156 \div (\dfrac{90}{36} + \dfrac{66}{x}) = 39$. This equation could be simplified to $36x/(90x + 2376) = 39/156$. Solving, $x = 44$. (Ans. C)

13. $A = kb^2/c^3$, where k = constant. Let b be replaced by 3b and c be replaced by 2c. Then, $A = k(3b)^2/(2c)^3$ or $A = \frac{9}{8}kb^2/c^3$. Thus, the new value of A has been obtained by multiplying the original A value by $\frac{9}{8}$.

14. $\frac{10}{\sqrt{3}} \cdot \frac{3\sqrt{2}}{\sqrt{5}} = \frac{30\sqrt{2}}{\sqrt{15}} = \frac{30\sqrt{2}}{\sqrt{15}} \cdot \frac{\sqrt{15}}{\sqrt{15}} = \frac{30\sqrt{30}}{15} = 2\sqrt{3}$. (Ans. D)

15. $2\sqrt{x} = x - 3$ Squaring both sides, $4x = x^2 - 6x + 9$. This becomes $x^2 - 10x + 9 = 0$, which factors as $(x-9)(x-1) = 0$. Only 9 is a root (1 does not check the original equation). (Ans. B)

16. $5(x+3) - 7 = 3x - 4(1+x)$ is equivalent to $5x + 15 - 7 = 3x - 4 - 4x$, which is equivalent to $5x + 15 = 3x + 7 - 4 - 4x$. (Ans. A)

17. Since 4 ordered pairs are given, let $y = Ax^3 + Bx^2 + Cx + D$. By substituting ordered pairs, we get the following: $-2 = -A + B - C + D$, $1 = 8A + 4B + 2C + D$.
$6 = 27A + 9B + 3C + D$, and $1 = -8A + 4B - 2C + D$.
Solving, $A = 0, B = 1, C = 0$, and $D = -3$.
Thus, $y = x^2 - 3$ or $y - x^2 = -3$. (Ans. B)

18. Let D = diameter of larger wheel, D - .5 = diameter of smaller wheel. The respective circumferences are πD and $\pi D - .5\pi$. Then, $100\pi D = 125(\pi D - .5\pi)$. Solving, D = 2.5 ft. (Ans. B)

19. The original mixture has 2 quarts each of alcohol and water. Let x = amount of water added.
Then $\frac{2}{4+x} = .40$. Solving, x = 1 (Ans. A)

20. For d dollars, $\frac{100d}{20} = 5d$ articles can be bought, but when the price per article increases to 25¢, the purchasing power of d dollars is $\frac{100d}{25} = 4d$ articles. The actual decrease is d articles. (Ans. D)

EXAMINATION SECTION
TEST 1

DIRECTIONS: Each question or incomplete statement is followed by several suggested answers or completions. Select the one that BEST answers the question or completes the statement. *PRINT THE LETTER OF THE CORRECT ANSWER IN THE SPACE AT THE RIGHT.*

1. Let b ε R, the set of real numbers.
   The solution set of $b^2 > b$ is

   A. {b|b>1}
   B. {b|b< 0 or b >}
   C. {b|b<-1 or b>1}
   D. R

   1.____

2. If k represents a positive integer, $2^{k+1} + 2^k$ is equal to

   A. 4^{2k+1}
   B. 2^{2k+1}
   C. $3(2^{k+1})$
   D. $3(2^k)$

   2.____

3. A function, f(x), is defined as $f(x) = 2x^2 - 5$.
   The value of f[f(2)] is

   A. 13
   B. 22
   C. 6
   D. 9

   3.____

4. If $\log_2 y = 5$, then y is equal to

   A. 7
   B. 10
   C. 25
   D. 32

   4.____

5. The graph of the equation $x^2 - 4x + y^2 = 12$ is a circle with radius _____, center _____.

   A. 4; (-2,0)
   B. 4; (2,0)
   C. 16, (-2,0)
   D. 16; (2,0)

   5.____

6. The TOTAL number of subsets of set {a,b,c,d} is

   A. 16
   B. 15
   C. 8
   D. 4

   6.____

7. If S represents the sum of the infinite geometric series
   $\frac{1}{4} + \frac{1}{8} + \frac{1}{16} + ...$, then

   A. S = 1
   B. S < 1
   C. 1 < S < 2
   D. S > 2

   7.____

8. Let R represent the set of real numbers.
   If a*b is defined as $\frac{a+b}{2}$ where a and b represent any two elements in R, then

   A. a*1=a
   B. a*0=0
   C. a*(2b)=(2a)*b
   D. 2+(a*b) =(2+a)*(2+b)

   8.____

9. A student observes that the same shaded part of a Venn diagram illustrates both sets $A \cap (B \cup C)$ and $(A \cap B) \cup (A \cap C)$. This suggests a property MOST closely resembling which property of real numbers?

   A. Commutative
   B. Distributive
   C. Associative
   D. Multiplicative inverse

   9.____

107

10. If c represents a real number and $c \neq 0$, then the product of the additive and multiplicative inverses of c is

    A. 1   B. -c   C. $\frac{1}{c}$ D. -1

11. For what value of k is 2 a root of the equation $2x^4 - 6x^3 + 4kx + 13 = 0$?

    A. $\frac{8}{3}$ B. $\frac{3}{8}$ C. $-\frac{3}{8}$ D. $-\frac{8}{3}$

12. The arithmetic mean between the roots of the equation $x^2 - 8x + 13 = 0$ is

    A. $-6\frac{1}{2}$ B. $6\frac{1}{2}$ C. -4   D. 4

13. The infinite repeating decimal of $0.0\overline{2}$ (where 2 is repeated) is equal to

    A. $\frac{2}{99}$ B. $\frac{11}{500}$ C. $\frac{1}{45}$ D. $\frac{22}{999}$

14. The relation between the Fahrenheit and Celsius readings may be stated $F = \frac{9}{5}C + 32$. The numerical readings on both scales are the same when the number of degrees is

    A. -8   B. -40   C. 8   D. 40

15. Which of the following pairs of equations represent parallel lines in a rectangular coordinate system?

    A. 3x-6y =9
       2x+4y = 6
    B. 3x-6y =9
       2x-4y = 6
    C. 3x-6y =9
       x-2y = 4
    D. 3x-6y = 9
       x+2y = 4

16. The graph below represents the solution set of which one of the following?

    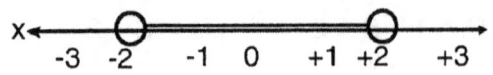

    A. $|x| < 2$ B. $|x| \leq 2$ C. $|x| = 2$ D. $|x| > 2$

17. Using the ordered pair (x,y) as an equivalent expression for $\frac{x}{y}$, the ordered pair representing the sum of (3, 8) and $\frac{x}{y}$ (2, 3) would be

    A. (1, 5)   B. (5, 11)   C. (25, 24)   D. (25, 6)

18. Solve for x: $4^{x-2} = 1$

    A. $\frac{1}{4}$ B. 2   C. -2   D. $2\frac{1}{4}$

19. Twelve identical machines can finish a job in 8 days. The number of machines needed to finish the same job in 6 days would be

    A. 18   B. 16   C. 14   D. 9

20. The reciprocal of $\sqrt{3}-\sqrt{2}$ is equal to

    A. 1   B. $\sqrt{3}+\sqrt{2}$ C. $\dfrac{1}{\sqrt{3}}-\dfrac{1}{\sqrt{2}}$ D. $-\sqrt{3}+\sqrt{2}$

KEY (CORRECT ANSWERS)

1.	B	11.	B
2.	D	12.	D
3.	A	13.	C
4.	D	14.	B
5.	B	15.	C
6.	A	16.	A
7.	B	17.	C
8.	D	18.	B
9.	B	19.	B
10.	D	20.	B

SOLUTIONS TO PROBLEMS

1. $b^2 > b$ implies $b(b-1) > 0$. If seen $b > 0$ and $b-1 > 0$, then a solution is $\{b|b > 1\}$. If $b < 0$ and $b-1 < 0$, then a solution is $\{b|b < 0\}$. Final answer: $\{b|b < 0 \text{ or } b > 1\}$. (Ans. B)

2. $2^{k+1} + 2^k = 2^k(2+1) = 3(2^k)$. (Ans. D)

3. $f[f(2)] = f[2(2^2)-5] = f[3] = 2(3^2)-5 = 13$. (Ans. A)

4. $\log y_2 = 5$ implies $2^5 = y$, so $y = 32$. (Ans. D)

5. Rewrite as $x^2 - 4x + 4 + y^2 = 12 + 4$, which becomes $(x-2)^2 + (y-0)^2 = 4^2$. Thus, the radius is 4 and the center is (2, 0). (Ans. B)

6. Given a set with n elements, the number of subsets = 2^n. In this example, $2^n = 2^4 = 16$. (Ans. A)

7. $S = \dfrac{a}{1-r}$, where a = first term, r = common ratio. Thus, $S = \dfrac{1}{4} \div (1 - \dfrac{1}{2}) = \dfrac{1}{2}$. The only correct choice is $S < 1$. (Ans. B)

8. $2 + (a*b) = 2 + \dfrac{a+b}{2} = \dfrac{4+a+b}{2}$. Also, $(2+a)*(2+b) = \dfrac{2+a+2+b}{2} = \dfrac{4+a+b}{2}$. (Ans. D)

9. The distributive property would be apparent in an example like $5 \cdot (3+7) = (5 \cdot 3) + (5 \cdot 7)$. The $\cap$ symbol replaces $\cdot$ and the $\cup$ symbol replaces +. (Ans. B)

10. The additive, multiplicative inverses of c are $-c$ and $\dfrac{1}{c}$, respectively. Then, $(-c)(\dfrac{1}{c}) = -1$. (Ans. D)

11. $2(2^4) - 6(2^3) + 4k(2) + 13 = 0$. Solving, $k = \dfrac{3}{8}$. (Ans. B)

12. The sum of the roots = 8. Thus, their average = 4. It should be noted that in the equation $Ax^2 + Bx + C = 0$, the sum of the roots is. (Ans. D)

13. Let $N = .0\overline{2}$. Then, $10N = .\overline{2}$ and $9n = .2$. Thus $N I = \dfrac{.2}{9} = \dfrac{2}{90} = \dfrac{1}{45}$. (Ans. C)

14. If F = C, then $C = \dfrac{9}{5}C + 32$. Solving, C = -40. (Ans. B)

15. Parallel lines have the same slope, but different y-intercepts. Both $3x - 6y = 9$ and $x - 2y = 4$ have slopes of $\dfrac{1}{2}$, but the y-intercepts are $-\dfrac{3}{2}$ and -2, respectively. (Ans. C)

5 (#1)

16. The graph translates to -2 < x < 2, which becomes |x| < 2. (Ans. A)

17. $\frac{3}{8}+\frac{2}{3}=\frac{25}{24}$, which corresponds to (25, 24). (Ans. C)

18. $4^{x-2}=1=4^0$. x-2 =0. x = 2 (Ans. B)

19. Let x = number of required machines. Then, $\frac{12}{x}=\frac{6}{8}$. x = 16. (Ans. B)

20. $\frac{1}{\sqrt{3}-\sqrt{2}}=\frac{1}{\sqrt{3}-\sqrt{2}}\frac{\sqrt{3}+\sqrt{2}}{\sqrt{3}+\sqrt{2}}=\frac{\sqrt{3}+\sqrt{2}}{1}=\sqrt{3}+\sqrt{2}$ (Ans. B)

16.____

17.____

18.____

19.____

20.____

TEST 2

DIRECTIONS: Each question or incomplete statement is followed by several suggested answers or completions. Select the one that BEST answers the question or completes the statement. *PRINT THE LETTER OF THE CORRECT ANSWER IN THE SPACE AT THE RIGHT.*

1. The graph of the equation $\dfrac{x^2}{9} - \dfrac{y^2}{16} = 1$ is a(n)

    A. parabola B. circle C. ellipse D. hyperbola

2. If $_{18}C_5 = {}_{18}C_{r+2}$ and $r \neq 3$, then $_rC_5 =$

    A. 18 B. 462 C. 7 D. 13860

3. If universal set U contains subsets A, B, and C, as shown in the accompanying Venn diagram below, then the shaded area may be represented by

    A. $A \cap B \cap C$
    B. $(A \cap C) \cup (B \cap C)$
    C. $(A \cup C) \cap (B \cup C)$
    D. $(A \cap C) \cup C$

4. The repeating decimal $0.\overline{314}$ may be represented by

    A. $\dfrac{.314314}{1000000}$ B. $\dfrac{314}{1000}$ C. $\dfrac{314}{990}$ D. $\dfrac{314}{999}$

5. An article was sold for m dollars at a gain of 15% on the cost. The cost, in dollars, of the article was

    A. $\dfrac{m}{.15}$ B. $\dfrac{m}{1.15}$ C. .15m D. 1.15m

6. A student takes six class tests during the term. If his arithmetic average was p for the first three tests and q for the next two tests, what mark on the sixth test will give him an average of 80 for all the tests?

    A. 480 - (3p+2q)
    C. 480 - (p+q)
    B. 80 - (3p+2q)
    D. 80 - (p+q)

7. The sum of a number, x, and its reciprocal is equal to the product of the same number and its reciprocal.
Which of the following equations can be used to find this number?

A. $x^2 + x + 1 = 0$ B. $x^2 + x - 1 = 0$
C. $x^2 - x + 1 = 0$ D. $x^2 - x - 1 = 0$

8. Two lines have equations $ax + by + c = 0$ and $dx + ey + f = 0$.
The graphs of these lines will be perpendicular to each other if and *only* if

A. $ae - bd = 0$ B. $ad - be = 0$
C. $ad + be = 0$ D. $ae + bd = 0$

9. A certain printing press can print an edition of a newspaper in 4 hours. After this press has been at work for 1 hour, a second press also starts to print the same edition. Working together, both presses require one more hour to finish the job.
How many hours would it have taken the second press to print the edition if it had worked alone?

A. 5 B. 2 C. 3 D. 4

10. The sum of the squares of the roots of the equation $x^2 - 6x + 4 = 0$ is

A. 28 B. 10 C. 18 D. 23

11. The fraction, $\dfrac{x^{-1} + y^{-1}}{x^{-1}}$ is equivalent to

A. $\dfrac{x}{x+y}$ B. $\dfrac{x+y}{x}$ C. $1 + \dfrac{1}{y}$ D. $1 + \dfrac{x}{y}$

12. When $x^{29} - 3x^{21} + 2$ is divided by $x-1$, the remainder is

A. -2 B. 0 C. 3 D. 4

13. If * is an associative binary operation such that $a*b = c$, $c*d = e$, and $b*d = f$, then $a*f$ equals

A. b B. c C. d D. e

14. Which of the following functions has an inverse relation which is NOT a function?

A. $f(x) = \dfrac{1}{2}x - 2$ B. $f(x) = x^2 + 3$
C. $f(x) = \log_{10} x$ D. $f(x) = \text{Arc sin } x$

15. On the curve $y = x^2$, two points P and Q are chosen having abscissas a and b, respectively.
The slope of $\overleftrightarrow{PQ}$ is

A. $a+b$ B. $a-b$ C. $b-a$ D. $\dfrac{a-b}{a+b}$

16. A can 3 inches in diameter contains 12 fluid ounces of water. A can filled to the same height but 4 inches in diameter contains _____ fluid ounces.

   A. 16   B. 18   C. $21\frac{1}{3}$ D. $28\frac{4}{9}$

17. The solution set of $x^2 < x$, where x is a real number, is

   A. $\{x|x < 0\}$ B. $\{x|0 < x < 1\}$
   C. $\{x|x > 0\}$ D. $\{x|x < 1\}$

18. If $\log V = t \log E + \log K$, then

   A. $V = (KE)^t$ B. $V = E^t + K$
   C. $V = KE^t$ D. $V = tE + K$

19. The number of distinct chords which can be drawn connecting 5 points on a circle is

   A. 20   B. 15   C. 10   D. 5

20. The equation of the axis of symmetry for the curve $y^2 = x - 6y$ is

   A. $y - 6 = 0$ B. $2x = 3y$
   C. $x - 3 = 0$ D. $y + 3 = 0$

KEY (CORRECT ANSWERS)

1.	D	11.	D
2.	B	12.	B
3.	B	13.	D
4.	D	14.	B
5.	B	15.	A
6.	A	16.	C
7.	C	17.	B
8.	C	18.	C
9.	B	19.	C
10.	A	20.	D

SOLUTIONS TO PROBLEMS

1. Any equation in the form, $\frac{x^2}{a^2} - \frac{y^2}{b^2} = 1$ is a hyperbola. Here, a, b are constants. (Ans. D)

2. $_{18}C_5 = \frac{18!}{5!\,13!}$ which $= \frac{18!}{13!\,5!} = {_{18}C_{13}}$

   Since r + 2 = 13, r = 11.

   Now, $_{11}C_5 = (11!)/[5! \cdot 6!] = 462$. (Ans. B)

3. Recognize that the shaded area can be illustrated as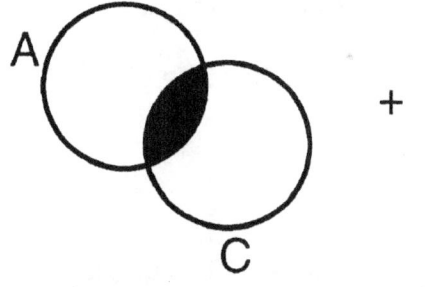

   = (A ∩ C + (B ∩ C) = (A ∩ C) ∪ (B ∩ C) (Ans. B)

4. Let N = 0.$\overline{314}$. Then, 1000N = 314.$\overline{314}$ and by subtraction 999N = 314. Thus, N = 314/999. (Ans. D)

5. Let C = cost. Then, m = C + .15C = 1.15C. Finally, C = m/1.15. (Ans. B)

6. An average of p for the first three tests implies a total of 3p. Likewise, an average of q for the next two tests implies a total of 2q. Let x = score on sixth test.

   Now, $\frac{3p + 2q + x}{6} = 80$, which means x = 480 - 3p - 2q. (Ans. A)

7. We have x + 1/x = (x)(l/x), which implies $(x^2+l)/x = 1$. This equation can be rewritten as $x^2 - x + 1 = 0$. (Ans. C)

8. The slope of the first line is $-\frac{a}{b}$, and the slope of the second line is $-\frac{d}{e}$. In order for the two lines to be perpendicular to each other, the slope of one line must equal the negative reciprocal of the other line. Thus, $-\frac{a}{b} = -1/-\frac{d}{e}$ which implies that ad + be = 0. (Ans. C)

9. Let x = number of hours the second press would need if it were to work alone. In performing the present job, the first press will have worked 2 hours and the second press will have worked 1 hour. The sum of the fractions representing the respective parts of the job done by each press equals 1. Thus, $2/4 + 1/x = 1$. Consequently, x = 2 hours. (Ans. B)

10. Let R_1, R_2 = the two roots. $R_1 + R_2 = 6$ and $R_1 R_2 = 4$.

    So, $(R_1 + R_2)^2 = R_1^2 + 2R_1R_2 + R_2^2 = 36$. Since $2R_1R_2 = 8$, this means $R_1^2 + R_2^2 = 28$. (Ans. A)

11. Rewrite the expression as $(\frac{1}{x} + \frac{1}{y}) / \frac{1}{x} = \frac{1}{x} / \frac{1}{x} + \frac{1}{y} / \frac{1}{x} = 1 + \frac{x}{y}$ (Ans. D)

12. By the Remainder Theorem, the remainder is the value of $x^{29} - 3x^{21} + 2$ when x = 1. Value = $x^{29} - 3(1)^{21} + 2 = 0$. (Ans. B)

13. $a*f = a*(b*d) = (a*b)*d = c*d = e$ (Ans. D)

14. The inverse of $f(x) = x^2 + 3$ is $g(x) = \pm\sqrt{x-3}$, and thus g(x) is NOT a function. (Ans. B)

15. The coordinates of P: (a, a^2) and the coordinates of Q (b, b^2). The slope of $\overleftrightarrow{PQ} = (b^2-a^2)/(b-a) = b+a = a+b$. (Ans. A)

16. Volume of first can $= (\pi)(\frac{3}{2})^2(H) = 27\pi H$ cubic inches.

    The volume of the second can = cubic inches. Thus, the ratio of volumes of the first can to the second Let x = number of fluid ounces in the second can. Then,

    $\frac{12}{x} = \frac{9}{16}$ and $x = 21\frac{1}{3}$. (Ans. C)

17. $x^2 < x$ becomes $x^2 - x < 0$. Then, $x(x-1) < 0$.
    Case 1: x < 0 and x-1 > 0 simultaneously. This is impossible
    Case 2: x > 0 and x-1 < 0 simultaneously. This implies 0 < x < 1. (Ans. B)

18. Rewrite the right side of the equation as $\text{Log } E^t + \text{Log } K = \text{Log }(E^t)(K)$. Now, Log V = Log $(E^t)(K)$, so $V = KE^t$.

19. The problem resolves into $_5C_2 = 5 \cdot 4 / 2 = 10$. (Ans. C)

20. Rewrite the equation as $x = y^2 + 6y$, which becomes $x = (y^2+6y+9) - 9$ which can be written as $x = (y+3)^2 - 9$. Axis of symmetry is y = -3 or y+3 = 0. (Ans. D)

TEST 3

DIRECTIONS: Each question or incomplete statement is followed by several suggested answers or completions. Select the one that BEST answers the question or completes the statement. *PRINT THE LETTER OF THE CORRECT ANSWER IN THE SPACE AT THE RIGHT.*

1. The series represented by the expression $\sum_{k=1}^{n}(2k-1)$ is equal to

   A. $\dfrac{n(n+1)}{2}$ B. n^2 C. $(n+1)^2$ D. $n(n+1)$

   1._____

2. The graph of $|x|+|y|=4$ is

   A. a square B. two intersecting lines
   C. two parallel lines D. one line

   2._____

3. If $x<b<0$ means that x and b are numbers such that x is less than b and b is less than zero, then

   A. $x^2 > bx > b^2$ B. $x^2 < b^5 < 0$
   C. $x^2 > bx$ but $bx<0$ D. $x^2>b^2$ but $b^2< 0$

   3._____

4. If x is positive and log log x, then

   A. x has no minimum or maximum value
   B. the maximum value of x is 1
   C. the maximum value of x is 4
   D. the minimum value of x is 4

   4._____

5. If the third term of a geometric progression is $\dfrac{1}{6}$ and the seventh term is $\dfrac{1}{6}$, the first, term is

   A. $\dfrac{1}{81}$ B. $\dfrac{1}{72}$ C. $\dfrac{1}{54}$ D. $\dfrac{1}{48}$

   5._____

6. Which values of x will satisfy the equation $3^{x^2-7x} = \left(\dfrac{1}{3}\right)^{4x+1}$

   A. $x=\dfrac{4\pm\sqrt{5}}{2}$ B. $x=\dfrac{3\pm\sqrt{3}}{2}$ C. $x=\dfrac{3\pm\sqrt{5}}{2}$ D. $x=\dfrac{2\pm\sqrt{3}}{2}$

   6._____

7. Which values of x satisfy the following equation involving a determinant?

   $\begin{vmatrix} x & 2 & 1 \\ -1 & 1 & -1 \\ 3 & 2 & 3x \end{vmatrix} = 0$

   7._____

117

A. $x = -\frac{11}{3}, x = 1$
B. $x = \frac{3}{4}, x = -1$
C. $x = -\frac{7}{8}, x = 2$
D. $x = 4, x = 3$

8. Which of the following expresses $x^3 - 2x^2 - 5x + 6$ as the product of three linear factors?

   A. $(x-1)(x-2)(x-3)$
   B. $(x-1)(x+2)(x+3)$
   C. $(x-1)(x-2)(x+3)$
   D. $(x-1)(x+2)(x-3)$

9. If $f(x) = 3^x$, then $f(x) + f(x+1) =$

   A. 4
   B. $f(x)$
   C. $3f(x)$
   D. $4f(x)$

10. The number of distinct points of intersection of the relations $x^2 + 9y^2 = 1$ and $x^2 + 9y^2 = 9$ is

    A. 1
    B. 2
    C. 3
    D. 0

11. Simplify the product $(256)^{.16} (256)^{.09}$

    A. 4
    B. 16
    C. 64
    D. 256.25

12. The sixth term of the expansion of $(\frac{2}{x\sqrt{3}} + \frac{x^2}{2})^9$ is

    A. $7x^6$
    B. $10x^6$
    C. $63x^7$
    D. $18x^7$

13. A man has five close friends. In how many ways may he invite one or more of them to accompany him on a hunting trip?

    A. 5
    B. 10
    C. 31
    D. 32

14. When $x^2 + 3x^2 + cx + 5$ is divided by x-2, the remainder is 13. The value of c is

    A. -6
    B. -2
    C. 2
    D. 6

15. The real values of x and y that satisfy the equation $3x + 2y + xi = 11 + 1 - 2yi$ may be described as follows:

    A. $x > 0$ and $y > 0$
    B. $x > 0$ and $y < 0$
    C. $x < 0$ and $y < 0$
    D. $x < 0$ and $y > 0$

16. The equation of the tangent to the curve $y = x^3 - x^2 + x - 1$ at the point on the curve where $x = 1$ is

    A. $y = 0$
    B. $2y + x = 1$
    C. $y = 2x + 2$
    D. $y = 2x - 2$

17. A group of boys and girls have an average (arithmetic mean) weight of 40 kg. 17.____
    If the average weight of the girls is 35 kg and the average weight of the boys is 50 kg,
    then the ratio of boys to girls is

    A. 2:3　　　　　B. 1:2　　　　　C. 3:2　　　　　D. 2:1

18. The value of the product $(\log_a b)(\log_b a)$, where (a>1, b>1) is 18.____

    A. 1　　　　　B. 0　　　　　C. ab　　　　　D. a+b

19. If $f(x) = 2x - 3$ and $g(x) = x^2 - 4$, find $f[g(x)] - g[f(x)]$. 19.____

    A. $-2(x^2-6x+8)$　　　　　B. $-x^2 + 2x + 1$
    C. $x^2 - 2x - 1$　　　　　D. $-2(x^2+6x+3)$

20. A plane makes the trip from City A to City B, traveling at an average rate of 380 miles per 20.____
    hour. On the return trip, the plane flies at an average of 420 miles per hour. The average
    rate of the plane for the roundtrip, in miles per hour, is

    A. 398　　　　　B. 401　　　　　C. 400　　　　　D. 399

KEY (CORRECT ANSWERS)

1.	B	11.	A
2.	A	12.	A
3.	A	13.	C
4.	D	14.	A
5.	C	15.	B
6.	C	16.	D
7.	A	17.	B
8.	D	18.	A
9.	D	19.	A
10.	D	20.	D

SOLUTIONS TO PROBLEMS

1. This summation is 1+3+5+ ... + 2n-1, which is an arithmetic progression whose sum can be written as $\frac{n}{2}[1+(2n-1)] = n^2$. (Ans. B)

2. The graph appears as: (Ans. A)

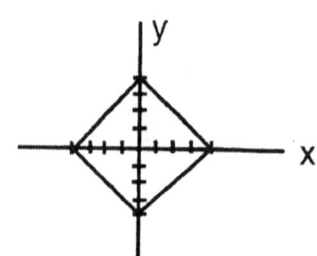

3. Since x < b < 0, both x and b are negative numbers.
   Using x < b, if both terms are multiplied by x, the order of inequality changes; thus, $x^2 >$ bx. Now, if both terms are multiplied by b (from x < b), then $bx > b^2$. Thus, $x^2 > bx > b^2$. Note that b^2, x^2, bx are all greater than 0. (Ans. A)

4. $\text{Log } 2 + \frac{1}{2}\text{Log } x = \text{Log } 2 + \text{Log}\sqrt{x} = \text{Log } 2\sqrt{x}$. Since x > 0 and $\text{Log } x \geq \text{Log } 2\sqrt{x}$, we get $x \geq 2\sqrt{x}$. This implies $x^2 \geq 4x$, which would yield (normally) $x \geq 4$ or $x \leq -4$; BUT since x is positive, the only acceptable answer is $x \geq 4$. Thus, 4 is the minimum value of x. (Ans. D)

5. $t_n = ar^{n-1}$, where tn = nth term, a = first term, r = ratio of each term to preceding term and n = number of terms. $\frac{1}{6} = ar^2$ and $\frac{27}{2} = ar^6$. Divide the second equation by the first equation to get $r^4 = 81$. Thus, r = 3 or -3, with either value of r, $a = \frac{1}{54}$. (Ans. C)

6. Rewrite as $3^{x^2-7x} = (3^{-1})^{4x+1} = 3^{-4x-1}$. Equating exponents, we get $x^2 - 7x = -4x - 1$ or $x^2 - 3x + 1 = 0$. Using the quadratic formula, $x = (3 \pm \sqrt{5})/2$. (Ans. C)

7.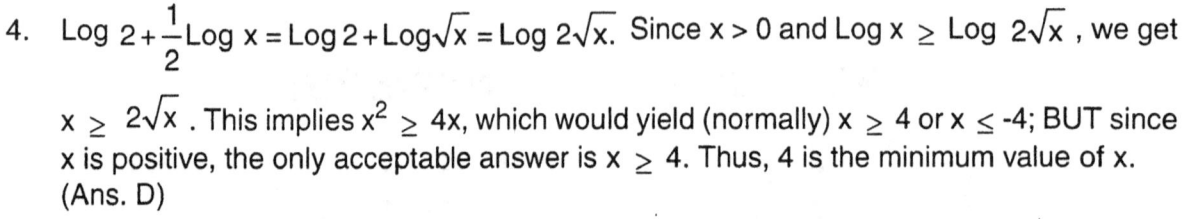

   Now solving $3x^2 + 8x - 11 = 0$ to get $(3x+11)(x-1) = 0$. Thus, $x = 1$ and $-\frac{11}{3}$. (Ans. A)

5 (#3)

8. Since -2 is a solution of $x^3 - 2x^2 - 5x + 6 = 0$, $x+2$ is a factor. Likewise, the numbers 1 and 3 are solutions of $x^3 - 2x^2 - 5x + 6$; so $(x-1)$ and $(x-3)$ are factors. The three factors are $(x-1)$, $(x+2)$, $(x-3)$. (Ans. D)

9. $f(x) + f(x+1) = 3^x + 3^{x+1} = 3x(1+3^1) = 4(3^x) = 4f(x)$. (Ans. D)

10. Substitute $x^2 = 1 - 9y^2$ into the second equation $(1-9y^2) + 9y^2 = 9$. This leads to $0y^2 = 8$. Thus, no solution. (Ans. D)

11. $(256)^{.16} (256)^{.09} = 256^{.25} = \sqrt[4]{256} = 4$. (Ans. A)

12. sixth term $= (_9C_5)(\frac{2}{x\sqrt{3}})^4 (\frac{x^2}{2})^5 = (126)(\frac{2^4}{9x^4})(\frac{x^{10}}{2^5}) = 7x^6$. (Ans. A)

13. $_5C_1 + _5C_2 + _5C_3 + _5C_4 + _5C_5 = 5 + 10 + 10 + 5 + 1 = 31$, where $_aC_b$ means combinations of a items taken b at a time. (Ans. C)

14. The polynomial $x^3 + 3x^2 + cx + 5$ must have a value of 13 when 2 is substituted for x. (Remainder Theorem). Thus, $8 + 12 + 2c + 5 = 13$. Then, $c = -6$. (Ans. A)

15. If $a + bi = c + di$, then $a = c$ and $b = d$. Thus, $3x + 2y = 12$ and $x = -2y$. Then, $x = 6$, $y = -3$. Choice B is CORRECT. (Ans. B)

16. Determine $\frac{dy}{dx} = 3x^2 - 2x + 1$. Evaluate $3x^2 - 2x + 1$ at $x = 1$ to get 2. Thus, the tangent has a slope of 2 and passes through $(\frac{1}{3}, 0)$. Note that the 0 y-value was obtained by evaluating $x^3 - x^2 + x - 1$ at $x = 1$. Finally, the equation of the tangent is $y = 2x - 2$. (Ans. D)

17. Let x = number of boys, y = number of girls. Realize that the total weight of the entire group of boys and girls can be expressed as either the total number of boys and girls times their average weight or the total weight of boys plus the total weight of the girls. Thus, $(x+y)(40) = 50x + 35y$. This reduces to $10x = 5y$ or $x:y = 1:2$. (Ans. B)

18. Let $\log_a b = x$ so that $a^x = b$. Let $\log_b a = y$ so that $b^y = a$. By substitution, $a^x = (b^y)^x = b$. This implies that $xy = 1$. (Ans. A)

19. $f[g(x)] = f(x^2-4) = 2(x^2-4) - 3 = 2x^2 - 11$
    $g[f(x)] = g(2x-3) = (2x-3)^2 - 4 = 4x^2 - 12x + 5$
    Now, $f[g(x)] - g[f(x)] = -2x^2 + 12x - 16 = -2(x^2-6x+8)$. (Ans. A)

20. Let distance from A to B be x miles. Average rate = total distance divided by total time = $(x+x) \div (\frac{x}{380} + \frac{x}{420}) = 2x \div [(x)(800)/159,600] = 399$ mph. (Ans. D)

TEST 4

DIRECTIONS: Each question or incomplete statement is followed by several suggested answers or completions. Select the one that BEST answers the question or completes the statement. *PRINT THE LETTER OF THE CORRECT ANSWER IN THE SPACE AT THE RIGHT.*

1. The values of x that satisfy the equation $|3x-4| = |5-4x|$ may be described as follows:

   A. 2 values of x < 0
   B. 2 values of x > 0
   C. 1 value of x > 0, 1 value of x < 0
   D. 2 values of x > 0, 2 values of x < 0

2. Two of the roots of the equation $2x^3 - 12x^2 + px + q = 0$ are 2 and 3. The third root is

   A. 1   B. 2   C. -1   D. -7

3. An equation with real coefficients has 2+i, 3, and 4 among its roots. The LOWEST possible degree of the equation is

   A. 5   B. 6   C. 3   D. 4

4. In the complex number system $\dfrac{1}{i} + \dfrac{1}{i^2} + \dfrac{1}{i^3}$ equals

   A. 1   B. -1   C. 2i   D. 1-i

5. The value of $[1-2(2-3)^{-1}]^{-1}$ is

   A. -1   B. 2   C. $\dfrac{1}{3}$ D. $-\dfrac{1}{3}$

6. An eleventh year mathematics class studying complex numbers was asked to express the quotient $\dfrac{\sqrt{36}}{\sqrt{-9}}$ in terms of i.

   Student A wrote $\dfrac{\sqrt{36}}{\sqrt{-9}} = \sqrt{\dfrac{36}{-9}} = \sqrt{-4} = 2i$

   Student B wrote $\dfrac{\sqrt{36}}{\sqrt{-9}} = \dfrac{6}{3i} = \dfrac{2}{i}$

   Student C wrote $\dfrac{\sqrt{36}}{\sqrt{-9}} = \dfrac{6}{3i} = \dfrac{2}{i} \cdot \dfrac{i}{i} = \dfrac{2i}{i^2} = \dfrac{2i}{-1} = -2i$

   The students who expressed this CORRECTLY were

   A. A and B *only*   B. A and C *only*
   C. B and C *only*   D. all three

7. The expression $\dfrac{1}{a^{-1}+b^{-1}}$ equals

   A. $a+b$ B. $\dfrac{1}{-a-b}$ C. $(a+b)^1$ D. $\dfrac{ab}{a+b}$

8. If $f(x) = 2^x$, where x is real, and if f^{-1} denotes the inverse function of f, then when $a > 1$ and $b > 1$, $\dfrac{f^{-1}(a)}{f^{-1}(b)} =$

   A. $\dfrac{2^b}{2^a}$ B. $\log_2 a - \log_2 b$ C. $\dfrac{\log_2 a}{\log_2 b}$ D. $2^{\frac{b}{a}}$

9. The x-intercept(s) of the graph $y = x^3 - 6x^2 + 12x - 8$ is(are)

   A. 1 and 2 B. 2 C. -8 and 2 D. -8

10. The third term in the expansion of $(x-2y)^8$ is

    A. $112x^6y^2$ B. $-112x^6y^2$ C. $28x^5y^3$ D. $-28x^5y^3$

11. How many hours does it take a train, traveling at an average rate of 30 mph between stops, to travel m miles if it makes s stops of t minutes each?

    A. $\dfrac{2m+st}{60}$ B. $\dfrac{m+st}{60}$ C. $30m + st$ D. $\dfrac{m}{30} + st$

12. When a positive integer x is divided by a positive integer y, the quotient is w and the remainder is z where w and z are integers.
    The remainder when x+3wy is divided by y is

    A. z B. w C. 3w D. 0

13. A train takes 12 seconds to pass through the entrance of a tunnel. Fifteen seconds later, the train is completely out of the tunnel. Assuming that the speed of the train remains constant and the tunnel is 435 yards long, the length of the train is _____ yards.

    A. 348 B. 360 C. 372 D. 384

14. The area of the circle whose equation is $x^2 + y^2 + 4x - 1 = 0$ is

    A. π B. 5π C. 16π D. 25π

15. The solution set of $|x+2| \leq 6$ is

    A. $-8 \leq x \leq 4$ B. $x \leq -8$ or $x \geq 4$
    C. $-4 \leq x \leq 8$ D. $x \leq -4$ or $x \geq 8$

16. In a class, three times as many students passed a test as failed. The arithmetic mean of grades on the test for the entire class was double the arithmetic mean of all failures on the test.
    If the arithmetic mean of all the passing grades was 84, then the arithmetic mean of all failing grades was

    A. 32 B. 36 C. 42 D. 46

17. The measure of a side of a square is 10. The radius of the circle circumscribed around the square is CLOSEST to

    A. 5 B. 6 C. 7 D. 9

18. Which of the following represents the solution set for x in the equation $\log_8(x-1) + \log_8(x+1) = 1$?

    A. {3, -3} B. {-3} C. {3} D. {8}

19. The expression in SIMPLEST form is

    A. $\dfrac{\sqrt{x}}{2}$ B. $\dfrac{\sqrt{x}+1}{3}$ C. $\dfrac{\sqrt{x}+2}{4}$ D. $\dfrac{2\sqrt{x}-1}{x-1}$

20. A person makes a deposit in a bank which gives 6.4% simple interest per year. After 270 days, his money has grown to 1,310 dollars from the interest.
    Assuming that the bank's interest is based on a year of 360 days, the amount that the person *initially* deposited was

    A. $1150 B. $1175 C. $1225 D. $1250

KEY (CORRECT ANSWERS)

1. B
2. A
3. D
4. B
5. C
6. C
7. D
8. C
9. B
10. A

11. A
12. A
13. A
14. B
15. A
16. B
17. C
18. C
19. A
20. D

SOLUTIONS TO PROBLEMS

1. Either $3x-4 = 5-4x$ or $3x-4 = -(5-4x)$. The solution becomes: $x = \frac{9}{7}$ and $x = 1$. Thus, we have 2 values of $x > 0$. (Ans, B)

2. Since 2 is a root, $16 - 48 + 2p + q = 0$. Since 3 is also a root, $54 - 108 + 3p + q = 0$. Solving, $p = 22$, $q = -12$. Now, $2x^3 - 12x^2 + 22x - 12 = 0$, which equals $x^3 - 6x^2 + 11x - 6 = 0$ can be written as $(x-2)(x-3)(x-R) = 0$. Solving, $R = 1$. Thus, 1 is the third root. (Ans. A)

3. If $2+i$ is a root, then so is $2-i$. Thus, there are at least 4 roots, and 4 must be the lowest possible degree. (Ans. D)

4. This expression can be written as is $\frac{i^2 + i + 1}{i^3} = \frac{i}{i^3} = \frac{i}{-i} = -1$

5. $[1 - 2(2-3)^{-1}]^{-1} = [1 - 2(\frac{1}{-1})]^{-1} = 3^{-1} = \frac{1}{3}$ (Ans. C)

6. Only students B and C CORRECTLY changed to $3i$ first. It should be noted that student C is expressing the answer in preferred form over the form that student B is submitting. (Ans. C)

7. $\frac{1}{a^{-1} + b^{-1}} = \frac{1}{\frac{1}{a} + \frac{1}{b}} = \frac{1}{\frac{b+a}{ab}} = \frac{ab}{b+a}$ or $\frac{ab}{a+b}$ (Ans. D)

8. To find $f^{-1}(x)$, interchange x and y and solve for y.
   Let $y = 2^x$. Change to $x = 2^y$, which is equivalent to $y = \log_2 x$. Thus, $f^{-1}(x) = \log_2 x$.
   Now, $\frac{f^{-1}(a)}{f^{-1}(b)} = \frac{\log_2 a}{\log_2 b}$. (Ans. C)

9. The x-intercept(s) are found by setting $y = x^3 - 6x^2 + 12x - 8 = 0$. But, $x^3 - 6x^2 + 12x - 8 = (x-2)^3$. The solution of $(x-2)^3 = 0$ is 2. (Ans. B)

10. The third term is $(\frac{8 \cdot 7}{1 \cdot 2}) x^6 (-2y)^2 = 112 x^6 y^2$. (Ans. A)

11. Total time = time to travel m miles with no stops + time to (in hours) make s stops of t minutes each $\frac{m}{30} + \frac{st}{60} = \frac{2m + st}{60}$ (Ans. A)

12. $\dfrac{x}{y} = w + \dfrac{z}{y}$ from the given information. Now,

$(x+3wy) \div y = \dfrac{x}{y} + 3w = (w + \dfrac{z}{y}) + 3w = 4w + \dfrac{z}{y}$. Thus, z is the remainder. (Ans. A)

13. The speed of the train is x/12, where the length of the train is x yards. Then, 435 ÷ (x/12) = 15, and thus x = 348. Note that in the 12 seconds required to pass through the tunnel's entrance, the train is traveling the distance of its own length. (Ans. A)

14. Rewrite as $(x+2)^2 + y^2 = 5$, which implies that the radius SQUARED equals 5. Thus, area = 5π. (Ans. B)

15. |x+2| ≤ 6 is equivalent to -6 ≤ x+2 ≤ 6, which yields -8 ≤ x ≤ 4. (Ans. A)

16. Let x = number of students who failed, 3x = number of students who passed, and y = mean of all failing grades. Now, 4x students took the test, and the mean for all 4x students is found as follows: $[(84)(3x) + (y)(x)] / 4x = 63 + \dfrac{y}{4}$. Since this value is double the mean of all failures, we get: $63 + \dfrac{y}{4} = 2y$. Thus, y = 36. (Ans. B)

17. The radius of the circumscribed circle = $(\dfrac{1}{2})$ (diagonal of the square) =

$= (\dfrac{1}{2})(10\sqrt{2}) = 5\sqrt{2} \approx 7.07$. The closest answer is 7. (Ans. C)

18. $\log_8(x-1) + \log_8(x+1) = \log_8(x^2-1)$. Now, $\log_8(x^2-1) = 1$ $x^2-1 = 81$. This leads to 3 and -3 as values of x. But Log (negative number) is undefined. Thus, x = 3 only. (Ans. C)

19. Simplifying the numerator

$\sqrt{x^2 + 2x\sqrt{x} + x} = \sqrt{x(x+2\sqrt{x}+1)} = \sqrt{x(\sqrt{x}+1)(\sqrt{x}+1)} = (\sqrt{x}+1)\sqrt{x}$. Now, the problem

becomes $\dfrac{(\sqrt{x}+1)(\sqrt{x})}{2(\sqrt{x}+1)} = \dfrac{\sqrt{x}}{2}$. (Ans. A)

20. D = initial deposit. 6.4% for a year = $(6.4)(\dfrac{270}{360})$ % = 4.8% for 270 days. Thus,

D + .048D = 1310. D = 1250. (Ans. D)

EXAMINATION SECTION
TEST 1

DIRECTIONS: Each question or incomplete statement is followed by several suggested answers or completions. Select the one that BEST answers the question or completes the statement. *PRINT THE LETTER OF THE CORRECT ANSWER IN THE SPACE AT THE RIGHT.*

1. If a*b is defined as a + 2b, where a and b are real numbers, then

    A. the operation * is commutative
    B. the operation * is associative
    C. the operation * has the closure property
    D. a*1 = a

2. If x is a real number, the solution set of $\{x \mid -x^2 + 3x - 2 < 0\}$ may be described in which one of the following ways?

    A. $\{x \mid x < 1 \text{ or } x > 2\}$
    B. $\{x \mid x < -2 \text{ or } x > -1\}$
    C. $\{x \mid -2 < x < -1\}$
    D. $\{x \mid 1 < x < 2\}$

3. If a car travels two equal distances with a different speed for each distance, then its average speed for the entire trip is (with consistent units) which one of the following? The _____ mean of the speeds involved.

    A. geometric
    B. arithmetic
    C. reciprocal of the arithmetic
    D. harmonic

4. If $\log_4 x + \log_4 1/3 = -5/2$, then x equals

    A. $\dfrac{3}{32}$
    B. $\dfrac{5}{8}$
    C. $\dfrac{3}{4}$
    D. 4

5. If r and s are the roots of $x^2 - px + q = 0$, then $r^2 + s^2$ equals

    A. $p^2 + 2q$
    B. $p^2 - 2q$
    C. $p^2 + q^2$
    D. $p^2 - q^2$

6. The number of terms in the simplified expansion of $[(x+2y)^2(x-2y)^2]^3$ is which one of the following?

    A. 6
    B. 7
    C. 12
    D. 13

7. If $0.3^x = 6$, log 2 = .3010, and log 3 = .4771, then the value of x to the nearest tenth is

    A. -1.6
    B. -1.5
    C. -.5
    D. -.3

8. The sum of the roots of the equation $|x|^2 + |x| - 6 = 0$ is

    A. -6
    B. -1
    C. 0
    D. 1

9. If the complex number a + bi is represented by the ordered pair (a,b), then the multiplicative inverse of the complex number (1,-1) may be represented by which one of the following?

    A. (-1,1)
    B. (1,-1)
    C. $(\dfrac{1}{2},\dfrac{1}{2})$
    D. $(\dfrac{1}{2},-\dfrac{1}{2})$

10. If x and y are real numbers, the area of the region containing the points defined by
$\{(x,y) | (x^2+4y^2 < 16) \cap (2y \geq x-2) \cap (x \geq 0) \cap y \leq 0\}$ is

    A. 1 B. 2 C. 4 D. 6

11. If line AB passes through points (6,0) and (2,3) and intersects the Y-axis at point P, then the line which is perpendicular to AB and passes through point P has a slope and Y-intercept, respectively, equal to

    A. $-\dfrac{3}{4}$ and $4\dfrac{1}{2}$
    B. $\dfrac{3}{4}$ and $4\dfrac{1}{2}$
    C. $\dfrac{4}{3}$ and -8
    D. $\dfrac{4}{3}$ and $4\dfrac{1}{2}$

12. If a plane parallel to the base of a cone divides the altitude into two segments from vertex to base in the ratio a:b, then which one of the following is the ratio of the volumes of the two parts into which this cone is divided?

    A. $a^3 : b^3$
    B. $a^3 : b(3a^2+3ab+b^2)$
    C. $a^3 : (a+b)^3$
    D. $b^3 : a(a^2+3ab+3b^2)$

13. Of the following, the equation of a circle which passes through (2,0) and (6,0) and is tangent to the Y-axis is

    A. $(x-4)^2 + (y-\sqrt{12})^2 = 4$
    B. $(x-\sqrt{12})^2 + (y-3)^2 = 8$
    C. $(x-4)^2 + (y-\sqrt{12})^2 = 16$
    D. $x^2 + (y-12)^2 = 16$

14. Which one of the following lines is NOT an asymptote of the graph of the equation $xy^2 - y^2 - 4x + 1 = 0$?

    A. $x = 1$ B. $x = -1$ C. $y = 2$ D. $y = -2$

15. The SHORTEST distance from the point (-8,2) to the curve $x^2 + y^2 - 8x - 14y + 40 = 0$ is

    A. 5 B. 8 C. 12 D. 13

16. The equation of the ellipse, the length of whose minor axis is 8 and whose foci are at the points in which the circle $x^2 + y^2 = 9$ intercepts the x-axis, is which one of the following?

    A. $\dfrac{x^2}{9} + \dfrac{y^2}{16} = 1$
    B. $\dfrac{x^2}{16} + \dfrac{y^2}{9} = 1$
    C. $\dfrac{x^2}{16} + \dfrac{y^2}{25} = 1$
    D. $\dfrac{x^2}{25} + \dfrac{y^2}{16} = 1$

17. The equation of the directrix of the parabola $y^2 - 4x - 6y + 9 = 0$ is

    A. $x = -2$ B. $x = -1$ C. $x = 1$ D. $x = 2$

18. The solution set of $2x^2 + 7x - 4 < 0$ consists of all real values of x, such that   18.____

    A. x>4 or x<1/2
    B. x < -4 or x > 1/2
    C. -4 < x < -1/2
    D. -4 < x < 1/2

19. The repeating decimal, .152525.., is equivalent to which one of the following fractions?   19.____

    A. $\dfrac{146}{957}$
    B. $\dfrac{151}{990}$
    C. $\dfrac{6,101}{40,000}$
    D. $\dfrac{610,101}{4,000,000}$

20. If $3x^3 - 9x^2 + kx - 12$ is exactly divisible by x - 3, then it is also exactly divisible by which one of the following   20.____

    A. $3x^2 - x + 4$
    B. $3x^2 - 4$
    C. $3x^2 + 4$
    D. x - 4

KEY (CORRECT ANSWERS)

1. C   11. D
2. A   12. C
3. D   13. C
4. A   14. B
5. B   15. B

6. B   16. D
7. B   17. B
8. C   18. D
9. C   19. B
10. A   20. C

SOLUTIONS TO PROBLEMS

1. $a*b = a+2b$, which is still a real number when a,b are reals. Note: $a*b \neq b*a$ since $a+2b \neq b+2a$ and that neither the associative property nor the statement $a*1 = a$ hold. (Ans. C)

2. $-x^2 + 3x - 2 < 0$ means $x^2 - 3x + 2 > 0$, which implies $(x-2)(x-1) > 0$. Case 1: both $(x-2)$ and $(x-1) > 0$, which implies $x > 2$. Case 2: both $(x-2)$ and $(x-1) < 0$, which implies $x < 1$. The final answer is $x > 2$ or $x < 1$. (Ans. A)

3. Let D = common distance. Let x_1 = 1st speed, x_2 = 2nd speed. Average speed = total distance total time = $(D+D) \div (\frac{D}{x_1} + \frac{D}{x_2}) = (2x_1x_2)/(x_1 + x_2)$. The harmonic mean of two numbers $x_1, x_2 = 1/(\frac{1}{x_1} + \frac{1}{x_2}) \div 2$, which can be shown to be equivalent to $(2x_1x_2)/(x_1+x_2)$. (Ans. D)

4. $Log_4 x + Log_4 \frac{1}{3} = Log_4 \frac{1}{3}x$ by a rule of logs. Now, $Log_4 \frac{1}{3}x = \frac{5}{2}$ means $\frac{1}{3}x = 4^{-\frac{5}{2}} = \frac{1}{32}$. Thus, $x = \frac{3}{32}$ (Ans. A)

5. $rs = q$ and $r + s = p$, since this follows as properties as the roots of a quadratic equation. $(r+s)^2 = r^2 + 2rs + s^2 = p^2$. Since $rs = q$, we have $r^2 + 2q + s^2 = p^2$. Now, $r^2 + s^2$ must be $p^2 - 2q$. (Ans. B)

6. $[(x+2y)^2 (x-2y)^2]^3 = \{[(x+2y)(x-2y)]^2\}^3 = (x^2-4y^2)^6$. This last expression has seven different terms. (Ans. B)

7. $.3^x = 6$ means $(x)(\log .3) = \log 6$. Then, $(x)[(\log 3) + \log .1] = [\log 3 + \log 2]$. $x(.4771 - 1) = .4771 + .3010$. Solving, $x = -1.488$ or approx. -1.5. (Ans. B)

8. If x is positive, this equation reads $x^2 + x - 6$ and if x is negative, the equation reads $x^2 - x - 6$. For x positive, the sum of the two roots; = -1, and for x negative, the sum of the two roots = 1. Thus, the sum of all four roots = 0. (Ans. C)

9. $(1,-1)$ means $1-i$. The multiplicative inverse is $\frac{1}{1-i}$ which $= (\frac{1}{1-i})(\frac{1+i}{1+i}) = \frac{1+i}{2} = \frac{1}{2} + \frac{1}{2i}$. This is represented by $(\frac{1}{2}, \frac{1}{2})$. (Ans. C)

10.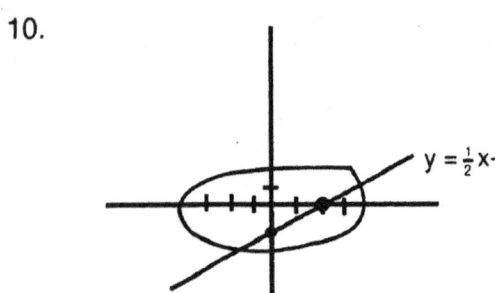

    $x^2 + 4y^2 < 16$ becomes $\frac{x^2}{4^2} + \frac{y^2}{2^2} < 1$, which represents the inside of an ellipse shown here. Shaded area = $(\frac{1}{2})(1)(2) = 1$. (Ans. A)

11.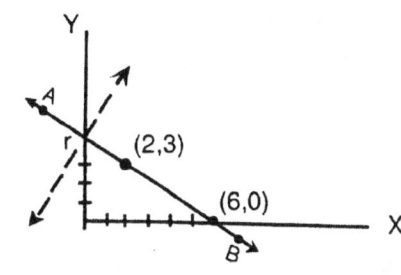

The equation of $\overleftrightarrow{AB}$ is $y = -\frac{3}{4}x + \frac{9}{2}$

Then, P is located at $(0, \frac{9}{2})$. Now, slope of dotted line $= \frac{4}{3}$. (Ans. D)

12.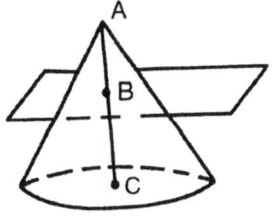

Let AB = a, BC = b, r = radius of circular base of small cone, R = radius of base of large cone. Note: a:a+b = r:R Volume of small cone = $\frac{1}{3}\pi r^2 a$ Volume of large cone $= \frac{1}{3}\pi R^2(a+b)$

Ratio of volumes = $r^2a/R^2(a+b) = a^3/(a+b)^3$ (Ans. C)

13.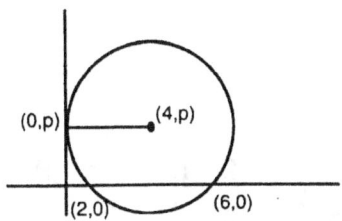

Let point of tangency be (0,p). Since a radius drawn to p must be parallel to the x-axis, the y coordinate of the center is p. Also, the x coordinate is 4 because the center must be equidistant from (2,0) and (6,0). Now, distance from (0,p) to (4,p) = 4 = distance from (4,p) to (2,0) = $\sqrt{p^4 + 4}$. Solving, $4 = \sqrt{p^4 + 4}$, $p = \sqrt{12}$ A circle with center at $(4, \sqrt{12})$ and radius of 4 has equation $(x-4)^2 + (y - \sqrt{12})^2 = 16$. (Ans. C)

14. $x = -1$ is NOT an asymptote since by substitution, $-y^2 - y^2 + 4 + 1 = 0$ and $y = \pm\sqrt{2.5}$. For the other choices, an unsolvable equation appears. (Ans. B)

15.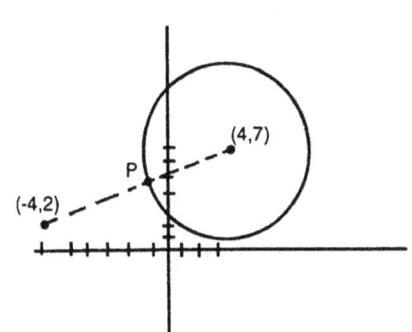

Rewrite $x^2 + y^2 - 8x - 14y + 40 = 0$ as $(x-4)^2 + (y-7)^2 = 2$. This is a circle with center at (4,7) and radius = 5. The shortest distance will be the distance from (-8,2) and p. The equation of the dotted line is $y = \frac{5}{2}x + \frac{64}{12}$ and p lies at the intersection of this dotted line and the circle, which is 5 units from (4,7). Since the distance from (-8,2) to (4,7) is 13, the distance from (-8,2) to p must be 8. (Ans. B)

16. 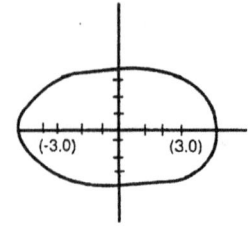 Foci are at ($\pm 3,0$), a = 5, b = 4, so the equation is $x^2/25 + y^2/16 = 1$. Here, a = 1/2 · length of major axis and b = 1/2 · length of minor axis. (Ans. D)

17. If the equation of a parabola is given by $(y-k)^2 = 4p(x-h)$ and the equation of the directrix is x = h-p. Transform $y^2 - 4x - 6y + 9 = 0$ to $(y-3)^2 = 4(x-0)$. Thus, p = 1, h = 0. The equation of the directrix is x = -1. (Ans. B)

18. By factoring, $(2x-1)(x+4) < 0$, which is solved by:

    Case 1: 2x-1 < 0 and x+4 > 0, which implies $-4 < x < \frac{1}{2}$.

    Case 2: 2x-1 > 0 and x+4 < 0, which has no answer. Final answer: $-4 < x < 4\frac{1}{2}$. (Ans. D)

19. Let N = .152525.., then 100N = 15.2525. Now, 99N = 15.1.

    Thus, N = $\frac{151}{990}$. (Ans. B)

20. 3 must be a solution of $3x^3 - 9x^2 + kx - 12 = 0$ if x-3 is a factor. $3(3)^3 - 9(3)^2 + k(3) - 12 = 0$. Then, k = 4. Since $3x^3 - 9x^2 + 4x - 12 = (x-3)(3x^2+4)$, then $3x^2 + 4$ must also divide evenly into $3x^3 - 9x^2 + 4x - 12$. (Ans. C)

TEST 2

DIRECTIONS: Each question or incomplete statement is followed by several suggested answers or completions. Select the one that BEST answers the question or completes the statement. *PRINT THE LETTER OF THE CORRECT ANSWER IN THE SPACE AT THE RIGHT.*

1. A, B, and C are the vertices of an equilateral triangle. A man traveled along its perimeter with the following average speeds: from A to B at r feet per minute, from B to C at s feet per minute, and from C to A at t feet per minute.
His average speed for the entire trip, in feet per minute, was

   A. $1/3(r+s+t)$
   B. $1/3(1/r+1/s+1/t)$
   C. $\dfrac{3rst}{rs+rt+st}$
   D. none of the above

   1.____

2. Given the three sets of coplanar points represented by: $3x + 4y \leq 24$, $x \geq 1$, and $y \geq 2$, then the area of the polygon common to the three sets of points is

   A. 2
   B. $\dfrac{169}{24}$
   C. 14
   D. $\dfrac{169}{12}$

   2.____

3. Other things being equal, the electrical resistance of a wire varies directly as its length and inversely as the square of its diameter.
If a wire 400 feet long and 2.5 mm in diameter has a resistance of 1.1 ohms, then the resistance of a wire of the same material whose length is 300 feet and whose diameter is 2 mm is, to the NEAREST tenth of an ohm,

   A. .5
   B. 1.0
   C. 1.3
   D. none of the above

   3.____

4. Consider the following sets of numbers: positive irrational numbers, complex numbers, positive real numbers, positive rational numbers, positive integers, positive even integers. These sets can be arranged in a nest of sets and subsets, with the exception of one of them.
The one which does NOT fit in such a nest is

   A. positive even integers
   B. complex numbers
   C. positive irrational numbers
   D. positive rational numbers

   4.____

5. If p, r, s, and t are non-negative real numbers; p, r, and s are in arithmetic progression; and r, s, and t are in geometric progression, which one of the following statements is NOT true?

   A. If $p \neq r$, then $s \neq t$
   B. $rt = (2r-p)^2$
   C. $rs = pt$
   D. If $p = 0, t = 4r$

   5.____

6. Of the following, the equation which represents the set of points such that the distance of each from the point (5,3) is twice its distance from the x axis is

   A. $x^2 - 3y^2 - 10x - 6y + 34 = 0$
   B. $x^2 - y^2 - 10x - 6y + 34 = 0$
   C. $x^2 - 3y^2 - 34 = 0$
   D. $x^2 - 3y^2 - 8x + 34 = 0$

   6.____

7. In the hyperbola $9x^2 - y^2 - 36 = 0$, the eccentricity is

   A. $2\sqrt{5}$ B. $\sqrt{10}$ C. $2\sqrt{10}$ D. 12

8. Which one of the following statements is TRUE concerning the graph of $xy - 2y = x$? It is

   A. continuous
   B. asymptotic only to the line $x = 2$
   C. asymptotic only to the line $y = 1$
   D. asymptotic to both lines $x = 2$ and $y = 1$

9. Given $\log 2 = 0.3010$, $\log 3 = 0.4771$, and $\log 7 = 0.8451$. Using these values, find $\log 46\ 2/3$.

   A. .6690 B. 1.6690 C. 1.6232 D. .6232

10. $x^2 - 6x + 8 > 0$ is TRUE for all values of x where

    A. $2 < x < 4$
    C. $x < 4$
    B. $x < 2$ or $x > 4$
    D. $x > 2$

11. The graph of $|x| + |y| = 8$ consists of

    A. one straight line
    C. the sides of a square
    B. a pair of straight lines
    D. a circle

12. The expansion of the determinant:

    $$\begin{vmatrix} x+a & x+2a & x+3a \\ x+2a & x+3a & x+4a \\ x+3a & x+4a & x+5a \end{vmatrix}$$

    is, when simplified,

    A. equal to 0
    B. a third degree expression in x
    C. a linear expression in x
    D. an expression that contains x, but does not contain x

13. The fraction $\dfrac{6}{x^2 - x}$ is equal to the sum of two other fractions whose denominators are x and x-1, respectively, and whose numerators are integers.
    Of the following, which one is one of the two fractions?

    A. $\dfrac{-6}{x-1}$ B. $\dfrac{-3}{x-1}$ C. $\dfrac{6}{x-1}$ D. $\dfrac{3}{x-1}$

14. A certain number is represented by $1+\dfrac{1}{x^2}$, with x a real number.

    If the sum of this number and its reciprocal is 2 1/6, then x MUST be either

    A. $\sqrt{-3} \cdot \sqrt{-3}$
    B. $\sqrt{3}$ or $-\sqrt{3}$
    C. 2 or -2
    D. $\sqrt{2}$ or $-\sqrt{2}$

15. The solution of the inequality $4^{2-2x} < 8x^2$ is

    A. x < -2
    B. x > 2/3
    C. x > 2/3 or x < -2
    D. x > 2/3 and x < -2

16. If the annual percent increase in population of a given community is known to have been constant, and if the population in 1990 was a, and in 2000 was b, then the expression below that represents the population for 1995 was

    A. $\dfrac{a+b}{2}$
    B. $\sqrt{ab}$
    C. $\dfrac{2ab}{a+b}$
    D. $\dfrac{ab}{a+b}$

17. The set of values satisfying the inequality $\left|\dfrac{10-x}{3}\right| < 2$ is

    A. 4 < x < 16
    B. 4 > x > -16
    C. -4 > x > -16
    D. x < 16

18. If the radius of a sphere is doubled, the percent increase in volume is

    A. 200
    B. 400
    C. 700
    D. 800

19. The sum of the reciprocals of the roots of the equation $x^2 + px + q = 0$ is

    A. $-\dfrac{p}{q}$
    B. $\dfrac{q}{p}$
    C. $\dfrac{p}{q}$
    D. $-\dfrac{q}{p}$

20. If $n \neq 0$, the expression $n\sqrt{\dfrac{20}{4^{n+2}+2^{2n+2}}}$ is equal to

    A. $\dfrac{1}{4}$
    B. $\dfrac{1}{2}n\sqrt{10}$
    C. $\dfrac{1}{4}n\sqrt{5}$
    D. $\dfrac{4}{n}$

KEY (CORRECT ANSWERS)

1. C
2. B
3. C
4. C
5. C

6. A
7. B
8. D
9. B
10. B

16. C
17. A
18. C
19. D
20. C

21. B
22. A
23. D
24. A
25. A

SOLUTIONS TO PROBLEMS

1. Let d = distance of each side. The times required to travel from A to B, B to C, and C to A are d/r, d/s, and d/t, respectively. Average speed = total distance ÷ total time = 3d/(d/r+d/s+d/t) = 3rst/(rs+rt+st). (Ans. C)

2. The vertices of A, B, C are $(1, 5\frac{1}{4})$, $(1,2)$ and $(5\frac{1}{3}, 2)$, respectively.

   Area = $(\frac{1}{2})$ (BC)(AB) = $(\frac{1}{2})(4\frac{1}{3})(3\frac{1}{4})$ = 169/24. (Ans. B)

3. $R = KL/D^2$, where R = resistance, L = length, D = diameter, K = constant.
   1.1 = (K)(400)/6.25, so that K = .0172. Now, R = (.0172)(300)/4 = about 1.3. (Ans. C)

4. The positive irrational numbers don't fit in the nest. From the smallest to largest set, we have: positive even integers, positive integers, positive rational numbers, positive real numbers, complex numbers. (Ans. C)

5. Let p = 1, r = 3, s = 5, t = $\frac{25}{3}$. Then, rs = 15 ≠ pt = $\frac{25}{3}$
   Algebraically, we must have r = (p+s)/2 and r/s = s/t. (Ans. C)

6. Let (x,y) be any point of the required equation. The distance from (x,y) to the x-axis is y. The distance from (x,y) to (5,3) is $\sqrt{(x-5)^2-(y-3)^2}$. Now, 2y = $\sqrt{x^2-10x+25+y^2-6y+9}$, which becomes $x^2-3y^2-10x-6y+34 = 0$. (Ans. A)

7. Rewrite as $\frac{x^2}{4} - \frac{y^2}{36} = 1$, so that a = 2, b = 6, c = $\sqrt{40}$ or $2\sqrt{10}$

   Eccentricity = $\frac{c}{a} = \frac{2\sqrt{10}}{2} = \sqrt{10}$. (Ans. B)

8. xy - 2y = x would be asymptotic to x = 2 (since 2y-2y ≠ 2) and to y = 1 (since x-2 ≠ x). (Ans. D)

9. $\text{Log } 46^{\frac{2}{3}} = \text{Log } \frac{140}{3} = \text{Log } 140 - \text{Log } 3 = (\text{Log } 10 + \text{Log } 7 + \text{Log } 2) - \text{Log } 3 = 1.6690.$ (Ans. B)

10. Factor into $(x-4)(x-2) > 0$.
    Case 1: Both factors are > 0, so that $x > 4$.
    Case 2: Both factors are < 0, so that $x < 2$.
    Final answer is $x < 2$ or $x > 4$. (Ans. B)

11. The vertices are: $A(0,8)$, $B(8,0)$, $C(0,-8)$, and $D(-8,0)$.
    The graph is actually a combination of 4 segments: $x+y = 8$, $y-x = 8$, $x+y = -8$, $y-x = -8$.
    This represents a square.
    (Ans. C)

12. This determinant can be reduced to $\begin{vmatrix} 1 & 2 & 3 \\ 2 & 3 & 4 \\ 3 & 4 & 5 \end{vmatrix}$
    The value becomes $(1)(3)(5) + (2)(4)(3) + (3)(4)(2) - (3)(3)(3) - (2)(2)(5) - (1)(4)(4) = 0$. (Ans. A).

13. Writing $\frac{6}{x^2 - x} = \frac{-6}{x} + \frac{6}{x-1}$ one of the fractions is $\frac{6}{x-1}$ (Ans. C)

14. The reciprocal of $1 + \frac{1}{x^2}$ is $\frac{x^2}{x^2 + 1}$. The sum of these two expressions is, which is equal to.
    This is equivalent to $6x^4 + 12x^2 + 6 + 6x^4 = 13x^4 + 13x^2$.
    Solving, $x = \pm\sqrt{2}$ and $\pm 3i$. Thus, only choice D is correct since $\pm 3i$ are imaginary numbers. (Ans. D)

15. $4^{2-2x} < 8^{x^2}$ can be rewritten as $2^{4-4x} < 2^{3x^2}$, which becomes $4-4x < 3x^2$. Now, $(3x-2)(x+2) > 0$, which leads to $x > \frac{2}{3}$ or $x < -2$. (Ans. C)

16. Let k = annual percent increase. Then, $a(1 + \frac{k}{100})^{10} = b$
    Thus, $k = \sqrt[10]{b/a} - 1$. Now, in 1995, the population can be denoted as
    $a(1 + \sqrt[10]{b/a} - 1)^5 = a \cdot \sqrt{b/a} = \sqrt{ab}$. (Ans. B)

17. $\left|\frac{10-x}{3}\right| < 2$ means $-2 < \frac{10-x}{3} < 2$, which is satisfied by $4 < x < 16$.
    (Ans. A)

18. Volume = $\frac{4}{3}\pi R^3$. If 2R replaces R, new volume = $\frac{32}{3}\pi^2 R^3$

    $2^3 = 8$. The percent increase is 800%. (Ans. D)

19. Let R_1, R_2 be the two roots. We require $\frac{1}{R_1} + \frac{1}{R_2}$, which equals $(R_2+R_1)/(R_1)(R_2)$ = Sum of roots/Product of roots = $-p/q$. (Ans. A)

20. $\sqrt[n]{\frac{20}{4^{n+2}+2^{2n+2}}} = \sqrt[n]{\frac{2^2 \cdot 5}{2^{2n+4}+2^{2n+2}}} = \sqrt[n]{\frac{2^2 \cdot 5}{2^{2n+2}(2^2+1)}} = \sqrt[n]{\frac{1}{2^{2n}}} = \frac{1}{4}$ (Ans. A)

TEST 3

DIRECTIONS: Each question or incomplete statement is followed by several suggested answers or completions. Select the one that BEST answers the question or completes the statement. *PRINT THE LETTER OF THE CORRECT ANSWER IN THE SPACE AT THE RIGHT.*

1. If log 2 = .301, log 3 = .477, and log 7 = .845, then log 14.4 =   1.___
   A. 1.158   B. 1.447   C. 2.158   D. 2.447

2. If $\dfrac{A}{x^2-1} + \dfrac{B}{x^2+2} = \dfrac{2x^2+3}{(x^2-1)(x^2+2)}$, the value of (A+B) is   2.___
   A. -2   B. $\dfrac{2}{3}$ C. $\dfrac{4}{3}$ D. 2

3. The product of $(1-1/6)(1-1/7)(1-1/8)\ldots(1-\dfrac{1}{n+4})(1-\dfrac{1}{n+5})$ is   3.___
   A. $\dfrac{3}{(n+4)(n+5)}$ B. $\dfrac{5}{n+4}$ C. $\dfrac{5}{n+5}$ D. ∞

4. The 8th term of $(\dfrac{2a}{3} - \dfrac{3}{2a})^{12}$ is   4.___
   A. $\dfrac{1782}{a^2}$ B. $-1782a^2$ C. $\dfrac{-1782}{a^2}$ D. $1782a^2$

5. If $f(x) = \dfrac{x}{x-1}$, then $f(x+1) =$ 5.___
   A. $\dfrac{1}{f(x)}$ B. $\dfrac{1}{f(x)}+2$ C. $\dfrac{1}{f(x)}+\dfrac{2}{x}$ D. $f(x)+2$

6. A 25-foot ladder is placed against a vertical wall so that the foot of the ladder is 7 feet from the bottom of the wall.   6.___
   If the top of the ladder slips 4 feet, then how many feet will the foot of the ladder slide?
   A. 4   B. 5   C. 8   D. 9

7. A regular octagon is formed by cutting off each corner of a square whose side is 6.   7.___
   The length of one side of the octagon is
   A. 2   B. $2\sqrt{2}$ C. $2\sqrt{2}-2$ D. $6\sqrt{2}-6$

8. The solution set for $x^2-x-2 > 0$ may be represented by which one of the following?   8.___
   A. $\{x|x>-1\} \cup \{x|x<2\}$ B. $\{x|x>-1\} \cap \{x|x<2\}$
   C. $\{x|x<-1\} \cup \{x|x>2\}$ D. $\{x|x<-1\} \cap \{x|x>2\}$

9. The figure below is the graph of which one of the following sentences?

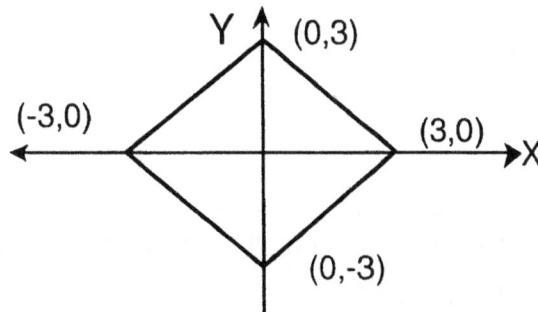

A. $x^2+y^2=9$
B. $|x|=3$ and $|y|=3$
C. $|x+y|=3$
D. $|x| + |y|=3$

10. If the operation * is defined as follows: a*b = 2a + 3b, and all other numerical operational rules hold as always, then the value of 1*(3*2) is equal to

A. 13
B. 22
C. 28
D. 38

11. If f = {(1,3), (2,5), (3,5)}, which one of the following statements is FALSE?

A. The domain of f is {1,2,3}
B. f(f[1]) = 5
C. f is a function
D. The inverse of f is a function

12. The integers, modulo 7, form a group under *multiplication x*.
The inverse of 4 x 6 is

A. 1
B. 3
C. 5
D. 6

13. If X and Y are subsets of the set I, and X^1 and Y^1 are the complements of X and Y, respectively, with respect to I, then the complement of X ∩ Y is

A. $X^1 \cap Y$
B. $X \cup Y^1$
C. $X^1 \cap Y^1$
D. $X^1 \cup Y^1$

14. An Abelian group is a group whose elements satisfy

A. the commutative law but not the associative law
B. the associative law but not the commutative law
C. both the commutative and the associative laws
D. neither the commutative nor the associative laws

15. The shaded portion below is

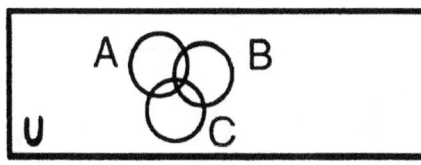

A. $C \cap (A \cup B)^1$
B. $C \cap (A \cup B)$
C. $C \cup (A \cup B)^1$
D. $C \cup (A \cup B)$

16. The equations of the asymptotes of $2x + 3y + 1 = xy$ are

    A. $x - 3 = 0$ and $y - 2 = 0$
    B. $x - 3 = 0$ and $3y + 1 = 0$
    C. $2x + 1 = 0$ and $y - 2 = 0$
    D. $2x + 1 = 0$ and $3y + 1 = 0$

17. The distance between point A(1,2,-1) and point B (x,-2,4) is $5\sqrt{2}$.
    Which one of the following pairs represents the possible values of x?

    A. 1 and 2   B. 1 and -2   C. 4 and 2   D. 4 and -2

18. Find the coordinates of the center of a circle whose equation is $x^2 + y^2 - 4x - 2y - 75 = 0$.

    A. (4,1)   B. (1,4)   C. (2,1)   D. (1,2)

19. The endpoints of a diameter of a circle are (-6,4) and (8,6).
    If A and B are the y-intercept points of the circle, then the length of AB is

    A. $5\sqrt{2}$ B. 10   C. 14   D. $10\sqrt{2}$

20. The equation $r = \dfrac{3}{1 - \cos\theta}$ represents a(n)

    A. circle   B. ellipse   C. hyperbola   D. parabola

KEY (CORRECT ANSWERS)

1.	A	11.	D
2.	D	12.	C
3.	C	13.	D
4.	C	14.	C
5.	C	15.	A
6.	C	16.	A
7.	D	17.	D
8.	C	18.	C
9.	D	19.	C
10.	D	20.	D

SOLUTIONS TO PROBLEMS

1. $\text{Log } 14.4 = \text{Log } \dfrac{144}{10} = \text{Log } 144 - \text{Log } 10 = \text{Log } 2^4 + \text{Log } 3^2 - \text{Log } 10 = (4)(.301) + (2)(.477) - 1 = 1.158$. (Ans. A)

2. $\dfrac{A}{x^2-1} + \dfrac{B}{x^2+2} = \dfrac{A(x^2+2) + B(x^2-1)}{(x^2-1)(x^2+2)}$

   Thus, since $Ax^2 + Bx^2 = 2x^2$, $A + B = 2$. (Ans. D)

3. This product can be rewritten as $(\dfrac{5}{6})(\dfrac{6}{7})(...)(\dfrac{n+3}{n+4})(\dfrac{n+4}{n+5})$.

   Through multiple cancellations, this becomes $\dfrac{5}{n+5}$. (Ans. C)

4. The eighth term $= -({}_{12}C_7)(\dfrac{2a}{3})^5(\dfrac{3}{2a})^7 = (-792)(\dfrac{9}{4a^2}) = -\dfrac{1782}{a^2}$

   This procedure is known as the binomial expansion. (Ans. C)

5. $f(x+1) = \dfrac{x+1}{x+1-1} = \dfrac{x+1}{x} = \dfrac{x-1}{x} + \dfrac{2}{x} = \dfrac{1}{f(x)} + \dfrac{2}{x}$ (Ans. C)

6. Using the Pythagorean Theorem, the top of the ladder is $\sqrt{25^2 - 7^2} = 24$ feet above the ground. If it slips 4 feet, the distance from the base of the ladder to the wall is $\sqrt{25^2 - 20^2} = 15$ feet. Thus, the ladder will have slid $15 - 7 = 8$ feet. (Ans. C)

7.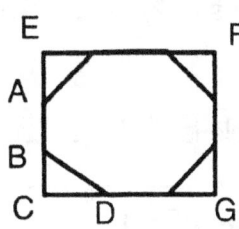

   Let C,E,F,G be vertices of the square. Let $BC = CD = EA = x$.

   Then, $BD = \sqrt{x^2 + x^2} = x\sqrt{2}$.

   Now, $AB = x\sqrt{2}$. Since $EC = 6 = EA + AB + BC = x + x\sqrt{2} + x$.

   Solving, $x = 6 - 3\sqrt{2}$.

   Thus, $AB = (6 - 3\sqrt{2})(\sqrt{2}) = 6\sqrt{2} - 6$ (Ans. D)

8. $x^2 - x - 2 > 0$ becomes $(x-2)(x+1) > 0$.
   Case 1: $x-2 > 0$ and $x+1 > 0$, which yields $x > 2$
   Case 2: $x-2 < 0$ and $x+1 < 0$, which yields $x < -1$
   Thus, either $x > 2$ or $x < -1$; i.e., $\{x|x<-1\} \cup \{x|x>2\}$ (Ans. C)

9. The four sides can be represented by $x+y = 3$, $y = x-3$, $y = -x-3$, and $y = x+3$. Condensing, this is equivalent to $|x| + |y| = 3$. (Ans. D)

10. 1 * (3*2) = 1 * [(2)(3)+(3)(2)] = 1 * 12 = 2(1)+3(12) = 38 (Ans. D)

11. Inverse of f = {(3,1),(5,2),(5,3)}, which is NOT a function. (Ans. D)

12. 4 x 6 = 24, which is 3(mod 7). The inverse n is such that 3 x n = 1. By trying different numbers, we find n = 5. (Ans. C)

13. 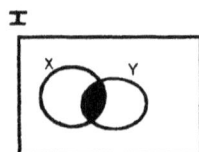 Complement of X ∩ Y is everything in I which is NOT shaded = $X^1 \cup Y^1$. (Ans. D)

14. A group must have the property of associativity. If it is an Abelian group, the commutativity property must also exist. (Ans. C)

15. 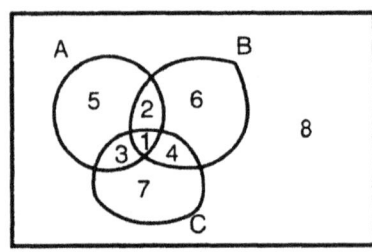 By numbering the regions, we seek region 7.
C = regions 1,3,4,7 and A ∪ B = regions 1,2,3,4,5,6.
Thus, $(A \cup B)^1$ = regions 7,8.
Now, C K (A ∪ B)1 = region 7. (Ans. A)

16. If x = 3, 2x+3y+1 = xy becomes 6+3y+1 = 3y (no value for y).
If y = 2, the above equation becomes 2x+6+1 = 2x (no value for x) (Ans. A)

17. Distance = $\sqrt{(1-x)^2 + (2-[-2])^2 + (-1-4)^2} = 5\sqrt{2}$
This reduces to $x^2 - 2x - 9 = 0$. Solving, x = 4 and x = -2. (Ans. D)

18. Rewrite as $x^2 - 4x + 4 + y^2 - 2y + 1 = 75 + 4 + 1$, which becomes $(x-2)^2 + (y-1)^2 = 80$. The center is located at (2,1). (Ans. C)

19. 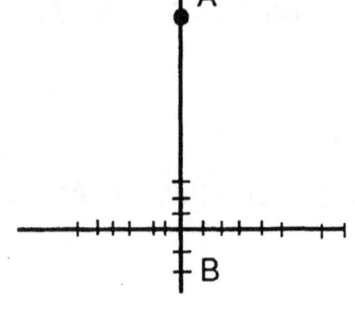 The center of the circle is $(\frac{-6+8}{2}, \frac{4+6}{2}) = (1,5)$
The radius is of length $\sqrt{(8-1)^2 + (6-5)^2} = \sqrt{50}$
Thus, the equation of the circle can be written as $(x-1)^2 + (y-5)^2 = 50$. The y-intercepts would be solutions to $(0-1)^2 + (y-5)^2 = 50$. So, the y-intercepts are 12 and -2. Length of AB = 14. (Ans. C)

20. Convert the equation to r - rcos θ = 3, which becomes
$\sqrt{x^2+y^2} - x = 3$. This simplifies to $y^2 = 6x+9$, which is a parabola. (Ans. D)

TEST 4

DIRECTIONS: Each question or incomplete statement is followed by several suggested answers or completions. Select the one that BEST answers the question or completes the statement. *PRINT THE LETTER OF THE CORRECT ANSWER IN THE SPACE AT THE RIGHT.*

1. What is the equation of the perpendicular bisector of the line segment whose end points are (2,6) and (-4,3)?   1.____

   A. $4x + 2y - 5 = 0$
   B. $x - 2y + 10 = 0$
   C. $4x - 2y + 13 = 0$
   D. $x + 2y - 8 = 0$

2. Which one of the following principles involving exponents that are natural numbers MOST directly suggests the definition that $x = 1$?   2.____

   A. $x^a \div x^b = x^{a-b}, x \neq 0, a \geq b$
   B. $(x^a)^b = x^{ab}$
   C. $x^a y^a = (xy)^a$
   D. $x^a \div y^a = (\frac{x}{y})^a, y \neq 0$

3. The first and second terms of a geometric series are x^{-4} and x^t, and ($x \neq 0$), respectively. If x^{52} is the eighth term of the series, t is equal to   3.____

   A. 5/2   B. 24/7   C. 4   D. 16/3

4. The resistance of a wire is directly proportional to the length and inversely proportional to the cross-sectional area. A 100-foot roll of a given size wire has a resistance of 4 ohms. A 250-foot roll of wire, whose diameter is one-third that of the wire on the first roll, will have a resistance, in ohms, of   4.____

   A. 3 1/3   B. 30   C. 54   D. 90

5. The multiplicative inverse of $1 + \sqrt{2}$ is which one of the following?   5.____

   A. $1 + \sqrt{2}$ B. $-1 + \sqrt{2}$ C. $-1 - \sqrt{2}$ D. $1 - \sqrt{2}$

6. Which one of the following describes the roots of the equation $x^2 - 2ix - 1 = 0$ (where $i = \sqrt{-1}$)?   6.____

   A. Imaginary and equal
   B. Imaginary and unequal
   C. Rational and equal
   D. Rational and unequal

7. Eliminating t from a parametric equations, $x = 1 - e^t$ and $y = 1 + e^{-t}$, yields   7.____

   A. $y = \frac{1}{x-1}$
   B. $y = \frac{x-2}{x-1}$
   C. $y = \frac{2-x}{x-1}$
   D. $y = \frac{x}{x-1}$

8. If $|2x+3| < 7$, then   8.____

   A. $-5 < x < -2$
   B. $-2 < x < 5$
   C. $2 < x < 5$
   D. $-5 < x < 2$

145

9. The solution set of $7x - 3 > (x+1)^2$ is which one of the following?

   A. $\{x|x < 1\} \cap \{x|x > 4\}$
   B. $\{x|x < 1\} \cup \{x|x > 4\}$
   C. $\{x|x > 1\} \cap \{x|x < 4\}$
   D. $\{x|x > 1\} \cup \{x|x < 4\}$

10. Two roots of the equation $x^3 + px + q = 0$ are -1 and 3. The third root is

    A. 1   B. -1   C. 2   D. -2

11. The ratio of $\log_2 15$ to $\log_8 225$ is

    A. 1/2   B. 2/1   C. 3/2   D. 2/3

12. If the logarithms in the equation $2 \log_{10} x - \log_{10}(30-2x) = 1$ are real numbers, then the solution set of this equation is which one of the following?

    A. $\{10, -30\}$ B. $\{10\}$ C. $\{-30\}$ D. $\{\ \}$

13. The determinant $\begin{vmatrix} a & 3 & 2 \\ 1 & 0 & 2 \\ 3 & 1 & -1 \end{vmatrix}$ has the value 19.

    The value of $\underline{a}$ is

    A. -19   B. -19/2   C. -2   D. 2

14. The line segment joining the points (-4,1) and (8,-8) is cut by the y-axis to form two line segments in the ratio

    A. 1:3   B. 1:2   C. 2:3   D. 2:5

15. If the lines whose equations are $2x + 3y = 7$ and $3x + ay = 12$ intersect at an angle of 90, then the value of a is

    A. $-\dfrac{9}{2}$ B. $+\dfrac{9}{2}$ C. -2   D. +2

16. In the figure at the right, line AB is perpendicular to line BC. Line segment XY slides into different positions so that X is always on AB, and Y is always on BC. If Z is the midpoint of XY, then the locus of Z is

    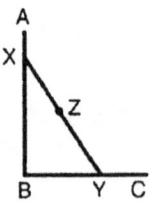

    A. a line
    B. an arc of a circle
    C. one branch of a hyperbola
    D. an arc of an ellipse

17. The area of the triangle, bounded by the lines whose equations are $5y = 4x - 5$ and $2x + 5y = 25$, respectively, and the y-axis, is

    A. 10   B. 15   C. 18   D. 20

18. The coordinates of the vertex of the parabola $y = x^2 + 8x - 3$ are   18.____

    A. (-8,-3)   B. (8,125)   C. (4,45)   D. (-4,-19)

19. If k is real and $ax + by + c = 0$ and $dx + ey + f = 0$ are the equations of two intersecting   19.____
    lines, then the equation of a system of lines passing through their intersection

    A. $(ax+by+c) + k(dx+ey+f) = 0$
    B. $k(ax+by+c)(dx+ey+f) = 0$
    C. $(ax+by+c) + (dx+ey+f) = k$
    D. $K(\dfrac{ax+by+c}{dx+ey+f}) = 0$

20. The graph of $|x| + |y| \geq 1$ includes points in quadrant(s)   20.____

    A. I but no other quadrants
    B. I and II but no other quadrants
    C. I, II, and III but no other quadrants
    D. I, II, III, and IV

KEY (CORRECT ANSWERS)

1.	A	11.	C
2.	A	12.	D
3.	C	13.	D
4.	D	14.	B
5.	B	15.	C
6.	A	16.	B
7.	B	17.	B
8.	D	18.	D
9.	C	19.	A
10.	D	20.	D

SOLUTIONS TO PROBLEMS

1. 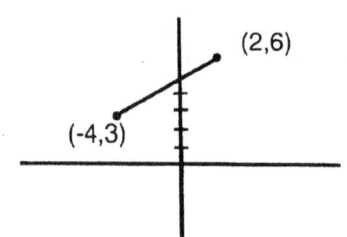 The midpoint of the line segment is (-1,4.5). Since the slope of this segment is 4, the slope of the perpendicular bisector is -2. The equation of the perpendicular bisector is y - 4.5 = -2(x+1), which becomes 4x + 2y -5 = 0. (Ans. A)

2. Since $x^a \div x^b = x^{a-b}$. Letting a = b, this can be written as $x^a \div x^a = x^0$ and $x^a \div x^a$ must be 1. Thus, $x^0 = 1$. Note: the correction in selection A from a > b to a ^ b. (Ans. A)

3. $x^t \div x^{-4} = x^{t+4}$ and this must be the common ratio of the geometric series. x^{52} = eighth term $(x^{-4})(x^{t+4})$ Now, 52 = 7t+24 and so t = 4. (Ans. C)

4. R = KL/A, where R = resistance, K = constant of proportionality, L = length, A = area. Let 9 = cross-sectional area of the first wire. Since the second wire has a diameter only 1/3 that of the first wire, its area would be $\frac{1}{9}(9) = 1$. 4 = (K)(100)/9 and K =.36. Now, resistant of second wire = (.36)(250)/1 = 90 ohms. (Ans. D)

5. $(1+\sqrt{2})(M) = 1$, where M = multiplicative inverse.
$M = 1/(1+\sqrt{2}) = [1/(1+\sqrt{2})][(1-\sqrt{2})/(1-\sqrt{2})] = -1 + \sqrt{2}$ (Ans. B)

6. The roots of $x^2 - 2ix - 1 = 0$ are $[2i \pm \sqrt{(2i)^2 - 4(1)(-1)}]/2 = (2i\pm)/2 = i$ (double root). This is an imaginary root. (Ans. A)

7. Since $e^t = 1 - x$, $e^{-t} \frac{1}{1-x}$ = So, $y = 1 + e^{-t} = 1 + \frac{1}{1-x} = \frac{2-X}{1-X} = \frac{X-2}{X-1}$ (Ans. B)

8. |2x+3| < 7 means -7 < 2x + 3 < 7, which yields -5 < x < 2. (Ans. D)

9. $7x - 3 > (x+1)^2$ simplifies to $x^2 - 5x + 4 < 0$ or (x-4)(x-1) < 0. The solution is 1 < x < 4, which means {x|x > 1}∩{x|x < 4}. (Ans. C)

10. $(-1)^3 + p(-1) + q = 0$ and $(3)^3 + p(3) + q = 0$. Solving these two equations yields p = -7 and q = -6. The original equation becomes $x^3 - 7x - 6 = 0$. Since $x^3 - 7x - 6 = (x+1)(x-3)(x+2)$, the third root is -2. (Ans. D)

11. $\text{Log}_2 15 = x$ means $2^x = 15$. $\text{Log}_8 225 = y$ means $8^y = 225$ or $(2^3)^y = 15^2$. This implies $2^{\frac{3}{2}y} = 15$ and so $x = \frac{3}{2}y$. Thus, the ratio of $\text{Log}_2 15$ to $\text{Log}_8 225 = x/y = 3/2$. (Ans. C)

12. $2\text{Log}_{10}x = \text{Log}_{10}x^2$. $2\text{Log}_{10}x - \text{Log}_{10}(30-2x) = \text{Log}_{10}(\frac{x^2}{30-2x})$. Now, if $\text{Log}_{10}(\frac{x^2}{30-2x}) = 120$, $\frac{x^2}{30-2x} = 10$. Thus, the solution becomes none of the given real numbers. In fact, because $30-2x$ must be > 0, this would force $x < 15$. Final answer is $\{\}$. (Ans. D)

13. The value of the determinant is gotten by: $(a)(0)(-1) + (3)(2)(3) + (2)(1)(1) - (2)(0)(3) - (3)(1)(-1) - (a)(1)(2)$ and this $= 19$ Thus, $18 + 2 + 3 - 2a = 19$, and so $a = 2$. (Ans. D)

14.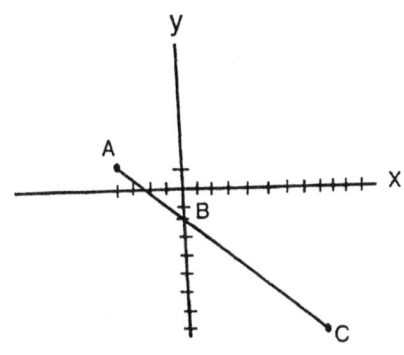

    Slope of $\overline{AC} = \frac{-8-1}{8-(-4)} = -\frac{3}{4}$ B is located at $(0,-2)$. $AB = \sqrt{4^2 + 3^2} = 5$ and $BC = \sqrt{8^2 + 6^2} = 10$. $5:10 = 1:2$ (Ans. B)

15. Two lines which intersect at 90 will have slopes which are negative inverses of each other. The slope of $2x + 3y = 7$ is $-\frac{2}{3}$, and so the slope of $3x + ay = 12$ must be $\frac{3}{2}$. Thus, $-\frac{3}{a} = \frac{3}{2}$ and $a = -2$. (Ans. C)

16.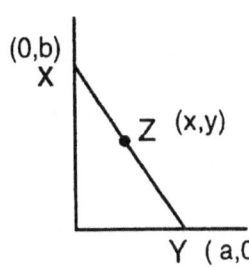

    Z = midpoint, distance of XY = constant. Thus, $\sqrt{a^2 + b^2}$ is a constant. Now, distance of XZ = distance of YZ.
    $\sqrt{x^2 + (y-b)^2} = \sqrt{(x-z)^2 + y^2}$.
    Simplifying, $x^2 + y^2 - 2by + b^2 = x^2 - 2ax + a^2 + y^2$. (Ans. B)

17.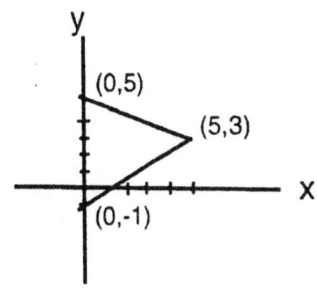

    Using the segment connecting $(0,-1)$ and $(0,5)$ as the base, the height would extend from $(5,3)$ to $(0,3)$. Area $= (\frac{1}{2})(\text{base})(\text{height}) = (\frac{1}{2})(6)(5) = 15$. (Ans. B)

18. Rewrite $y = x^2 + 8x - 3$ as $y = (x+4)^2 - 19$. The vertex is $(-4,-19)$, and this represents the lowest point of the parabola. (Ans. D)

19. Since $ax + by + c = 0$ and $dx + ey + f = 0$, the sum of these two equations would also be zero. Also, $k(dx+ey+f) = 0$. Thus, $(ax+by+c) + k(dx+ey+f) = 0$. (Ans. A)

20. 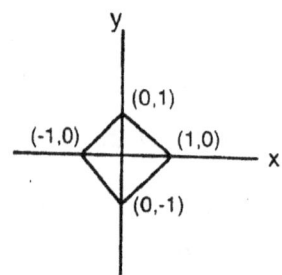 The square on the left is identifiec by: $|x| + |y| = 1$. The graph of $|x| + |y| \geq 1$ would also include everything exterior to the square, and so would include points in all four quadrants. (Ans. D)

EXAMINATION SECTION
TEST 1

DIRECTIONS: Each question or incomplete statement is followed by several suggested answers or completions. Select the one that BEST answers the question or completes the statement. *PRINT THE LETTER OF THE CORRECT ANSWER IN THE SPACE AT THE RIGHT.*

1. In the regular sequence $5\frac{1}{3}$, $8\frac{23}{24}$, $11\frac{7}{12}$, $14\frac{5}{24}$, ..., the next term is

    A. $16\frac{1}{6}$ B. $16\frac{11}{24}$ C. $16\frac{5}{8}$ D. $16\frac{5}{6}$

    1.____

2. 6, 12, 14, 28, 30, 60, _____
    Assuming that the above numerical series continues in the same pattern, which one of the following is the missing numeral?

    A. 120   B. 32   C. 62   D. 90

    2.____

3. If the probability that an event will occur is 3/5, then the probability that it will NOT occur is

    A. 1/5   B. 1/3   C. 2/5   D. 5/3

    3.____

4. If a number is increased by 400%, it is multiplied by

    A. 3   B. 4   C. 5   D. 400

    4.____

5. The LOWEST common multiple of 18 and 24 is equal to

    A. 1/4 the product of 18 and 24
    B. 1/3 the product of 18 and 24
    C. the product of the highest common factor and the smaller of the numbers
    D. the product of the numbers divided by the highest common factor

    5.____

6. In the multiplication example at the right, the value of the second partial product is

    A. 269
    B. 2,690
    C. 26,900
    D. 269,000

    ```
        538
      X 257
      -----
       3766
       2690
       1076
      ------
      138,266
    ```

    6.____

7. Of the following statements about operations involving the terms of a fraction, which one is NOT true?

    A. Multiplying the numerator multiplies the fraction.
    B. Multiplying the denominator divides the fraction.
    C. Dividing the denominator divides the fraction.
    D. Dividing the numerator divides the fraction.

    7.____

8. If A is 2/3 as large as B and C is 1/2 as large as B, then it is TRUE that

   A. A + C is smaller than B
   B. three times C is smaller than twice A
   C. twice A is larger than twice C by 1/3 of the latter
   D. twice B is smaller than A + C

9. In a number system with the base 7, what number is equivalent to 269 in the decimal system?

   A. 524   B. 533   C. 542   D. 623

10. What is the number in the decimal system which is equivalent to 1011 in the binary system?

    A. 3   B. 11   C. 22   D. 1011

11. The intersection of the set of boys in the sixth grade of a given school with the set consisting of class 6-1 in that school is composed of

    A. the boys in class 6-1
    B. the girls in class 6-1
    C. all of class 6-1
    D. all boys in the sixth grade except for those in class 6-1

12. The operation under which the set of positive integers is closed and has the identity element 1 is

    A. addition   B. subtraction
    C. multiplication   D. division

13. 8 x 57 = (8 x 50) + (8 x 7)
    The above equation is an application of which one of the following mathematical concepts?

    A. Distributive law
    B. Associative law for addition
    C. Commutative law for multiplication
    D. Multiplicative identity

14. If ten pupils get the test scores 10, 20, 20, 55, 70, 70, 70, 80, 90, 100, then the

    A. mode of their scores is 20
    B. median of their scores is 70
    C. arithmetic mean of their scores is 70
    D. range of their scores is 80

15. Of a class of 35 pupils who took a given test, 8 scored 80%, 9 scored 70%, 14 scored 60%, and 4 were absent.
    The four absent children were given a special test a few days later.
    If the arithmetic mean is to be used as the average score, in order for the entire class to average 70%, the average score in the special test MUST be

    A. 75%   B. 82%   C. 83%   D. 85%

16. In order to get to his destination, Mr. Stone walked for 1/2 hour at 3 miles per hour, rode by bus for 3/4 hour at 30 miles per hour, and then traveled the remaining distance by train for hours at 55 miles per hour.
    Using the arithmetic mean as the average, the average speed of travel for the entire journey, in miles per hour, is CLOSEST to which one of the following?

    A. 43   B. 44   C. 47   D. 51

    16._____

Questions 17-25.

DIRECTIONS: METHOD I - Write the letter of the CORRECT answer in the space at the right.

METHOD II - In the space at the right, write the letter of the number which corresponds to the number of the CORRECT answer.

17. The value of $x + x + x + 2x$ is

    A. $2x^4$ B. $4x^2$
    C. $5x^4$ D. $5x$
    E. none of the above is correct

    17._____

Questions 18-20.

DIRECTIONS: For Questions 18 to 20, find the value of each expression if $a = 2$, $b=3$, $c = -4$.

18. $4a + 2b$

    A. 11   B. 10   C. 6
    D. 14   E. none of the above is correct

    18._____

19. $3b^2 - 2ac$

    A. 43   B. 11   C. 97
    D. 65   E. none of the above is correct

    19._____

20. $\sqrt{c^2 - 3(a+b)}$

    A. -31   B. 1   C. 13
    D. 9   E. none of the above is correct

    20._____

21. $x^3 \cdot x^2 =$

    A. x^6 B. $2x^3$ C. $3x^2$
    D. x^5 E. none of the above is correct

    21._____

22. Simplify as much as possible: $\dfrac{x - \dfrac{1}{x}}{1 - \dfrac{1}{x}}$ $(X \neq 0)$

    A. $x-1$ B. $x+1$ C. $\dfrac{1}{x} - 1$

    22._____

D. $\dfrac{1}{x+1}$ E. none of the above is correct

23. Simplify: $\sqrt{9x^2y^4}$

    A. $3x^2y^2$ B. $9xy^2$ C. $3xy^3$
    D. $3xy$ E. none of the above is correct

24. Simplify: $\sqrt{4a^2 + 4ab^2 + b^4}$

    A. $2(a+b^2)$ B. $a + 2b^2$ C. $2a(a+b)$
    D. $2a + b^2$ E. none of the above is correct

25. Multiply: $(\sqrt{6} - \sqrt{3})(\sqrt{6} + \sqrt{3})$

    A. 27   B. 45   C. 3
    D. 9   E. none of the above is correct

23. ___
24. ___
25. ___

KEY (CORRECT ANSWERS)

1. D
2. C
3. C
4. C
5. D
6. C
7. C
8. C
9. B
10. B

11. A
12. C
13. A
14. B
15. D
16. A
17. D
18. D
19. A
20. B

21. D
22. B
23. E
24. D
25. C

SOLUTION TO PROBLEM

1. The difference between successive numbers is $2\frac{5}{8}$. Thus, the fifth number is $14\frac{5}{24} + 2\frac{5}{8} = 16\frac{20}{24} = 16\frac{5}{6}$

2. Beginning with 6, the pattern is double the given number to get the next number, then add 2 to get the following number. Since 30 was doubled to get 60, the next number is 62.

3. The probability that an event will not occur = 1 - the probability it will occur = $1 - \frac{3}{5} = \frac{2}{5}$

4. Let x = original number. An increase of 400% means x + 4x = 5x, and 5x is 5 times the original number.

5. The L.C.M. of 18 and 24 is 72, and the G.C.F. is 6. Their product, 432, divided by 6 equals 72. Choice D is correct.

6. The 2nd partial product corresponds to the line 2690_, which actually represents 26,900.

7. Choice C is the INCORRECT statement, since dividing the denominator actually increases the fraction. For example, if the fraction 1/6 is changed by dividing the denominator by 2, we get 1/3. of course, 1/3 is twice as large as 1/6.

8. Since $A = \frac{2}{3}B$ and C = 1/2B, then twice $A(\frac{4}{3}B)$ is larger than twice C(B) by 1/3 of twice C. Thus, $\frac{4}{3}B = B + \frac{1}{3}B$.

9. 269(base 10) = $5 \times 7^2 + 3 + 7^1 + 3 \times 7^0$, so this becomes 533(base 7)

10. 1011(base 2) means, in base 10, $1 \times 2^3 + 0 \times 2^2 + 1 \times 2^1 + 1 \times 2^0 = 8 + 0 + 2 + 1 = 11$

11. The intersection must lead to a common set, which is the boys in class 6-1.

12. For positive integers, the identity element of 1 is used in multiplication. Thus, n x 1 = n, where n is any number.

13. 8 x 57 = 8(50+7) = (8x50) + (8x7). This illustrates the distributive law.

14. The median for 10 scores is the average of the 5th and 6th scores, provided the scores are arranged in order. In this example, both 5th and 6th scores are 70. Thus, the median is 70.

15. Let x = average score of the 4 absent children. An average of 70 for all 35 pupils means the total of all 35 scores is (70)(35) = 2450. The total of the scores for the pupils present is (8)(80) + (9)(70) + (14)(60) = 2110.
    Then, 2110 + 4x = 2450. Solving, x = 85.

16. Average speed = total distance ÷ total time
    $$= [(\tfrac{1}{2})(3) + (\tfrac{3}{4})(30) + (2\tfrac{1}{2})(55)] \div [\tfrac{1}{2} + \tfrac{3}{4} + 2\tfrac{1}{2}] = 161.5 \div 3.75 = 43.06 \approx 43 \text{ mph}$$

17. $x + x + x + 2x = 5x$, since each $x = 1x$

18. $4a + 2b = (4)(2) + (2)(3) = 14$

19. $3b^2 - 2ac = (3)(9) - (2)(2)(-4) = 27 + 16 = 43$

20. $\sqrt{c^2 - 3(a+b)} = \sqrt{16 - (3)(5)} = \sqrt{1} = 1$

21. $x^3 \cdot x^2 = x^5$. When common bases are multiplied, the exponents are added.

22. $(x - \tfrac{1}{x}) \div (1 - \tfrac{1}{x}) = \dfrac{x^2 - 1}{x} \div \dfrac{x - 1}{x} = \dfrac{(x-1)(x+1)}{x} \cdot \dfrac{x}{x-1} = x + 1$

23. $\sqrt{9x^2y^4} = 3xy^2$, which is none of choices A, B, C, or D.

24. $\sqrt{4a^2 + 4ab^2 + b^4} = \sqrt{(2a + b^2)^2} = 2a + b^2$

25. $(\sqrt{6} - \sqrt{3})(\sqrt{6} + \sqrt{3}) = \sqrt{36} + \sqrt{18} - \sqrt{18} - \sqrt{9} = 6 - 3 = 3$

TEST 2

DIRECTIONS: Each question or incomplete statement is followed by several suggested answers or completions. Select the one that BEST answers the question or completes the statement. *PRINT THE LETTER OF THE CORRECT ANSWER IN THE SPACE AT THE RIGHT.*

1. In the proportion $2\frac{1}{3} : 3\frac{1}{2} = 1\frac{1}{4} : ?$, the missing term is

   A. $1\frac{5}{8}$ B. $1\frac{7}{8}$ C. $2\frac{1}{6}$ D. $2\frac{5}{6}$

2. The value of is $\frac{1}{16^{-2}} + 10^0 \times 10^2$ is

   A. 1 B. 100.01 C. 200 D. 10,100

3. If x varies inversely as y, and x = 75 when y = 15, then what is x when y = 3?

   A. 15 B. 225 C. 375 D. 1125

4. Of the following, the reciprocal of is $(\frac{1}{x} + \frac{x}{2})$ is

   A. $\frac{x}{1} + \frac{2}{x}$ B. $\frac{x+2}{1+x}$ C. $\frac{2x+x^2}{2x}$ D. $\frac{2x}{x^2+2}$

5. In making six revolutions a long a straight path, a wheel covers a distance of 90 feet. Assuming no slipping or sliding, the radius of the wheel is

   A. 30π B. 15π C. $\frac{15}{\pi}$ D. $\frac{15}{2\pi}$

6. If the dimensions of a rectangular solid are 12, 16, and 20, the diagonal of the solid is

   A. 20 B. $16\sqrt{5}$ C. $20\sqrt{2}$ D. $8\sqrt{10}$

7. If the side of an equilateral triangle is equal to the side of a square, then the ratio of the area of the triangle to the area of the square is

   A. $\frac{1}{3}$ B. $\frac{\sqrt{3}}{4}$ C. $\frac{\sqrt{3}}{6}$ D. $\frac{\sqrt{3}}{9}$

8. Of five brothers, John is older than Harry, Paul is older than Sam, Harry is older than Paul, and Sam is older than Charles.
   Which one of the five brothers is third in order of age?

   A. John B. Harry C. Sam D. Paul

1.____
2.____
3.____
4.____
5.____
6.____
7.____
8.____

9. If 1/3 of a number is 1/5, what is 1/7 of the number?

   A. 3/35 B. 3/7 C. 5/7 D. 7/5

10. A man sold his farm for $15,000, thereby making a gross profit of 25% on his investment. If he had sold the farm for $16,000, what percent of gross profit on his investment would he have realized?

    A. 26 B. 30 C. 33 1/3 D. $37\frac{1}{2}$

11. A house was insured against fire for 4/5 of its assessed valuation. If the premium on the insurance policy was $64, which was of one percent of the face of the policy, the assessed valuation of the house was

    A. $20,480 B. $24,500 C. $25,600 D. $32,000

12. Solve for x: $\frac{5x}{8} - 9 = 11$

    A. $\frac{1}{3}$
    B. $2\frac{1}{2}$
    C. 32
    D. 4
    E. none of the above is correct

13. Solve for x: x - 2y = 2
                 2x + 3y = 25

    A. 3 B. 7 C. 8
    D. 11 E. none of the above is correct

14. Factor 10x + 4y

    A. 5(2x+y) B. 10(x+y) C. 2(5x+2y)
    D. 7(x+y)   E. none of the above is correct

15. Reduce to lowest terms: $\frac{x^2 - 25}{x^2 + x - 20}$

    A. $\frac{x+5}{x-4}$ B. $\frac{x-5}{x-4}$ C. $\frac{25}{x-20}$

    D. $\frac{x+5}{x+4}$ E. none of the above is correct

16. Combine: $5 - \frac{6}{x}$

A. $\dfrac{5x-6}{x}$ B. $\dfrac{5x+6}{x}$ C. $30x$

D. $\dfrac{6x-5}{x}$ E. none of the above is correct

17. What is the simplified form of 15x - 18 - (4x-2)?   17.____

    A. 11x-16   B. 19x-20   C. 19x-16
    D. 11x-20   E. None of the above is correct

18. The difference between two numbers is d.   18.____
    If the *larger* of the numbers is x, what is the other?

    A. x+d   B. y   C. x-d
    D. d-x   E. None of the above is correct

19. If both the length and the width of a rectangle are doubled, the effect is to multiply the area by   19.____

    A. 4   B. 2   C. 3

    D. $2\dfrac{1}{2}$ E. none of the above is correct

20. If x articles cost 2y cents, at the same rate how many cents would five of the articles cost?   20.____

    A. 10y   B. 10xy   C. $\dfrac{10y}{x}$

    D. $\dfrac{10x}{y}$ E. None of the avbove is correct

21. In the formula $r = \dfrac{3dk^2m}{5}$, the value of k is multiplied by 4, while the values of d and m remain unchanged.   21.____
    The ratio of the *new* value of r to the original value of r is _____ to 1.

    A. 16   B. 4   C. 64
    D. 32   E. none of the above is correct

22. If the population of a city increases x% every ten years and it is now n, what will the population be in ten years?   22.____

    A. $n + \dfrac{xn}{10}$ B. 100xn   C. $n + \dfrac{x}{100}$

    D. $n + \dfrac{xn}{100}$ E. None of the avbove is correct

23. The sum of three numbers is 69. The second number is twice the first, and the third is 17 more than the first. What are the numbers?

    A. 13, 26, 30   B. 11, 22, 28   C. 7, 21, 24
    D. 14, 27, 28   E. None of the above is correct

24. The second of three numbers is 11 more than the first, and the third is 5 more than twice the first. Twice the third number is 33 more than the sum of the first and second numbers. What are the numbers?

    A. 19, 30, 41   B. 2, 13, 35   C. 17, 28, 39
    D. 10, 21, 35   E. None of the above is correct

25. A baseball manager bought 10 bats and 21 balls for $47.60. Later in the season, at the same price, he paid $27.60 for six bats and one dozen balls.
How much did he pay for *each* ball and *each* bat?

    A. Bat $1.50, ball $1.50   B. Bat $1.75, ball $1.25
    C. Bat $1.60, ball $1.40   D. Bat $1.40, ball $1.60
    E. None of the above is correct

KEY (CORRECT ANSWERS)

1.	B	11.	D
2.	C	12.	C
3.	C	13.	C
4.	D	14.	C
5.	D	15.	B
6.	C	16.	A
7.	B	17.	A
8.	D	18.	C
9.	A	19.	A
10.	C	20.	C

21.	A
22.	D
23.	A
24.	C
25.	D

SOLUTIONS TO PROBLEMS

1. $2\frac{1}{3} : 3\frac{1}{2} = 1\frac{1}{4} : ?$ Call the ? x. Then, by cross-multiplying $2\frac{1}{3}x = (3\frac{1}{2})(1\frac{1}{4}) \cdot \frac{7}{3}x = \frac{35}{8}$.

   Solving, $x = \frac{15}{8} = 1\frac{7}{8}$

2. $\frac{1}{10^{-2}} + 10^0 \times 10^2 = 100 + 1 \times 100 = 200$. Recall, multiplication before addition.

3. $\frac{75}{x} = \frac{3}{15}$. $3x = 1125$. Solving, $x = 375$

4. $1 \div (\frac{1}{x} + \frac{x}{2}) = 1 \div \frac{2+x^2}{2x} = \frac{2x}{x^2 + 2}$

5. Six revolutions = (6)(circumference of the wheel) = $(6)(2\pi R) = 12\pi R = 90$ ft. Solving, $R = 90/12\pi = 15/2\pi$ ft.

6. The diagonal of a face (with length, width) is $\sqrt{12^2 + 16^2} = 20$. The diagonal of the solid is $\sqrt{20^2 + 20^2} = \sqrt{800} = 20\sqrt{2}$

7. Let x = side of equilateral triangle = side of square. Their respective areas are $\frac{x^2}{4}\sqrt{3}$ to $x^2 = \frac{\sqrt{3}}{4} : 1$ or $\frac{\sqrt{3}}{4}$

8. The 5 brothers, from youngest to oldest, are Charles, Sam, Paul, Harry, John. Then, Paul is the third oldest.

9. Let x = missing number. $\frac{1}{3}x = \frac{1}{5}$, so $x = \frac{3}{5}$. Then, we get $(\frac{3}{5})(\frac{1}{7}) = \frac{3}{35}$

10. Let x = investment. Then, $1.25x = \$15,000$, so $x = \$12,000$. If he had sold the farm for $16,000, his profit would be $4000/$12,000 = 33 1/3%

11. Let x = face value of policy. Then, $\$64 = .0025x$, so that $x = \$25,600$. Now, the assessed valuation = $\$25,600 \div .80 = \$32,000$

12. Add 9 to each side of equation to get $\frac{5}{8}x = 20$. Then, $x = 20 \div \frac{5}{8} = 32$

13. Multiplying the top equation by 3 and the bottom equation by 2, we have $3x - 6y = 6$ and $4x + 6y = 50$. Adding these new equations, $7x = 56$, so $x = 8$.

14. $10x + 4y = (2)(5x+2y)$. This is Common Term Factoring.

15. $(x^2-25) \div (x^2+x-20) = [(x-5)(x+5)] \div [(x+5)(x-4)] = (x-5)/(x-4)$

16. $5 - \dfrac{6}{x} = \dfrac{5x}{x} - \dfrac{6}{x} = \dfrac{5x-6}{x}$

17. $15x - 18 - (4x-2) = 15x - 18 - 4x + 2 = 11x - 16$

18. If the larger number is x, the smaller number is x-d

19. Let L,w = original length, width, so that the area is Lw.
    If 2L, 2w = new length, width, the area becomes 4Lw, so that the area has been multiplied by 4

20. If x articles cost 2y cents, then 1 article costs 2y/x cents. Thus, 5 articles cost 10y/x cents

21. Given $r = 3dk^2m/5$, if the value of k is multiplied by 4, then the value of r is multiplied by $4^2 = 16$. The ratio of the new r to the old r is 16:1.

22. n = current population. An increase of x% means the new population will be

    $$n + (\dfrac{x}{100})n = n + \dfrac{xn}{100}$$

23. Let x, 2x, x+17 be the three numbers. Then, x + 2x + x + 17 = 69. Simplifying, 4x + 17 = 69, so x = 13. The three numbers must be 13, 26, 30.

24. Let x, x+11, 2x+5 be the three numbers. Then, 2(2x+5) = x + x + 11 + 33. Simplifying, 4x + 10 = 2x + 44. Solving, x = 17. The three numbers are 17, 28, 39.

25. Let x = price of 1 bat, y = price of 1 ball. Then, 10x + 21y = $47.60 and 6x + 12y = $27.60. Multiply the 1st equation by 3 and the 2nd equation by 5 to get 30x + 63y = $142.80 and
    30x + 60y = $138. Subtracting, 3y = $4.80, so y = $1.60. Substitute into the original 1st equation to get 10x + (21)($1.60) = $47.60. Simplifying, 10x + $33.60 = $47.60. Then, x = $1.40

TEST 3

DIRECTIONS: Each question or incomplete statement is followed by several suggested answers or completions. Select the one that BEST answers the question or completes the statement. *PRINT THE LETTER OF THE CORRECT ANSWER IN THE SPACE AT THE RIGHT.*

1. Rational numbers are a subset of

   A. transcendental numbers B. irrational numbers
   C. real numbers D. integers

   1.____

2. $2^n + 1$ is a prime number when n is

   A. 3 B. 4 C. 5 D. 6

   2.____

3. An exercise in which the associative rule is illustrated is

   A. 5x4+3 B. 5x4x3= 5x(4x3)
   C. 5+(4x3) D. (5+4) x 3

   3.____

4. If $|x-3| < 7$, then

   A. -4<x <10 B. 10< x< 10
   C. 4<x <10 D. -4< x < 7

   4.____

5. If $2x^2 - 12x + K = 4$, the two roots of the equation are equal when K equals

   A. 9 B. 18 C. 22 D. 26

   5.____

6. The equation of a line passing through the point (0,5) and parallel to $2x + y = 8$ is

   A. y = 2x + 5 B. y + 5 = -2x
   C. y + 5 = 2x D. y = -2x + 5

   6.____

7. A figure consists of a semicircle resting on a square whose side equals 14 inches. If the diameter of the semicircle equals the side of the square, the TOTAL area of the figure, in square inches, is $(\pi = \frac{22}{7})$

   A. 273 B. 350 C. 504 D. 812

   7.____

8. The amount (A) of light at a point varies directly as the intensity (I) of the source and inversely as the square of the point's distance (d) from the source. If I is quadrupled and d is multiplied by 2, then A is

   A. doubled B. unaffected
   C. halved D. multiplied by 4

   8.____

9. The ratio of 10 meters to 0.1 millimeters is

   A. $10^3:1$ B. $10^4:1$ C. $10^5:1$ D. $10^6:1$

   9.____

10. The arithmetic mean of the set of quantities, 15, 12, 3, -4, -17, can be changed to

    A. +2 B. -2 C. +6 D. -6

    10.____

11. If then to three decimals is

    A. 0.707 B. 0.354 C. 0.177 D. 0.089

12. The sum of an arithmetic progression is given by the formula $S = \frac{n}{2}[2a+(n-1)d]$. The sum of 15 terms of the series 2,5,8,11... is

    A. 322 B. 330 C. 345 D. 405

13. The difference between a two digit number (in which the tens' digit is larger than the units' digit) and the number with the same digits reversed is a multiple of

    A. 6 B. 7 C. 9 D. 11

14. A linear relation between the variables r and s in the table is $\dfrac{r\ 1\ 2\ 3\ 4}{s\ 2\ 5\ 8\ 11}$ is

    A. $r = \dfrac{s}{2}$ B. $r = s - 1$ C. $s = 2r + 1$ D. $s = 3r - 1$

15. The theoretic basis of multiplication by means of the slide rule is

    A. addition of logarithms
    B. multiplication of logarithms
    C. use of base 2
    D. use of base 8

16. A theorem states that if P is true, then Q follows as a result. Consequently, another theorem that must also be TRUE is

    A. if Q is not true, then P is not true
    B. if Q is true, then P is true
    C. if P is not true, then Q is not true
    D. none of these is necessarily true

17. If b is greater than a (a and b are both positive), then $\dfrac{a+1}{b+1}$ is less than

    A. $\dfrac{a}{b}$ B. $\dfrac{a+1}{b}$ C. $\dfrac{a}{b+1}$ D. $\dfrac{a+1}{b+2}$

18. When 2 quarts of an 8% strength solution is mixed with 4 quarts of a 2% solution, the resulting mixture is a solution of

    A. 3% B. 4% C. 5% D. 6%

19. Trains A and B travel toward each other from points 150 miles apart at 50 and 60 miles per hour, respectively. To meet midway, the headway needed by train A is _____ minutes.

    A. 10 B. 15 C. 25 D. 30

20. A 350 ft. length on a blueprint is represented by a line inches long. The distance, in yards, represented by a line on the blueprint 2 3/4 inches long is

   A. 65 1/3   B. 75   C. 91 2/3   D. 95

21. The statement $x - 6 \leq 6$ is equivalent to

   A. $x \geq -36$ B. $x \leq 0$ C. $C \leq 12$
   D. $x \leq 36$ E. $x \geq 12$

22. An automobile is moving at r miles per hour, and an airplane is moving three times as fast. How many hours will the plane require for a 500 mile flight?

   A. $\dfrac{1500}{r}$ B. $\dfrac{500}{3r}$ C. $\dfrac{3r}{500}$
   D. $500-3r$ E. $1500r$

23. If $4x + 5y = 13$ and $2x + 3y = 7$, then $x =$

   A. -2   B. -1   C. $\dfrac{1}{2}$ D. 2   E. 4

24. Which of these is the graph of $2x + 3y = 6$?

A. 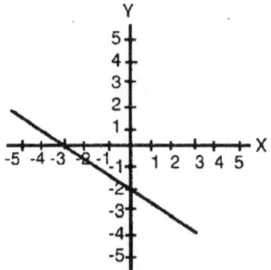   B. 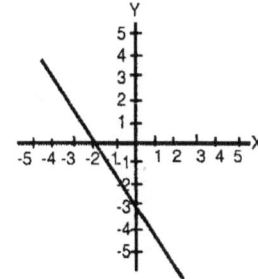   C.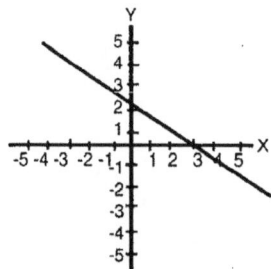

D. 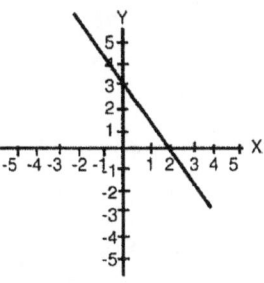   E.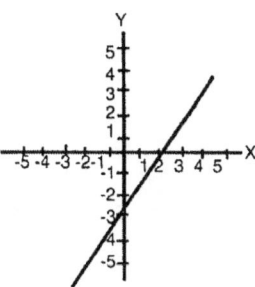

25. If x is a real number, what are ALL the values of x for which $x^4 + 16$ is a positive number? All

   A. x greater than -2   B. x greater than zero
   C. x greater than 2   D. x between -2 and 2
   E. All values of x

4 (#3)

KEY (CORRECT ANSWERS)

1.	C	11.	B
2.	B	12.	C
3.	B	13.	C
4.	A	14.	D
5.	C	15.	A
6.	D	16.	A
7.	A	17.	B
8.	B	18.	B
9.	C	19.	B
10.	A	20.	C

21. C
22. B
23. D
24. C
25. E

———

SOLUTIONS TO PROBLEMS

1. Rational numbers can always be represented as p/q, where p and q are integers. As such, they are a subset of the real numbers.

2. When n = 4, $2^n + 1 = 17$, which is prime.

3. 5 x 4 x 3 = 5x (4 x 3) illustrates the Associative Rule.

4. |x-3| < 7 means x - 3 < 7 and x - 3 > -7. Solving, we get x < 10 and x > -4. This can be written as -4 < x < 10.

5. If k = 22, then $2x^2 - 12x + k = 4$ can be simplified to $2x^2 - 12x + 18 = 0$. Rewriting as $2(x-3)^2 = 0$, we note that this equation has two equal roots.

6. A line parallel to 2x + y = 8 is 2x + y = k, k a constant. Since (0,5) is on the line given by 2x + y = k, 2(0) + 5 = k, so k = 5. The equation is 2x + y = 5 or y = -2x + 5

7. The area of the square is $14^2 = 196$. Since the semicircle has a radius of 7, its area is $(\frac{1}{2})(\frac{22}{7})(7^2) = 77$. The combined area is 196 + 77 = 273 sq.in.

8. Based on the given, we can write $A = Kl/d^2$, k a constant. If l is quadrupled and d is doubled, the value of A remains the same.

9. 10 meters: .1 millimeters = 10,000 millimeters: .1 millimeters = 10^4: .1 = 10^5:1

10. Arithmetic mean $(15 + 12 + 3 - 4 - 17) \div 5 = 9 \div 5 \approx 2$

11. $\sqrt{1/8} = 1/2\sqrt{2} \approx 1/(2)(1.4142) \approx .354$

12. $s = \frac{15}{2}[4 + (14)(3)] = \frac{15}{2}(46) = 345$

13. Let 10t+u = original number and 10u+t = number with digits reversed. Their difference is 9t-9u, which is always a multiple of 9.

14. Let s = a+br, a,b constants. Using the first two entries, 2 = a + b and 5 = a + 2b. Subtracting, 3 = b. Then, a = -1. Thus, s = -1+3r or s = 3r-1.

15. When multiplying using a slide rule, the addition of logs is engaged.

16. The contrapositive of *If P is true, then Q is true* is *If Q is not true, then P is not true*. If a statement is true, so is its contrapositive.

17. (a+1)/(b+1) must be less than (a+1)/b if b > a and a,b > 0. An increase in denominator, from b to b+1, will reduce the value of the fraction.

6 (#3)

18. The amount of solution in the result is (.08)(2) + (.02)(4) = .24 quarts out of a total of 6 quarts. This is then a .24/6 = .04 = 4% strength solution in the mixture.

19. Each train must travel 75 miles in order to meet midway. If they leave at the same time, train A would travel for 1 hr. 30 min.; train B for 1 hr. 15 min. Thus, train A needs a head-start of 15 nin.

20. $350' : 3\frac{1}{2}" \ x' : 2\frac{3}{4}"$. Then, $3\frac{1}{2}x = 962\frac{1}{2}$. Solving, x = 275'. Since we need yards, 275' = 275 ÷ 3 = 91 2/3 yds.

21. x - 6 ≤ 6 is equivalent to x ≤ 12, by just adding 6 to both sides of the inequality.

22. The plane's speed is 3r mph. For a 500 mile flight, the time needed is 500/3r.

23. Multiply the 1st equation by 3 to get 12x + 15y = 39. Multiply the 2nd equation by 5 to get 10x + 15y = 35. Subtracting, 2x = 4, so x = 2.

24. For the graph of 2x + 3y = 6, note that the intercepts are (0,2) and (3,0). Choice C has both points on the line given.

25. Since the lowest value of x^4 is 0, if x is real, then x^4+16 is a positive number 16 for all values of x.

TEST 4

DIRECTIONS: Each question or incomplete statement is followed by several suggested answers or completions. Select the one that BEST answers the question or completes the statement. *PRINT THE LETTER OF THE CORRECT ANSWER IN THE SPACE AT THE RIGHT.*

1. A motorist travels 120 miles to his destination at the average speed of 60 miles per hour and returns to the starting point at the average speed of 40 miles per hour. His average speed for the entire trip is _____ per hour.   1.____

    A. 53 B. 50 C. 48 D. 45

2. A snapshot measures 2 1/2 inches by 1 7/8 inches. It is to be enlarged so that the longer dimension will be 4 inches. The length of the enlarged shorter dimension will be   2.____

    A. $2\frac{1}{2}$ inches
    B. 3 inches
    C. 3 3/8 inches
    D. none of the above

3. Fron a piece of tin in the shape of a square 6 inches on a side, the largest possible circle is cut out. Of the following, the ratio of the area of the circle to the area of the original square is CLOSEST in value to   3.____

    A. 4/5 B. 2/3 C. 3/5 D. 1/2

4. The approximate distance s in feet that an object falls in t seconds when dropped from a height is obtained by use of the formula $s = 16t^2$. In 8 seconds, the object will fall   4.____

    A. 15,384 feet
    B. 1,024 feet
    C. 256 feet
    D. none of the above

5. A pound of water is evaporated from 6 pounds of sea water containing 4% salt. The percentage of salt in the remaining solution is   5.____

    A. 3 1/3
    B. 4
    C. 4 4/5
    D. none of the above

6. The product of 75^3 and 75^7 is   6.____

    A. $(75)^{10}$ B. $(150)^{10}$ C. $(75)^{21}$ D. $(5,625)^{10}$

7. The scale of a map is: 3/4 inch = 10 miles. If the distance on the map between two towns is 6 inches, the ACTUAL distance is   7.____

    A. 45 miles
    B. 60 miles
    C. 80 miles
    D. none of the above

8. If $d = m - \frac{50}{m}$ and m is a positive number which increases in value, d   8.____

    A. increases in value
    B. decreases in value
    C. remains unchanged
    D. fluctuates up and down in value

9. If a cubic inch of a metal weighs 2 pounds, a cubic foot of the same metal weighs

    A. 8 pounds
    B. 24 pounds
    C. 288 pounds
    D. none of the above

10. According to the Federal income tax law, if the taxable income in the case of a separate return is over $14,000 but not over $16,000, the tax is $840 + 20% of the excess over $14,000.
    If a taxpayer files a separate tax return and his taxable income is $15,500, the tax is

    A. $690
    B. $1,230
    C. $1,360
    D. none of the above

11. If the number of square inches in the area of a circle is equal to the number of inches in its circumference, the diameter of the circle is

    A. 4 inches
    B. 2 inches
    C. 1 inch
    D. none of the above

12. The LEAST common multiple of 20, 24, 32 is

    A. 960
    B. 1,920
    C. 15,360
    D. none of the above

13. Six quarts of a 20% solution of alcohol in water are mixed with 4 quarts of a 60% solution of alcohol in water. The alcoholic strength of the mixture is

    A. 80%
    B. 40%
    C. 36%
    D. none of the above

14. To find the radius of a circle whose circumference is 60",

    A. multiply 60 by π
    B. divide 60 by 2π
    C. divide 30 by 2π
    D. divide 60 by and extract the square root of the result

15. A micromillimeter is defined as one millionth of a millimeter.
    A length of 17 micromillimeters may be represented as

    A. .00017 mm.
    B. .0000017 mm.
    C. .000017 mm.
    D. .00000017 mm.

16. If $9x + 5 = 23$, the numerical value of $18x + 5$ is

    A. 46
    B. 41
    C. 32
    D. 23+9x

17. When the fractions 2/3, 5/7, 8/11, and 9/13 are arranged in ascending order of size, the result is

    A. 8/11, 5/7, 9/13, 2/3
    B. 5/7, 8/11, 2/3, 9/13
    C. 2/3, 8/11, 5/7, 9/13
    D. 2/3, 9/13, 5/7, 8/11

18. If the outer diameter of a metal pipe is 2.84 inches and the inner diameter is 1.94 inches, the thickness of the metal is

   A. .45 of an inch
   B. .90 of an inch
   C. 1.94 inches
   D. 2.39 inches

19. The sum of the squares of the first n integers is given by the formula
$$S = \frac{1}{6}n(n+1)(2n+1).$$
By use of this formula, the sum of the squares of the first 50 integers is

   A. 2,500
   B. 63,750
   C. 42,925
   D. none of the above

20. By the common logarithm of a number is meant

   A. a method of performing a quick computation
   B. the power of 10 which is equivalent to the number
   C. an arrangement of the solution of an arithmetic problem involving the number
   D. the exponent of the number

21. Solve for x: 5x - 2 = 18

   A. 20
   B. 2
   C. -4
   D. 3 1/5
   E. none of the above is correct

22. Solve for x: 8+3x-2=x

   A. -3
   B. $2\frac{1}{2}$
   C. 3
   D. -4
   E. none of the above is correct

23. In the figure at the right, what is the slope of line *l* ?

   A. $\frac{-3}{2}$
   B. $\frac{-2}{3}$
   C. $\frac{2}{3}$
   D. $\frac{3}{2}$

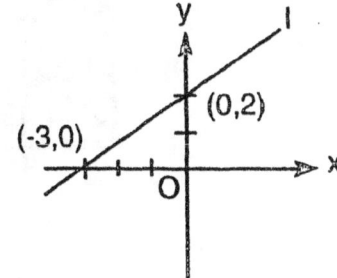

24. Which one of the following could be the graph of the equation y = -x + 1?   24.____

   A.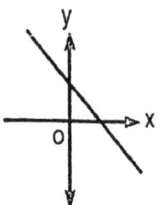
   B.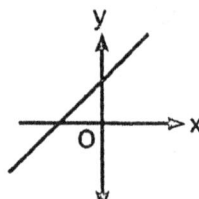

   C.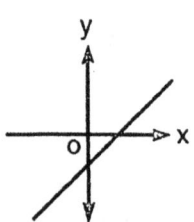
   D.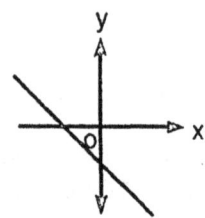

25. Which one of the following could be the graph of (x, y) : x ≥ 3, and y ≤ -1?   25.____

   A.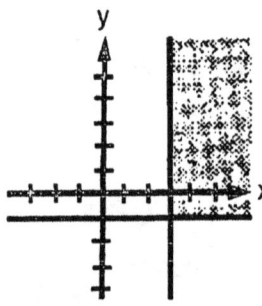
   B.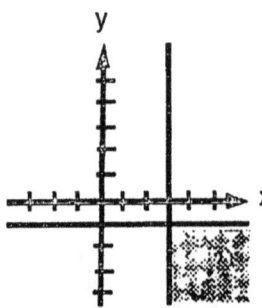

   C.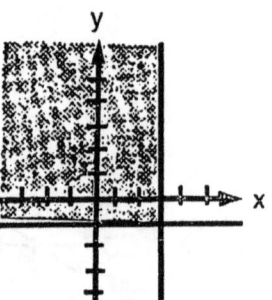
   D.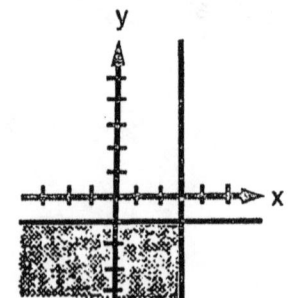

KEY (CORRECT ANSWERS)

1.	C	11.	A
2.	B	12.	D
3.	A	13.	C
4.	B	14.	B
5.	C	15.	C
6.	A	16.	B
7.	C	17.	D
8.	A	18.	A
9.	D	19.	C
10.	D	20.	B

21. E
22. A
23. C
24. A
25. B

SOLUTIONS TO PROBLEMS

1. Average speed is total distance ÷ total time = (120+120) ÷ (2+3) = 240 ÷ 5 = 48 mph

2. Let x = enlarged width. Then, $2\frac{1}{2}/1\frac{7}{8} = 4/x$. $2\frac{1}{2x} = 7\frac{1}{2}$.
   Solving, x = 3 in.

3. Area of the circle = $(\pi)(3^2) \approx 28.286$. Area of the square = $6^2 = 36$. Then, 28.286 ÷ 36 ≈ .7857 ≈ 4/5

4. $S = (16)(8^2) = (16)(64) = 1024$ ft.

5. The amount of pure water initially was (6)(.96) = 5.76 lbs., so that after a pound is extracted (of pure water), 4.76 lbs. remains. The amount of salt is still (6)(.04) = .24 lbs. Since the new mixture is 5 lbs. (water and salt), the salt content is .24/5 = .048 or 4 4/5%

6. $(75^3)(75^7) = 75^{10}$. When two numbers with the same bases are multiplied, the exponents are added.

7. Let x = actual distance. Then, $\frac{3}{4}/10 = 6/x$. $\frac{3}{4x} = 60$.
   Solving, x = 80 miles

8. $d = m - \frac{50}{m}$, where m > 0. As m increases, $\frac{50}{m}$ will decrease, and this will increase the value of d. Example: For m = 10, d = 5. For m = 20, d = 17.5.

9. 12^3 = 1728 cu.in. = 1 cu.ft. Then, (2)(1728) = 3456 lbs.

10. Tax = $840 + (.20)($15,500 - $14,000) = $840 + $300 = $1140

11. Area of circle = πR^2. Circumference of circle = $2\pi R$.
    If these are equal, $R^2 = 2R$, so R = 2. The diameter must be 4 in.

12. $20 = 2^2.5$, $24 = 2^3.3$, $32 = 2^5$. Thus, the L.C.M. = $2^5.3.5 = 480$

13. The amount of alcohol in the mixture of 10 quarts is (.20)(6) + (.60)(4) = 3.6 quarts. Then, 3.6/10 = 36%

14. $C = 60 = 2\pi R$. Then, the radius is $60/2\pi$.

15. 17 micromillimeters = 17 millionths of a millimeter = .000017 mm.

16. If 9x + 5 = 23, x = 2. Then, 18x + 5 is worth 41.

17. The corresponding decimals are $.\overline{6}, .71, .\overline{72}, .69$

    Arranged in ascending order, we have $.\overline{6}, .69, .71, .\overline{72}$, corresponding to 2/3, 9/13, 5/7, 8/11

18. Let x = thickness. Then, 2.84 = 1.94 + 2x. Solving,
    x = .45" (The outer diameter includes the inner diameter plus twice the thickness.)

19. $S = (\frac{1}{6})(50)(101) = 42,925$

20. The common logarithm of a number is the power of 10 equivalent to that number. For example, Log 1000 = 3, since $10^3 = 1000$

21. Add 2 to both sides to get 5x = 20. Then, x = 4

22. Simplify to 6 + 3x = x. Subtract 3x from both sides to get 6 = -2x. Solving, x = -3

23. Slope = (2-0)/(0-(-3)) = $\frac{2}{3}$

24. For y = -x+1, the intercepts are (1,0) and (0,1). This is illustrated in Choice A.

25. For x ≥ 3, y ≤ -1, the shaded area must lie to the right of the vertical line x = 3 and below the horizontal line y = -1. This is illustrated in choice B.

EXAMINATION SECTION
TEST 1

DIRECTIONS: Each question or incomplete statement is followed by several suggested answers or completions. Select the one that BEST answers the question or completes the statement. *PRINT THE LETTER OF THE CORRECT ANSWER IN THE SPACE AT THE RIGHT.*

1. If $2x + 1 = 7$, then $x =$

   A. $\frac{1}{4}$ B. $\frac{1}{3}$ C. 3   D. 4   E. 11

   1.____

2. The statement, *A certain number f increased by twice another number n is equal to 30,* can be written

   A. $f + 2n = 30$ B. $f + 2f = 30$ C. $2f + n = 30$
   D. $2f + 2n = 30$ E. $2nf = 30$

   2.____

3. $(-5) - (-9) =$

   A. -14   B. -4   C. 4   D. 14   E. 45

   3.____

4. If $x = y = z = 1$, then $= \frac{x-y}{x+z} =$

   A. -2   B. -1   C. 0   D. 1/2   E. 1

   4.____

5. $-2x + 5x - 9x =$

   A. $-16x$ B. $-14x$ C. $-11x$ D. $-6x$ E. $-2x$

   5.____

6. If n is an even number, what is the next larger even number?

   A. $n-2$ B. $n-1$ C. $n+1$ D. $n+2$ E. $2n$

   6.____

7. What is the coefficient of y in the expression $2y^5 + 6y^4 - 4y^2 - 5y + 1$?

   A. -5   B. -1   C. 1   D. 2   E. 3

   7.____

8. If $A = LW$ and if $A = 12$ and $L = 3$, then $W =$

   A. $\frac{3}{4}$ B. 3   C. 4   D. 12   E. 36

   8.____

9. $\frac{x^7}{x^3} =$

   A. $x^{3.5}$ B. x^4 C. x^{10} D. x^{21} E. 3.5

   9.____

10. Which of these is equivalent to $x(x+a) - a(x-a)$?

    A. $(x+a)(x-a)^2$ B. $(x+a)^2(x-a)$ C. $(x+a)^3$
    D. $(x+a)^2$ E. x^2+a^2

    10.____

11. $-11x^2y + 5x^2y =$

    A. -6 B. $-6x^2y$ C. $-6x^4y^2$

    D. $16x^2y$ E. $16x^4y^2$

11._____

12. If $x = -2$, then $5x^3 =$

    A. $1,000$ B. 40 C. 30 D. -40 E. $-1,000$

12._____

13. $\dfrac{5}{x} - \dfrac{3}{2x} =$

    A. $-\dfrac{2}{x}$ B. $\dfrac{2}{2x}$ C. $\dfrac{7}{2x}$ D. $7x$ E. 7

13._____

14. $\dfrac{7x^6}{42x^2} =$

    A. $\dfrac{x^6}{6x^2}$ B. $6x^4$ C. $\dfrac{x^4}{6}$ D. $6x^3$ E. $\dfrac{x^3}{6}$

14._____

15. $\dfrac{20x^3y^3}{7} \div \dfrac{35x^3}{4y^3} =$

    A. $\dfrac{16x^6}{49}$ B. $\dfrac{16y^6}{49}$ C. $25x^6$ D. $25y^6$ E. $\dfrac{16}{49x^3y^3}$

15._____

16. $(r+5)(r-3) =$

    A. r^2-15 B. $r^2-2r-15$ C. r^2-2r-8

    D. r^2+2r-8 E. $r^2+2r-15$

16._____

17. $5y^3(2y+4xy) =$

    A. $10y^3 + 20xy^3$ B. $2y^4 + 4xy^4$ C. $10y^4 + 4xy^4$

    D. $10y^4 + 20xy^4$ E. $10y^4 + 10xy^4$

17._____

18. $3(2-3a) - (5-a) =$

    A. $1 - 10a$ B. $1 - 8a$ C. $1 - 4a$

    D. $11 - 8a$ E. $11 - 10a$

18._____

19. If $3x - 7 = x$, then $x =$

    A. 4 B. 3.5 C. 1 D. -3.5 E. -4

19._____

20. Every fifth degree polynomial with real coefficients must have _____ real root(s).

    A. 0 B. at least 1   C. at least 2

    D. 3 E. 5

20._____

21. If $\dfrac{a}{c^2} = 5$, $c^2 = 2ax$, then $x =$

   A. $\dfrac{1}{10}$ B. $\dfrac{1}{5}$ C. $\dfrac{2}{5}$ D. $\dfrac{5}{2}$ E. 10

22. If $px^3 + qx - 2 = 0$ when $x = -1$, what is the value of $px^3 + qx - 2$ when $x = 1$?

   A. -4   B. -2   C. 0   D. 2   E. 4

23. If $\log x = \log 1 + \log 2 + \log 3 + \log 4 + \log 5$, then $x =$

   A. 6   B. 15   C. 36   D. 55   E. 120

24. If $\begin{cases} y - x^2 - 5 = 0 \\ y - x = 7 \end{cases}$, then $x =$

   A. -1 or 2   B. -2 or 2   C. -3 or 4
   D. $-\sqrt{5}$ or $\sqrt{5}$ E. $-\sqrt{2}$ or $\sqrt{2}$

25. Which of these is the graph of the set of points (x,y) in the plane for which the y-coordinate of each point is one *less* than twice the x-coordinate?

A. 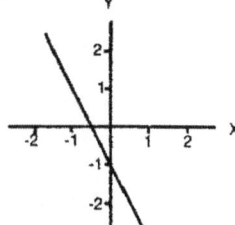   B. 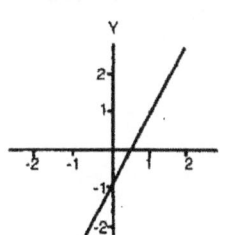   C.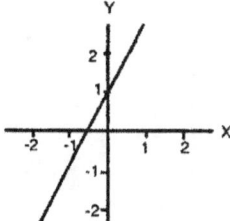

D. 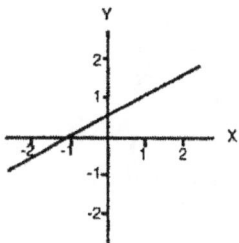   E.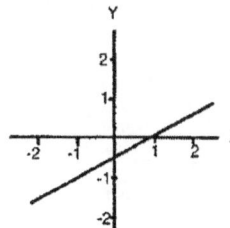

KEY (CORRECT ANSWERS)

1.	C	11.	B
2.	A	12.	D
3.	C	13.	C
4.	C	14.	C
5.	D	15.	B
6.	D	16.	E
7.	A	17.	D
8.	C	18.	B
9.	B	19.	B
10.	E	20.	B

21. A
22. A
23. E
24. A
25. B

SOLUTIONS TO PROBLEMS

1. Given 2x+1 = 7, subtract 1 from both sides to get 2x = 6. Solving, x = 3

2. f increased by twice n equals 30: f + 2n = 30

3. (-5) -(-9) = -5 + 9 = 4

4. (x-y)/(x+z) = (1-1)/(1+1) = 0

5. -2x + 5x - 9x = -6x

6. The next largest even number is n+2, when n is even

7. For the term -5y, -5 is the coefficient

8. 12 = 3W, then W = 4

9. $x^7/x^3 = x^4$. When dividing with like bases, subtract the exponents.

10. x(x+a) - a(x-a) = x^2 + ax - ax + a^2 = x^2 + a^2

11. $-11x^2y + 5x^2y = -6x^2y$

12. $5x^3 = 5(-2)^3 = 5(-8) = -40$

13. $\dfrac{5}{x} - \dfrac{3}{2x} = \dfrac{10-3}{2x} = \dfrac{7}{2x}$

14. $\dfrac{7x^6}{42x^2} = \dfrac{x^4}{6}$

15. $(20x^3y^3/7)(4y^3/35x^3) = (4y^3/7)^2 = 16y^6/49$

16. (r+5)(r-3) = r^2 - 3r + 5r - 15 = r^2 + 2r - 15

17. $5y^3(2y+4xy) = 10y^4 + 20xy^4$

18. 3(2-3a) - (5-a) = 6 - 9a - 5 + a = 1 - 8a

19. 3x - 7 = x. Subtract 3x from each side to get -7 = -2x. Solving, x = 3.5

20. A polynomial of 5th degree needs to have at least 1 real root. Note that if any of the roots are complex, they always appear as paired conjugates in the form a+bi and a-bi.

21. c^2 = 2ax, so x = c^2/2a. Since a/c^2 = 5, a/2c^2 = $2\dfrac{1}{2} = \dfrac{5}{2}$. Finally, x = c^2/2a = 1 ÷ (2a/c2) = 1 ÷ [4(a/2c2)] = $1 \div [(4)(\dfrac{5}{2})] = \dfrac{1}{10}$

22. $p(-1)^3 + q(-1) - 2 = 0$ becomes $-p - q - 2 = 0$, or $p + q = -2$. Then, $p(1)^3 + q(1) - 2 = p + q - 2 = -2 - 2 = -4$

23. $\text{Log } x = \text{Log } 1 + \text{Log } 2 + \text{Log } 3 + \text{Log } 4 + \text{Log } 5 = \text{Log}(1.2.3.4.5) = \text{Log } 120$. So, $x = 120$.

24. Since $y = x + 7$, $x + 7 - x^2 - 5 = 0$ simplifies to $x^2 - x - 2 = 0$. Factoring, $(x-2)(x+1) = 0$, so $x = 2$ or $x = -1$

25. For $y = 2x-1$, the intercepts are $(0,-1)$ and $(\frac{1}{2}, 0)$. Choice B is then the appropriate graph.

TEST 2

DIRECTIONS: Each question or incomplete statement is followed by several suggested answers or completions. Select the one that BEST answers the question or completes the statement. *PRINT THE LETTER OF THE CORRECT ANSWER IN THE SPACE AT THE RIGHT.*

1. $x^2 - 4x - 12 =$

   A. $(x-6)(x+2)$ B. $(x-3)(x+4)$ C. $(x+3)(x-4)$
   D. $(x+6)(x-2)$ E. $(x-4)(x-3)$

   1.____

2. $\dfrac{3y^2 - 7y^2 + y}{y} =$

   A. $3y^2 - 7y^2 + y$ B. $3y^3 - 7y^2$ C. $3y^2 - 7y$
   D. $3y^2 - 7y + 1$ E. $3y^3 - 7y + 0$

   2.____

3. $\dfrac{6m^2}{n} \cdot \dfrac{2n}{3m} =$ (reduced completely)

   A. $\dfrac{12m^2n}{3mn}$ B. $\dfrac{12m}{3}$ C. $\dfrac{2m^3}{2n^2}$ D. $4m$ E. $6m$

   3.____

4. If $c - ax = b$, then $x =$

   A. abc B. $\dfrac{b+ax}{c}$ C. $\dfrac{c-b}{a}$ D. $\dfrac{1}{a}$ E. $\dfrac{c-a}{b}$

   4.____

5. $\sqrt{125} - \sqrt{20} =$

   A. $5\sqrt{3}$ B. $3\sqrt{5}$ C. $21\sqrt{5}$ D. $\sqrt{105}$ E. 105

   5.____

6. If $\dfrac{3}{n} - 2 = \dfrac{5}{2n} - \dfrac{3}{2}$, then $n =$

   A. -4 B. -3 C. -2 D. -1 E. 1

   6.____

7. $\sqrt{45x} \cdot \sqrt{3x^3} =$

   A. $135x^4$ B. $135x^2$ C. $x^2\sqrt{135}$ D. $3x^2\sqrt{15}$ E. $5x^2\sqrt{3}$

   7.____

8. What is $\sqrt{126}$ to the nearest tenth?

   A. 63.0 B. 12.6 C. 11.9 D. 11.2 E. 10.8

   8.____

9. What is the slope of the line $3x + 2y = 6$?

   A. $-\dfrac{3}{2}$ B. $-\dfrac{2}{3}$ C. $\dfrac{2}{3}$ D. 2   E. 3

10. If $x + y = 4$ then $x =$
    $x - y = 2$

    A. 0   B. 1   C. 2   D. 3   E. 6

11.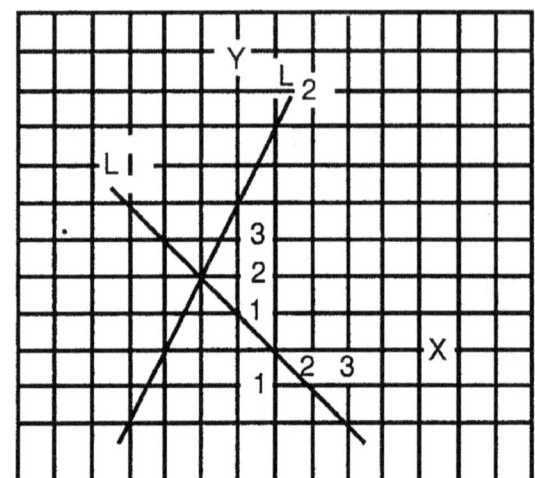

    The figure above shows the graphs of two linear equations. What is the solution of these equations?

    A. (-2,4)   B. (-1,2)   C. (-2,1)   D. (1,4)   E. (1,1)

12. If $9x - 63 = 18$, then $x =$

    A. -9   B. -5   C. 0   D. 5   E. 9

13. What is the square root of $16b^8$?

    A. $2b^2$ B. $4b^2$ C. $4b^4$ D. $8b^2$ E. $8b^4$

14. $2x^2(3x+4xy) =$

    A. $6x^2 + 8x^2y$ B. $3x^3 + 4x^3y$ C. $6x^3 + 4x^3y$
    D. $6x^3 + 8x^3y$ E. $6x^3 + 6x^3y$

15. Solve $R = \dfrac{K}{\pi D}$ for d. d =

    A. $\dfrac{\pi R}{k}$ B. $\dfrac{KR}{\pi}$ C. $\dfrac{\pi K}{R}$ D. $\dfrac{K}{\pi R}$ E. πKR

16. Two of a student's test marks are 68 and 84. A third mark is at least 40. What is his LOWEST possible average for the three tests?

    A. 40   B. 58   C. 62   D. 64   E. 76

17. When factored, $4a^2 + 12ab^2 =$

   A. $4a(a+3b^2)$ B. $4a(a+12b^2)$ C. $4ab(a+3b)$
   D. $4ab(a+12b)$ E. $4a^2(1+3b^2)$

18. A boy who has q quarters and d dimes buys p pencils at 5 cents each. How many cents does he have left?

   A. q+d-p B. q+d-5p C. 25q + 2(d-p)
   D. 25q + 10d - p E. 25q + 10d - 5p

19. If x + y = 5 and x - y = 3, then x =

   A. 1 B. 2 C. 4 D. 8

20. If $\dfrac{9}{n} - \dfrac{7}{n} = \dfrac{1}{6}$, then n =

   A. $\dfrac{1}{12}$ B. $\dfrac{1}{3}$ C. 6 D. 12

21. $k = \dfrac{3}{5}(n+60)$, which of these gives n in terms of k?

   A. $\dfrac{5k}{3} - 60$ B. $\dfrac{5k}{3} - 12$ C. $\dfrac{3k}{5} + 60$ D. $\dfrac{3k}{5} + 12$

22. $8a^2b + 12b^2 =$

   A. $4b(2a^2+3b)$ B. $8b(a^2+4b)$
   C. $4b^2(2a^2+3)$ D. $4ab(2a+3b)$

23. If p = 2 and r = -5, then $\dfrac{p+r}{p} =$

   A. -5 B. $\dfrac{-5}{2}$ C. $\dfrac{-3}{2}$ D. $\dfrac{3}{2}$

24. $(m+3n)(2m-n) =$

   A. $2m^2 - 3n^2$ B. $2m^2 - 3n^2 + 6$
   C. $2m^2 + 5mn - 3n^2$ D. $m^2 + 6mn - 3n^2$

25. Which of the following is the graph of 2x ≤ 6?

A.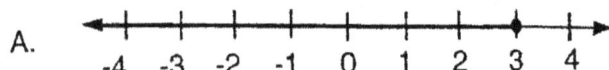

B.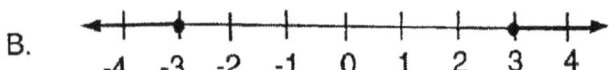

C.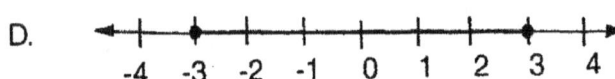

D.

KEY (CORRECT ANSWERS)

1. A
2. D
3. D
4. C
5. B

6. E
7. D
8. D
9. A
10. D

11. B
12. E
13. C
14. D
15. D

16. D
17. A
18. E
19. C
20. D

21. A
22. A
23. C
24. C
25. A

SOLUTIONS TO PROBLEMS

1. $x^2 - 4x - 12$ can be factored as $(x-6)(x+2)$

2. $(3y^3 - 7y^2 + y) \div y = 3y^2 - 7y + 1$

3. $(6m^2/n)(2n/3m) = (12m^2n/3mn) = 4m$

4. $c - ax = b$. Subtract c from both sides to get $-ax = b-c$. Divide by -a to get $x = (b-c)/-a$ or $(c-b)/a$.

5. $\sqrt{125} - \sqrt{20} = \sqrt{25}\sqrt{5} - \sqrt{4}\sqrt{5} = 5\sqrt{5} - 2\sqrt{5} = 3\sqrt{5}$

6. $\dfrac{3}{n} - 2 = \dfrac{5}{2n} - \dfrac{3}{2}$ Multiply every term by 2n to get $6 - 4n = 5 - 3n$. Simplifying, $-n = -1$, so $n = 1$.

7. $\sqrt{45x} \cdot \sqrt{3x^3} = \sqrt{135x^4} = x^2\sqrt{9}\sqrt{15} = 3x^2\sqrt{15}$

8. $\sqrt{126} \approx 1.225 \approx 11.2$

9. $3x + 2y = 6$ can be written as $y = -\dfrac{3}{2}x + 3$. In this form, the slope corresponds to the coefficient of x, which is $-\dfrac{3}{2}$.

10. Add the given equations to get $2x = 6$. Then, $x = 3$.

11. The solution is the intersection point $(-1, 2)$.

12. Add 63 to both sides to get $9x = 81$. Then, $x = 9$.

13. $\sqrt{16b^8} = 4b^4$, since $(4b^4)^2 = 16b^8$

14. $2x^2(3x + 4xy) = 6x^3 + 8x^3y$

15. $R = k/(\pi d)$. Then, $\pi R d = k$, so $d = k/(\pi R)$

16. $(68 + 84 + 40) \div 3 = 192 \div 3 = 64$

17. $4a^2 + 12ab^2 = 4a(a + 3b^2)$

18. q quarters and d dimes is worth $25q + 10d$ cents.
    p pencils at 5 cents each cost 5p cents. After buying these pencils, he has $25q + 10d - 5p$ cents left.

19. Add the given equations to get $2x = 8$. Then, $x = 4$.

20. $\dfrac{9}{n} - \dfrac{7}{n} = \dfrac{2}{n}$. Now, $\dfrac{2}{n} = \dfrac{1}{6}$. Cross-multiply to get $n = 12$.

21. Rewrite as $k = \dfrac{3}{5}n + 36$. Then, $\dfrac{3}{5}n = k - 36$. solving, $n = (k-36)/\dfrac{3}{5} = \dfrac{5}{3}k - 60$

22. $8a^2b + 12b^2$ can be factored as $4b(2a^2+3b)$

23. $(p+r)/p = (2-5)/2 = -\dfrac{3}{2}$

24. $(m+3n)(2m-n) = 2m^2 - mn + 6mn - 3n^2 = 2m^2 + 5mn - 3n^2$

25. Given $2x \leq 6$, then $x \leq 3$. The graph corresponding to this inequality would show a dot on 3 and an arrow going to the left, as in choice A.

TEST 3

DIRECTIONS: Each question or incomplete statement is followed by several suggested answers or completions. Select the one that BEST answers the question or completes the statement. *PRINT THE LETTER OF THE CORRECT ANSWER IN THE SPACE AT THE RIGHT.*

1. Which of these is a factor of $x^2 - 36$?

   A. x-4   B. x-2   C. x+6   D. x+9

   1.____

2. If x is an integer greater than 2, which formula is GREATEST?

   A. $\dfrac{2}{x}$ B. $\dfrac{x}{2}$ C. $\dfrac{2}{x+1}$ D. $\dfrac{x+1}{2}$

   2.____

3. If $-2x + 5 > -11$, it must be TRUE that

   A. x > -3   B. x > 8   C. x < 3   D. x < 8

   3.____

4. $\dfrac{x^{10}}{x^2} =$

   A. 5   B. x^5 C. x^8 D. x^{12}

   4.____

5. Which of the following is a factor of $2x^2 - 4x - 6$?

   A. x+1   B. x+3   C. 2x-1   D. 2x+3

   5.____

6. Consider these two equations:
   $2x + y = 5$
   $2x - y = 7$
   At what point will the graphs of these two equations cross each other?

   A. (2,1)   B. (3,-1)   C. (3,0)   D. (3,1)

   6.____

7. $(a-3b)^2 =$

   A. a^2-9b^2
   C. $a^2-3ab-9b^2$
   B. a^2+9b^2
   D. $a^2-6ab+9b^2$

   7.____

8. During a soccer game, Jose scored 3 more than twice as many points as Carlos scored. If Carlos scored c points, which of the following represents the number of points Jose scored?

   A. 2c+3   B. 3c+2   C. 2(c+3)   D. 3(c+2)

   8.____

9. If $y = x^2 + kx - 5$ and $y = 0$ when $x = 3$, then $k =$

   A. -4   B. $\dfrac{-4}{3}$ C. $\dfrac{4}{3}$ D. 4

   9.____

10. Which of these is an equation of the line that passes through the origin and has a slope of 7?

    A. $y = \dfrac{x}{7}$ B. $y = 7x$ C. $y = x - 7$ D. $y = x + 7$

11. Solve the equation $x^2 + 10x - 24 = 0$ for x.
    x equals

    A. 12 or x = -2
    B. 12 or x = 2
    C. 6 or x = -4
    D. 6 or x = 4
    E. -12 or x = 2

12. On which of these number lines does the heavy line represent all numbers x such that $-3 \leq x \leq 3$?

    A. [number line from -4 to 4]
    B. [number line from -4 to 4]
    C. [number line from -4 to 4]
    D. [number line from -4 to 4]
    E. [number line from -4 to 4]

13. If $Y = \dfrac{1}{X}$ and x is greater than 0, which of these statements is TRUE?

    A. As x increases, y increases.
    B. As x increases, y decreases.
    C. As x decreases, y decreases.
    D. When x is greater than 1, y is greater than 1.
    E. When x is less than 1, y is less than 1.

14. What number MUST be added to $x^2 - 6x + 4$ in order to make it a perfect square?

    A. -4   B. 0   C. 2   D. 5   E. 32

15. For what values of x is $\dfrac{x}{6} = \dfrac{1}{2}(x-3) - \dfrac{x}{3}$ a true statement?

    A. 0 *only*
    B. 3 *only*
    C. 0 and 3 *only*
    D. All values
    E. No value

16. Solve the formula $E = \dfrac{ar}{a+r}$ for r. r =

    A. $\dfrac{aE}{a-E}$ B. $\dfrac{aE}{a+E}$ C. $aE - a + E$ D. $aE - a - E$ E. $a - \dfrac{E}{a-E}$

17. If x is greater than 3, which of the following is the SMALLEST?

    A. $\dfrac{3}{x}$ B. $\dfrac{3}{x+1}$ C. $\dfrac{3}{x-1}$ D. $\dfrac{x}{3}$ E. $\dfrac{x+1}{3}$

18. $2(x+5) =$

    A. $x+10$ B. $2x+5$ C. $2x+7$ D. $2x+10$

19. $-8 - (-7) =$

    A. -15 B. -1 C. 1 D. 15

20. $(x^2+x+2) + (2x+2) =$

    A. x^2+3x+2 B. x^2+3x+4 C. $3x^2+2x+4$ D. $3x^2+3x+2$

21. $5 + 3(n+5) - 2n =$

    A. $n+10$ B. $n+20$ C. $6n+5$ D. $6n+40$

22. If $k(k-1)(k+2) = 0$, then $k =$

    A. 0 *only*
    B. 1 and -2 *only*
    C. -1 and 2 *only*
    D. 0, -1, 2
    E. 0, 1, -2

23. What value of k will make $x^2 - 10x + k$ a perfect square trinomial?

    A. -25   B. -5   C. 5   D. 25   E. 100

24. If $\dfrac{x-5}{8x} = \dfrac{3}{x+5}$, then the solution set for x is

    A. {1,-5,5}   B. {0,-5,5}   C. {-5,5}
    D. {-25,1}   E. {25,-1}

25.

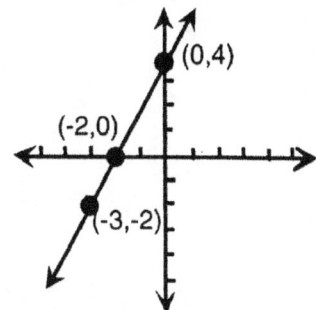

What equation represents the line above?

   A. y = 1/2x-2   B. y = 1/2x+4   C. y = 2x-2
   D. y = 2x+4   E. y = -3x-2

KEY (CORRECT ANSWERS)

1. C
2. D
3. D
4. C
5. A

6. B
7. D
8. A
9. B
10. B

11. E
12. A
13. B
14. D
15. E

16. A
17. B
18. D
19. B
20. B

21. B
22. E
23. D
24. E
25. D

SOLUTIONS TO PROBLEMS

1. $x^2 - 36 = (x-6)(x+6)$, so $x+6$ is one of the factors.

2. The value of $x = 2$ will yield the values $1, 1, \frac{2}{3}, \frac{3}{2}$ for choices A, B, C, D, respectively. Choice D is largest.

3. $-2x + 5 > -11$. Subtract 5 from each side to get $-2x > -16$. Now, $x < 8$. Remember to change the order of inequality when dividing or multiplying by a negative number.

4. $x^{10}/x^2 = x^8$. When dividing numbers with like bases, subtract the exponents.

5. $2x^2 - 4x - 6 = 2(x^2 - 2x - 3) = 2(x-3)(x+1)$, so $x+1$ is one of the factors.

6. Add the given equations to get $4x = 12$, so $x = 3$. Substitute $x = 3$ into the 1st equation to get $(2)(3) + y = 5$. Solving, $y = -1$. The point of intersection is $(3, -1)$.

7. $(a-3b)^2 = (a-3b)(a-3b) = a^2 - 3ab - 3ab + 9b^2 = a^2 - 6ab + 9b^2$

8. 3 more than twice c becomes $2c+3$

9. $0 = 3^2 + k(3) - 5$. Simplifying, $0 = 9 + 3k - 5$. Solving, $k = -4/3$

10. A slope of 7 means $y = 7x+k$, k a constant. Since the line passes through $(0,0)$, $0 = 7(0) + k$, so $k = 0$. Thus, $y = 7x$

11. $x^2 + 10x - 24 = 0$ becomes $(x+12)(x-2) = 0$. Thus, $x = -12$ or 2

12. If $-3 \leq x \leq 3$, then graphically a solid line segment should be drawn from -3 to 3. Choice A has the right graph.

13. As x increases, the value of y decreases (for $x>0$).
    Example: When $x = 5$, $y = \frac{1}{5}$. But when $x=10$, $y = \frac{1}{10}$

14. $x^2 - 6x + 9$ is a perfect square since it equals $(x-3)^2$.
    Given $x^2 - 6x + 4$, a 5 must be added.

15. $\frac{x}{6} = \frac{1}{2}(x-3) - \frac{x}{3}$. Multiply every term by 6 to get $x = 3(x-3) - 2x$.
    Simplifying, $x = 3x - 9 - 2x$. Then, $x = x - 9$ and thus no value of x is correct.

16. $E = ar/(a+r)$. Multiply both sides by $a+r$ to get $Ea + Er = ar$. Then, $Ea = ar - Er = r(a-E)$. Then, $r = Ea/(a-E)$ or $aE/(a-E)$.

17. The five choices have values of $\frac{3}{4}, \frac{3}{5}, 1, \frac{4}{3}, \frac{5}{3}$, if $x = 4$.
    Evidently, choice B is the smallest.

18. $2(x+5) = 2x + 10$

19. $-8 - (-7) = -8 + 7 = -1$

20. $(x^2+x+2) + (2x+2) = x^2 + 3x + 4$

21. $5 + 3(n+5) - 2n = 5 + 3n + 15 - 2n = n + 20$

22. If $k(k-1)(k+2) = 0$, then $k = 0$, $k-1 = 0$, or $k+2 = 0$. The values of k are 0, 1, -2.

23. Let $k = 25$. Then, $x^2 - 10x + 25$, which equals $(x-5)^2$, is a perfect square trinomial

24. $(x-5)/8x = 3/(x+5)$. Cross-multiply to get $x^2 - 25 = 24x$. Then, $x^2 - 24x - 25 = 0$. Factoring, $(x-25)(x+1) = 0$. Solving, $x = 25$ or $x = -1$

25. Slope of line is $(4-0)/(0-(-2)) = 2$. So, $y = 2x + k$. Substituting (0,4), $4 = 2(0) + k$, so $k = 4$. Then final equation is $y = 2x + 4$

TEST 4

DIRECTIONS: Each question or incomplete statement is followed by several suggested answers or completions. Select the one that BEST answers the question or completes the statement. *PRINT THE LETTER OF THE CORRECT ANSWER IN THE SPACE AT THE RIGHT.*

1. If $2x + y = 7$ and $x - 4y = 4$, then $y =$

   A. -15/9   B. -1/9   C. 7/16   D. 11/9   E. 7

2. $\dfrac{1}{y} + \dfrac{2}{3+y} =$

   A. $\dfrac{3}{3+2y}$ B. $\dfrac{3y+3}{3+2y}$ C. $\dfrac{y+1}{y+y^2}$ D. $\dfrac{y+3}{3y+y^2}$ E. $\dfrac{3y+3}{3y+y^2}$

3. For what real numbers x does $3x^2 - x - 4 = 0$?

   A. -4 and 3   B. -4/3 and 1   C. -2/3 and 2
   D. 2/3 and 2   E. 4/3 and -1

4. If $\dfrac{x}{3} + \dfrac{5}{6} = 2$, then $x =$

   A. -3   B. 6/5   C. 7/2   D. 7   E. 17/2

5. If $f(x) = 2x^3 - 3x^2 - x + 2$, then $f(-1) =$

   A. -4   B. -2   C. 0   D. 2   E. 4

6. If $\dfrac{3}{3k+x} = \dfrac{1}{k+1}$ and $k \neq -1$, then $x=$

   A. 1/3   B. 1   C. 3   D. 3k   E. 6k+3

7. The LOWEST common denominator of the fractions $\dfrac{1}{s^2 + s - 12}$ and $\dfrac{1}{s^2 - 5s + 6}$ is

   A. (s-2)(s-3)(s+4)   B. (s-2)(s-3)²(s+4)
   C. (s-2)(s+3)(s-4)   D. (s-2)(s-3)(s+3)(s-4)
   E. (s+2)(s-3)(s+3)(s-4)

8. Which equation states that the average of the numbers x, y, and z is 4 *more* than z?

   A. $x+y+z = z-4$ B. $\dfrac{x+y+z}{3} = z-4$
   C. $\dfrac{x+y+z}{3} = z+4$ D. $3x+3y+3z = z+4$

9. What is the solution set of the equation $x^2 - 2x = 0$?

   A. {0}   B. {0,2}   C. {-2,2}   D. {-2,0,2}

10. Jean, Paul, and Terry shared the driving on a trip. Jean drove 50 miles less than one-third the total distance, and Paul drove 40 miles more than one-third the total distance. If Terry drove the remaining 200 miles, how many miles did they drive?

    A. 570   B. 590   C. 610   D. 630

11. A team played 70 games and won 20 more games than it lost. If there were no ties, how many games did the team win?

    A. 25   B. 40   C. 45   D. 50

12. To mail some letters, Jane used only 20-cent and 25-cent stamps. If she used a total of 22 stamps that cost a total of $5.00, how many of the stamps were 20-cent stamps?

    A. 5   B. 10   C. 12   D. 15

13. If $6x - 2 = 10x$, then $x =$

    A. $\dfrac{-1}{2}$ B. $\dfrac{-1}{8}$ C. 1/2   D. 2

14. The length of a rectangular room is 4 feet greater than its width. If the area of the room is 96 square feet, what is the width of the room in feet?

    A. $2\sqrt{6}$ B. 6   C. 8   D. $8\sqrt{6}$

15. If $x = \sqrt{b^2 - 9}$, for which one of the following values of b will x be a *real* number?

    A. -1   B. 0   C. 2   D. 4

16. What is the solution set for the equation $|x| - 2 = 8$?

    A. {10}   B. {-6,6}   C. {6,10}   D. {-10,10}

17. If $x = 2$, then $x^0 + x^{-2} =$

    A. -4   B. $1\dfrac{1}{4}$ C. $2\dfrac{1}{4}$ D. 6

18. If $\log_b 10 = p$ and $\log_b 2 = q$, then $\log_b 20 =$

    A. pq   B. p+q   C. p^q D. q^p E. 2(p+q)

19. If $x - 7$ is a factor of $x^2 - 3x + p$, what is the value of p?

    A. -28   B. -21   C. -10   D. 21   E. 28

20. $-16^{\frac{1}{2}} + 8^{\frac{2}{3}} =$

A. $-\frac{8}{3}$ B. 0   C. $3\frac{3}{4}$ D. $4\frac{1}{4}$ E. 8

21. If $f(x) = 2x^4 - 3x^3 - 2x - 4$, then $f(2) =$

A. -10   B. -7   C. -4   D. 0   E. 4

22. The two solutions of the equation $2x^2 - x - 4 = 0$ are

A. opposite in sign
B. both positive and equal
C. both negative and equal
D. both positive but unequal
E. both negative but unequal

23. The equation $ax^2 + bx + c = 0$ has imaginary roots whenever $b^2 - 4ac$ is negative. What are ALL the values of c for which $x^2 + 2x + c = 0$ has imaginary roots?

A. $c < -1$ B. $c < 1$ C. $c > -1$
D. $c > 0$ E. $c > 1$

24.

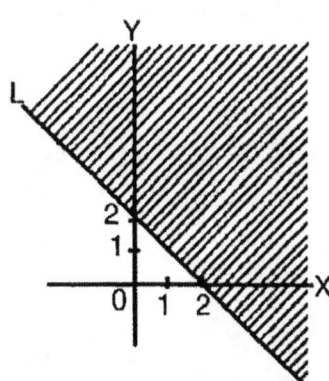

The equation of line L in the figure above is $x + y = 2$. Which of these conditions is satisfied by *every* point (x,y) in the shaded region?

A. $x \geq 2$ B. $y \geq 2$ C. $x + y \geq 2$

D. $x + y \leq 2$ E. $x \leq y + 2$

25. Which of these is the graph of y = |x|?   25.____

A.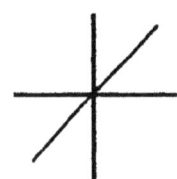

B.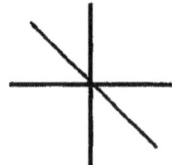

C.

D.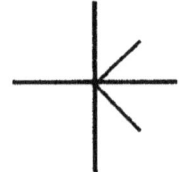

E.

KEY (CORRECT ANSWERS)

1. B   11. C
2. E   12. B
3. E   13. A
4. C   14. C
5. B   15. D

6. C   16. D
7. A   17. B
8. C   18. B
9. B   19. A
10. A   20. B

21. D
22. A
23. E
24. C
25. C

SOLUTIONS TO PROBLEMS

1. Double the 2nd equation to get 2x - 8y = 8. Subtract the 1st equation to get -9y = 1. Solving, y = - 1/9

2. $\dfrac{1}{y}+\dfrac{2}{3+y}=\dfrac{3+y+2y}{y(3+y)}=\dfrac{3y+3}{3y+y^2}$

3. $3x^2 - x - 4 = 0$ can be written as (3x-4)(x+1) = 0.
   Then, $x = \dfrac{4}{3}$ and -1.

4. $\dfrac{x}{3}+\dfrac{5}{6} = 2$. Multiply equation by 6 to get 2x + 5 = 12.
   Then, 2x = 7. Solving, x = 7/2

5. $f(-1) = 2(-1)^3 - 3(-1)^2 - (-1) + 2 = -2 - 3 + 1 + 2 = -2$

6. Cross-multiply to get 3(k+1) = 3k + x. 3k + 3 = 3k + x. By inspection, k = 3

7. Since $s^2 + s - 12 = (s+4)(s-3)$ and $s^2 - 5s + 6 = (s-3)(s-2)$, the L.C.D. must be (s+4)(s-3)(s-2)

8. The average of x, y, z is (x+y+z)/3, and since this is 4 more than z, (x+y+z)/3 = z + 4

9. $x^2 - 2x = 0$ can be factored as x(x-2) = 0. Thus, x = 0, 2

10. Let d = total distance. The distances Jean, Paul, and Terry drove were $\dfrac{1}{3}d - 50$, $\dfrac{1}{3}d + 40$, and 200, respectively. Now, $\dfrac{1}{3}d - 50 + \dfrac{1}{3}d + 40 + 200 = d$.
    Then, $\dfrac{2}{3}d + 190 = d$. This reduces to $\dfrac{1}{3}d = 190$. Solving, d = 570 miles.

11. Let x = games won, x-20 = games lost. Then, x + x - 20 = 70. 2x = 90. Solving, x = 45.

12. Let x = number of 20-cent stamps, 22-x = number of 25-cent stamps. Then, .20x + .25(22-x) = 5.00. .20x + 5.50 - .25x = 5.00. Simplifying, -.05x = =.50. Solving, x = 10

13. 6x - 2 = 10x. Subtract 6x from both sides to get -2 = 4x.
    Solving, $x = -\dfrac{2}{4} = -\dfrac{1}{2}$

14. Let w = width, w+4 = length. Then, w(w+4) = 96. $w^2 + 4w - 96 = 0$. Factoring, (w+12)(w-8) = 0. Using only the positive w value, w = 8.

15. If b = 4, then $x = \sqrt{4^2 - 9} = \sqrt{7}$ which is a real number.

16. $|x| - 2 = 8$ becomes $|x| = 10$. Thus, $x = -10$ and 10

17. $2^0 + 2^{-2} = 1 + \dfrac{1}{4} = 1\dfrac{1}{4}$

18. $\log_b 20 = \log_b(10 \cdot 2) = \log_b 10 + \log_b 2 = p + q$

19. $x-7$ is a factor of $x^2 - 3x - 28$, which equals $(x-7)(x+4)$. Thus, $p = -28$

20. $-16^{\frac{1}{2}} + 8^{\frac{2}{3}} = -\sqrt{16} + (\sqrt[3]{8})^2 = -4 + 4 = 0$

21. $f(2) = 2(2^4) - 3(2^3) - 2(2) - 4 = 32 - 24 - 4 - 4 = 0$

22. The solutions to $2x^2 - x - 4 = 0$ are $(1+\sqrt{33})/4$ and $(1-\sqrt{33})/4$, which are approximately 1.69 and -1.19. These solutions are opposite in sign.

23. For $x^2 + 2x + c = 0$ to have imaginary (or complex) roots, $2^2 - (4)(1)(c) < 0$. Then, $4 < 4c$. Solving, $c > 1$.

24. $x + y = 2$ can be written as $y = 2 - x$. Since the shaded region is above this line, $y \geq 2 - x$, which is equivalent to $x + y \geq 2$

25. If $y = |x|$, then $y = x$ when $x \geq 0$ and $y = -x$ when $x < 0$. The graph shown in choice C fits this description.

EXAMINATION SECTION
TEST 1

DIRECTIONS: Each question or incomplete statement is followed by several suggested answers or completions. Select the one that BEST answers the question or completes the statement. *PRINT THE LETTER OF THE CORRECT ANSWER IN THE SPACE AT THE RIGHT.*

1. What must be added to $5x - 3y + 2$ for it to equal $2x + y$?

    A. $3x+4y$
    B. $7x-2y-2$
    C. $-3x-2y+2$
    D. $-3x-2y-2$
    E. $-3x+4y-2$

    1.____

2. Which of the following statements about EVEN and ODD integers must be false?

    A. (ODD + EVEN) x ODD = ODD
    B. ODD x ODD + EVEN = ODD
    C. EVEN x EVEN + ODD = ODD
    D. (ODD + EVEN) x EVEN = ODD
    E. ODD + ODD x EVEN = ODD

    2.____

3. If $d = rt$ and $d = 60$ when $r = 30$, then $t =$

    A. $\frac{1}{2}$
    B. 2
    C. 20
    D. 90
    E. 1,800

    3.____

4. What is the product of $5x^2$ and $3x^5$?

    A. $15x^7$
    B. $8x^7$
    C. $2x^3$
    D. $8x^{10}$
    E. $15x^{10}$

    4.____

5. Which sentence is equivalent to $3 + 2x > 5$?

    A. $x < 1$
    B. $x > 1$
    C. $x < 4$
    D. $x > 4$
    E. $x\ 4$

    5.____

6. How can the following statement be written?
   A certain number n decreased by half of a second number t is equal to 50.

    A. $n - \frac{1}{2}t = 50$
    B. $2n - t = 50$
    C. $\frac{1}{2}n - t = 50$
    D. $\frac{1}{2}nt = 50$
    E. $\frac{1}{2}n + t = 50$

    6.____

7. What is the area of a square whose side is $2a + 5$?

    A. $8a+20$
    B. $2a^2+25$
    C. $4a^2+25$
    D. $4a^2+10a+25$
    E. $4a^2+20a+25$

    7.____

8. If $x - 2y = 7$ and $x + 2y = 5$, then $x =$

    A. $\frac{1}{2}$
    B. 0
    C. 5
    D. 6
    E. 7

    8.____

9. Sara has q quarters and 2 more dimes than quarters. What is the value of her coins in cents?

   A. q+2
   B. q+(q+2)
   C. 25q+20
   D. 25q+(q+2)
   E. 25q+10(q+2)

10. The equation 2(3x+5) = 2(5+3x) is true for all real numbers x because it is an example of the

    A. commutative property of multiplication
    B. commutative property of addition
    C. associative property of addition
    D. addition property of equality
    E. distributive property

11. If $3x^2 + bx + 1 = 0$ when x = 1, what is b?

    A. -4
    B. -1
    C. 1
    D. 4
    E. It cannot be determined from the information given.

12. Which of the following expressions is equal to (1+x)(1+y)?

    A. x+y
    B. 1+x+y
    C. 1+xy
    D. x+y+xy
    E. 1+x+y+xy

13. $(-2)^3(-3)^2 =$

    A. -72   B. -54   C. 36   D. 54   E. 72

14. If $\frac{x}{3} - 1 = \frac{x}{5} + 2$, then x =

    A. -15   B. $-\frac{2}{3}$ C. $\frac{3}{2}$ D. 15   E. $\frac{45}{2}$

15. Factor $3x^2 - 4x - 4$.

    A. (3x-2)(x+2)
    B. (3x+2)(x-2)
    C. (3x+1)(x-4)
    D. (3x-4)(x+1)
    E. (3x-4)(x-1)

16. What is the result when $x^3 - x^2 - 17x + 20$ is divided by $x^2 + 3x - 5$?

    A. x-4   B. x-2   C. x-1   D. x+1   E. x+4

17. If a = 3 and b = 2, then $\frac{ab^3}{(a-b)^2} =$

    A. $\frac{18}{5}$ B. $\frac{24}{5}$ C. 18   D. 24   E. 210

18. What value of x, when substituted in $\frac{1}{x-2}$, will make this fraction meaningless?

   A. -2
   B. 0
   C. 2
   D. Any number between -2 and 0
   E. Any number between 0 and 2

19. $\frac{5a^2b}{4} \div \frac{10b^2}{3a^2} =$

   A. $\frac{3b^4}{8}$ B. $\frac{3a^4}{8b}$ C. $\frac{25b^4}{6}$ D. $\frac{25a^4}{6}$ E. $\frac{3}{8a^2b^2}$

20. If $\log_{10} n = 1.9682$, then $\log_{10} 100n =$

   A. 1.0316   B. 2.9682   C. 3.9682
   D. 3.9364   E. 196.82

21. $\frac{3+2i}{i} =$

   A. 1   B. 5   C. 5i   D. -2+3i   E. 2-3i

22. If the graphs of $x + y = 3$ and $x + ky = 12$ intersect on on the Y-axis, then k =

   A. 0   B. 3   C. 4   D. 6   E. 12

23. What is the sum of the infinite geometric series $1 - \frac{1}{2} + \frac{1}{4} - \frac{1}{8} + \ldots ?$

   A. -1   B. 0   C. $\frac{2}{3}$ D. 1   E. $\frac{3}{2}$

24. If $f(x) = 4x+3$ and $g(x) = x^2-2$, then $f(g(x)) =$

   A. $-x^2+4x+5$ B. x^2+4x+1 C. $4x^2-8$
   D. $4x^2-5$ E. $4x^2+1$

25. For each of the graphs below, the lines are y = x and y = x+2. The shaded region in which   25. ____
of the graphs is the portion of the plane where y ≥ x and y ≤ x+2?

A.
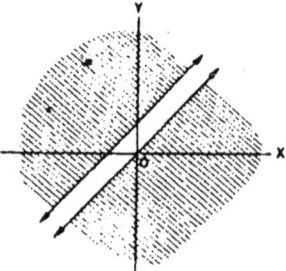

B.
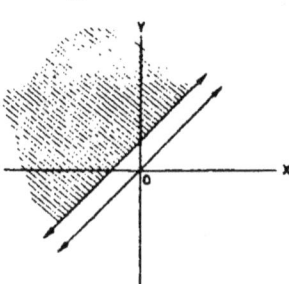

C.
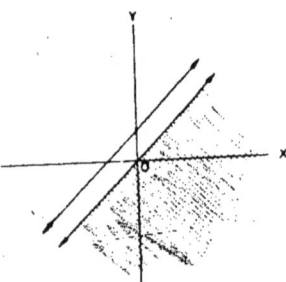

D.
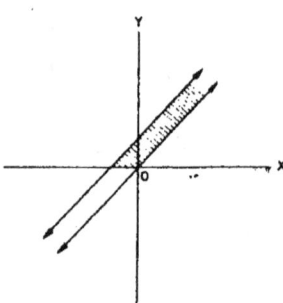

E.
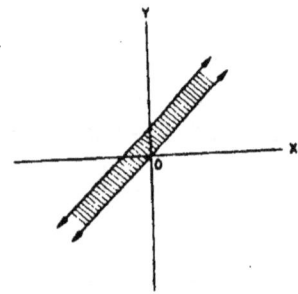

KEY (CORRECT ANSWERS)

1. E
2. D
3. B
4. A
5. B

6. A
7. E
8. D
9. E
10. B

11. A
12. E
13. A
14. E
15. B

16. A
17. D
18. C
19. B
20. C

21. E
22. C
23. C
24. D
25. E

SOLUTIONS TO PROBLEMS

1. $2x + y - (5x-3y+2) = -3x + 4y - 2$

2. Choice D is the false statement. Odd + even = odd, but odd x even = even.

3. $60 = 30t$, so $t = 60/30 = 2$

4. $(5x^2)(3x^5) = 15x^7$

5. $3 + 2x > 5$. Subtracting 3, $2x > 2$, so $x > 1$

6. $n - \frac{1}{2}t = 50$ is the equivalent mathematical expression.

7. $(2a+5)^2 = 4a^2 + 10a + 10a + 25 = 4a^2 + 20a + 25$

8. Adding the equations, $2x = 12$, so $x = 6$

9. q quarters = 25q, q+2 dimes = 10(q+2). Then, the total value = $25q + 10(q+2)$

10. $3x + 5 = 5 + 3x$ due to the commutative property of addition. An example of the commutative property of multiplication is $(3)(5) = (5)(3)$.

11. $3(1^2) + b(1) + 1 = 0$. Then, $3 + b + 1 = 0$. Thus, $b = -4$

12. $(1+x)(1+y) = 1+y+x+xy = 1+x+y+xy$

13. $(-2)^3(-3)^2 = (-8)(9) = -72$

14. Multiply equation by 15: $5x - 15 = 3x + 30$. $2x + 45$. So, $x = \frac{45}{2}$

15. $3x^2 - 4x - 4$ can be factored as: $(3x+2)(x-2)$

16. By long division, $(x^3-x^2-17x+20) \div (x^2+3x-5) = x - 4$

17. $(3)(2^3) \div 1^2 = (3)(8) \div 1 = 24$

18. The value $x = 2$ will render the fraction $\frac{1}{x-2}$ meaningless.

19. $(5a^2b/4) \div 10b^2/3a^2) = 15a^4b \div 40b^2 = 3a^4/8b$

20. $\text{Log}_{10}100n = \text{Log}_{10}100 + \text{Log}_{10}n = 2 + 1.9682 = 3.9682$

21. $(3+2i) \div i = [(3+2i) \div i] \cdot [i/i] = (3i+2i^2)/i^2 = (3i-2)/-1 = -3i + 2$ or $2 - 3i$

22. An intersection on the y-axis means $x = 0$. Then, $0 + y = 3$ and $0 + ky = 12$. The 1st equation yields $y = 3$. Thus, $0 + 3k = 12$, so $k = 4$

23. $1 - \frac{1}{2} + \frac{1}{4} - \frac{1}{8} + \ldots = \frac{1}{1-(-\frac{1}{2})} = \frac{1}{\frac{3}{2}} = \frac{2}{3}$

24. $f(g(x)) = f(x^2-2) = 4(x^2-2) + 3 = 4x^2 - 5$

25. The correct shaded area will lie between y = x + 2 and y = x, which is choice E.

TEST 2

DIRECTIONS: Each question or incomplete statement is followed by several suggested answers or completions. Select the one that BEST answers the question or completes the statement. *PRINT THE LETTER OF THE CORRECT ANSWER IN THE SPACE AT THE RIGHT.*

1. Phil has 15 coins; some are quarters and the rest are nickels. If he has $2.95 in coins, how many nickels does he have?

   A. 4   B. 5   C. 6   D. 9   E. 11

   1._____

2. If $x = \dfrac{3}{4}$, then $x^{-2} =$

   A. $-\dfrac{16}{9}$ B. $-\dfrac{6}{8}$ C. $-\dfrac{9}{16}$ D. $\dfrac{8}{6}$ E. $\dfrac{16}{9}$

   2._____

3. What is the slope of the line whose equation is $3y - 6x = 4$?

   A. -6   B. $\dfrac{4}{3}$ C. 2   D. 3   E. 4

   3._____

4. If $a - b = -4x - 7y$ and $a = 3x - 5y$, solve for b in terms of x and y.

   A. -7x-2y   B. -x-12y   C. x+12y
   D. 7x+2y   E. $\dfrac{4x+7y}{3x-5y}$

   4._____

5. Which of these sequences is a geometric progression?

   A. $1, \dfrac{1}{2}, \dfrac{1}{3}, \dfrac{1}{4}, \dfrac{1}{5}, ...$ B. 1, 3, 6, 10, 15,...

   C. $\dfrac{1}{2}, \dfrac{1}{4}, \dfrac{1}{6}, \dfrac{1}{8}, ...$ D. $1, \dfrac{1}{3}, \dfrac{1}{9}, \dfrac{1}{27}, ...$

   E. $1, \dfrac{1}{3}, \dfrac{1}{6}, \dfrac{1}{9}, ...$

   5._____

6. When simplified, $\dfrac{t^6}{t^4 + t^2} =$

   A. t^2 B. $t^2 + t^4$ C. 1   D. $\dfrac{t^3}{t^4+1}$ E. $\dfrac{t^4}{t^2+1}$

   6._____

7. If $\log_{10} x = 2$, then $x =$

   A. 2   B. 4   C. 12   D. 20   E. 100

   7._____

8. If a and b are integers and $\frac{a}{b}$ is negative, then

   A. both a and b are negative
   B. neither a nor b is negative
   C. a is negative and b is positive
   D. a is positive and b is negative
   E. either a or b is positive and the other is negative

9. What must K be if (5,K) is on the graph of 2x + 3y = 7?

   A. 7   B. 3   C. 2   D. 1   E. -1

10. The graph of $-3 \leq x < 3$ is

    A.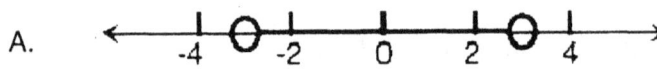

    B.

    C.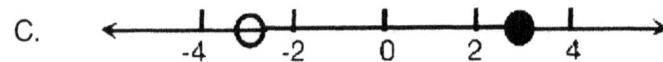

    D.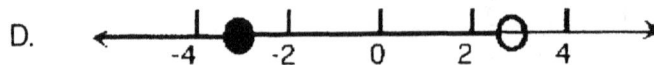

    E.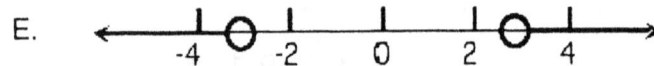

11. Jane weighs 45 kilograms on Earth but would weigh 18 kilograms on Mars. Her brother George weighs 70 kilograms on Earth.
    How many kilograms would he weigh on Mars?

    A. 12   B. 28   C. 43   D. 45   E. 175

12. What is the solution to the system below?
    2x + 3y = 7
    x + y = 3

    A. (2,1)   B. (1,2)   C. (5,-1)   D. (-1,5)   E. (0,3)

13. Bill requires 6 hours to complete the same job that John can complete in 4 hours. What part of the job can they complete in one hour working together?

    A. $\frac{1}{10}$ B. $\frac{1}{5}$ C. $\frac{1}{3}$ D. $\frac{5}{12}$ E. $\frac{1}{2}$

14. What value of x will make the expression $\frac{2(x+1)}{x-4}$ meaningless?

    A. -4 B. -1 C. 1 D. 2 E. 4

15. What is the remainder when $n^2 + 7n - 9$ is divided by $n+1$?

    A. -15 B. -3 C. 1 D. 3 E. 6n-9

16. $\sqrt[3]{-125} =$

    A. -25 B. -5 C. 5 D. 25 E. ±5

17. $(2x^2)(3x^3) =$

    A. $5x^5$
    B. $6x^6$
    C. $5x^6$
    D. $6x^5$
    E. None of the above

18. If $\frac{5}{n} - \frac{3}{n} = \frac{1}{4}$, then n =

    A. $\frac{1}{8}$ B. $\frac{1}{2}$ C. 2 D. 4 E. 8

19. Solve the equation $x^2 - 7x + 12 = 0$ for x.
    x equals _____.

    A. -3; -4 B. -3; 4 C. 3; 4 D. 2; -6 E. 2; 6

20. Which of these, when added to m+n, gives n-m?

    A. 2m B. -2m C. 2m-2n D. m-n E. n-m

21. $2\sqrt{2} + 3\sqrt{48} - 5\sqrt{27} =$

    A. $\sqrt{3}$ B. $\sqrt{12}$ C. $\sqrt{27}$ D. $\sqrt{48}$ E. $\sqrt{58}$

22. Solve the following system of equations for x: $\begin{cases} x + y = 4 \\ x - y = 2 \end{cases}$

    A. 0 B. 1 C. 3 D. 4 E. 6

23. $5^0 =$

    A. $-\frac{1}{5}$ B. 0 C. $\frac{1}{5}$ D. 1 E. 5

24. Which of these expressions is equivalent to $x(x-a) + a(x+a)$?

    A. $(x+a)^2(x-a)$
    B. $(x+a)(x-a)^2$
    C. $(x+a)^3$
    D. $(x+a)^2$
    E. x^2+a^2

25. Which of these could be the graph of $y = 2x^2+3x+2$?   25._____

A.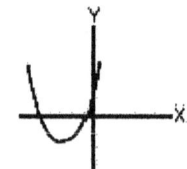

B.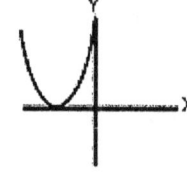

C.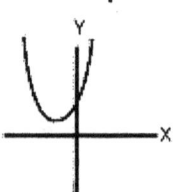

D.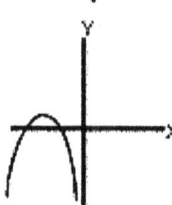

E.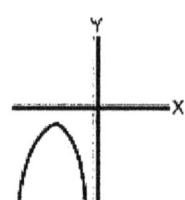

KEY (CORRECT ANSWERS)

1. A
2. E
3. C
4. D
5. D

6. E
7. E
8. E
9. E
10. B

11. B
12. A
13. D
14. E
15. A

16. B
17. D
18. E
19. C
20. B

21. A
22. C
23. D
24. E
25. C

210

SOLUTIONS TO PROBLEMS

1. Let x = number of nickels, 15-x = number of quarters. Then, .05x + .25(15-x) = $2.95. So, -.20x + 3.75 = 2.95. Simplifying, -.20x = -.80. Solving, x = 4

2. $(\frac{3}{4})^{-2} = 1 \div (\frac{3}{4})^2 = 1 \div \frac{9}{16} = \frac{16}{9}$

3. Rewrite 3y - 6x = 4 as $y = 2x + \frac{4}{3}$. The slope of the line is given by the coefficient of x, which is 2.

4. 3x - 5y - b = -4x - 7y, by substituting the expression for a. Subtracting 3x - 5y, we get -b = -7x - 2y, so b = 7x + 2y

5. In a geometric progression, each term must be a <u>constant</u> multiple of the preceding term. Choice D is correct, where the constant multiplier is 1/3.

6. $t^6 / (t^4 + t^2) = t^6 / t^2(t^2 + 1) = t^4 / (t^2 + 1)$

7. $\log_{10} x = 2$, so $x = 10^2 = 100$

8. If $\frac{a}{b}$ is negative, either a is negative or b is negative (but <u>not</u> both negative simultaneously).

9. 2(5) + 3k = 7. Then, 10 + 3k = 7. Solving, k = -1

10. The graph of $-3 \leq x < 3$ is a line segment from -3 to 3, with a dot on -3 and an open circle on 3.

11. Let x = George's weight on Mars. Then, $\frac{45}{70} = \frac{18}{x}$. Cross-multiplying, 45x = 1260. Solving, x = 28

12. Multiply the 2nd equation by 3 to get 3x + 3y = 9. Now, subtract the 1st equation to get x = 2. Substituting in the original 2nd equation, 2+y=3. So, y = 1.

13. In one hour, Bill does $\frac{1}{6}$ of the job while John does $\frac{1}{4}$. Together, they complete $\frac{1}{6} + \frac{1}{4} = \frac{5}{12}$ of the job.

14. If x = 45 the denominator of 2(x+1)/(x-4) becomes 0. This makes the fraction meaningless.

15. $(n^2+7n-9) \div (n+1) = n + 6 + \frac{-15}{n+1}$. Thus, the remainder is -15.

16. $\sqrt[3]{-125} = -5$, since $(-5)^3 = -125$

17. $(2x^2)(3x^3) = 6x^5$

18. $\dfrac{5}{n} - \dfrac{3}{n} = \dfrac{2}{n}$. Then, $\dfrac{2}{n} = \dfrac{1}{4}$. Cross-multiplying, $n = 8$

19. Factor to get $(x-4)(x-3) = 0$. Then, $x = 4, 3$

20. $n - m - (m+n) = n-m-m-n = -2m$

21. $2\sqrt{12} + 3\sqrt{48} - 5\sqrt{27} = 2\sqrt{4}\sqrt{3} + 3\sqrt{16}\sqrt{3} - 5\sqrt{9}\sqrt{3}$
    $= 4\sqrt{3} + 12\sqrt{3} - 15\sqrt{3} = \sqrt{3}$

22. Add the equations to get $2x = 6$. So, $x = 3$

23. $5^0 = 1$. Any real number, except 0, raised to the zero exponent yields 1.

24. $x(x-a) + a(x+a) = x^2 - ax + ax + a^2 = x^2 + a^2$

25. For the graph of $y = 2x^2 + 3x + 2$, first note that the coefficient of x^2 is positive. This means the graph must have a minimum y value. Only choices A,B,C satisfy this requirement. Next, if we let $y = 0$, $0 = 2x^2 + 3x + 2$ has non-real roots (namely, $-\dfrac{3}{4} \pm \sqrt{-7/4}$). This implies that the graph must not intersect the x-axis, where y would be 0. Only choice C fulfills this requirement also.

TEST 3

DIRECTIONS: Each question or incomplete statement is followed by several suggested answers or completions. Select the one that BEST answers the question or completes the statement. *PRINT THE LETTER OF THE CORRECT ANSWER IN THE SPACE AT THE RIGHT.*

1. If $m = \sqrt{3}$, then $m^{-4} =$

   A. -9   B. $\dfrac{1}{81}$ C. $\dfrac{1}{9}$ D. 3   E. 9

2. If $\dfrac{a^2}{r+t} = m$ and if $m \neq 0$, then $r =$

   A. $a^2 - t^2$ B. $\dfrac{m}{a^2} - t$ C. $\dfrac{a^2 - t}{m}$ D. $\dfrac{a^2 - mt}{m}$ E. $\dfrac{a^2 + mt}{m}$

3. If $x^3 - 8x^2 = 0$, then $x =$

   A. 0 *only*   B. 2 *only*   C. 8 *only*   D. 0 or 2   E. 0 or 8

4. For what value of k is $x-1$ a factor of $3x^5 - k$?

   A. -3   B. $\dfrac{1}{3}$ C. $\dfrac{5}{3}$ D. 3   E. 5

5. Which of these could be a term in the expansion of $(a+b)^{12}$?

   A. $220ab^{12}$ B. $220a^3b^2$ C. $220a^3b^{10}$
   D. $220a^6b^2$ E. $220a^9b^3$

6. $(1+i)^2 =$

   A. 0   B. 2   C. 2i   D. 1+i   E. 2+2i

7. If x and y are real numbers and if $y = \sqrt{3x^2 - 4}$, what is the MINIMUM value of y?

   A. $-\infty$ B. -4   C. -2   D. 0   E. 2

8. If $x = -3$ is one solution of the equation $x^2 + x + c = 0$, then $c =$

   A. -12   B. -6   C. 2   D. 3   E. 6

9. $\log_2 8 =$

   A. $\dfrac{1}{4}$ B. 3   C. 4   D. 16   E. 64

10. $\begin{vmatrix} 4 & 2 & 1 \\ 0 & 0 & 1 \\ 1 & 1 & 0 \end{vmatrix} =$

   A. -2   B. 0   C. 2   D. 7   E. 9

11. The solution set of $y^4 + y^2 - y - 1 = y(y^3-1)$ is

   A. [1,-1,i,-i]   B. [0,1,-1]   C. [1,-1]
   D. [1]   E. [0]

12. If the graph of the equation $cy = dx^2 - 4$ passes through the points (2,0) and (-4,3), then $c =$

   A. 4   B. 0   C. $-\frac{9}{2}$ D. $-\frac{20}{3}$ E. -20

13. If the system of equations $\begin{cases} x = \frac{2}{3}k \\ y - 6x = 6K \\ y = 6 - 2k \end{cases}$ is consistent, then $k =$

   A. $-\frac{3}{4}$ B. $\frac{1}{2}$ C. 1   D. $\frac{3}{2}$ E. 3

14. If the two solutions of $x^2 + 4x + c = 0$ are real and unequal, which of these describes ALL possible values of the constant c?

   A. $c \neq 0$ B. $c = 0$ C. $c > 1$
   D. $c < 4$ E. $c > 4$

15. $|x-2| < 4$ if and *only* if

   A. $x < 2$ B. $x < 6$
   C. $x > -2$ D. $-2 < x < 6$
   E. $x < -2$ and $x > 6$

16. If $x^2 - y^2 = 5$ and $x^2 + y^2 = 13$, then $x^4 - y^4 =$

   A. 1   B. 18   C. 25   D. 64   E. 65

17. The graph of $5x^2 + 5y^2 = 25$ is a circle with center at

   A. (5,5)   B. (-5,-5)   C. (0,0)   D. (5,0)   E. (0,5)

18. What are ALL the numbers which satisfy the equation $x^2 - 5x - 14 = 0$ and also satisfy the inequality $x > 5$?

   A. -2 *only*   B. 7 *only*   C. -2 and 7
   D. $x > 5$ E. $x \geq 7$

19. What are ALL real numbers x for which (x-3)(x+1) > 0?

    A. x < -1
    B. x > 3
    C. -1 < x < 3
    D. -3 < x < 1
    E. x < -1, x > 3

20. If determinants are used to solve the system of equations

    $\begin{cases} 2x + y = 3 \\ 1x + 4y = 7 \end{cases}$

    then y =

    A. $\dfrac{\begin{vmatrix} 2 & 3 \\ 1 & 7 \end{vmatrix}}{\begin{vmatrix} 2 & 1 \\ 1 & 4 \end{vmatrix}}$
    B. $\dfrac{\begin{vmatrix} 2 & 1 \\ 1 & 4 \end{vmatrix}}{\begin{vmatrix} 3 & 1 \\ 7 & 4 \end{vmatrix}}$
    C. $\dfrac{\begin{vmatrix} 2 & 1 \\ 1 & 4 \end{vmatrix}}{\begin{vmatrix} 2 & 3 \\ 1 & 7 \end{vmatrix}}$
    D. $\dfrac{\begin{vmatrix} 3 & 1 \\ 7 & 4 \end{vmatrix}}{\begin{vmatrix} 2 & 1 \\ 1 & 4 \end{vmatrix}}$
    E. $\dfrac{\begin{vmatrix} 3 & 7 \\ 2 & 1 \end{vmatrix}}{\begin{vmatrix} 2 & 1 \\ 1 & 4 \end{vmatrix}}$

21. If $25^x = 5$ and $3^{x+y} = 81$, then y =

    A. 2
    B. $\dfrac{5}{2}$
    C. 3
    D. $\dfrac{7}{2}$
    E. $\dfrac{9}{2}$

22. What are ALL real numbers x for which
    $x^2 - x - 1 < x^2 - 1$?

    A. x < 0
    B. x > 0
    C. 0 < x < 1
    D. -1 < x < 1
    E. -1 < x < 2

23. If (2,-3) and (-6,9) are ordered pairs of real numbers of the form (x, mx+b), then m =

    A. $-\dfrac{3}{2}$
    B. $-\dfrac{2}{3}$
    C. $-\dfrac{1}{2}$
    D. $\dfrac{2}{3}$
    E. $\dfrac{3}{2}$

24. If 2, 6, 18, 3x+3 are the first four terms of a geometric sequence, then x =

    A. 5
    B. 7
    C. 9
    D. 11
    E. 17

25.

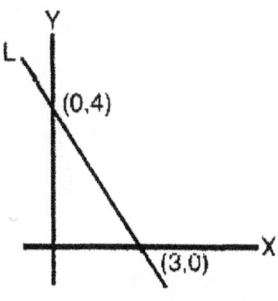

    What is the equation of line L which crosses the X-axis and the Y-axis at the points indicated in the figure above?

    A. 3y+4x = 0
    B. 4y+3x = 0
    C. x + y = 12
    D. 3y+4x = 12
    E. 4y+3x = 12

4 (#3)

KEY (CORRECT ANSWERS)

1. C
2. D
3. E
4. D
5. E

6. C
7. D
8. B
9. B
10. A

11. C
12. A
13. B
14. D
15. D

16. E
17. C
18. B
19. E
20. A

21. D
22. B
23. A
24. E
25. D

SOLUTIONS TO PROBLEMS

1. $(\sqrt{3})^{-4} = 1 \div (\sqrt{3})^4 = \frac{1}{9}$

2. $a^2/(r+t) = m$. Multiply by $r+t$ to get $a^2 = mr + mt$. Subtract mt to get $a^2 - mt = mr$. Finally, $r = (a^2-mt)/m$

3. $x^3 - 8x^2 = x^2(x-8) = 0$. Then, $x = 0$ or 8

4. If $k = 3$, $3x^5 - 5 = 3(x^5-1) = 3(x-1)(x^4+x^3+x^2+x+1)$. Then, $x-1$ becomes a factor.

5. Note that $220 = (12)(11)(10)/3!$, where $3! = (3)(2)(1) = 6$. In expanding $(a+b)^{12}$, the fourth term would be $(12)(11)(10)/3! a^9 b^3$ or $220 a^9 b^3$

6. $(1+i)^2 = 1 + 2i + i^2 = 2i$, since $i^2 = -1$

7. Since $y = \sqrt{3x^2 - 4}$, the minimum value of y is 0, since the lowest value of a square root is 0. (Incidentally, when $x = \pm\sqrt{4/3}$, $y = 0$)

8. $(-3)^2 - 3 + c = 0$. Then, $9 - 3 + c = 0$. Solving, $c = -6$

9. Let $x = \log_2 8$. Then, $2^x = 8$, so $x = 3$

10. The value of this determinant is $(4)(0)(0) + (2)(1)(1) + (1)(1)(0) - (1)(0)(1) - (2)(0)(0) - (4)(1)(1) = -2$.

11. $y^4 + y^2 - y - 1 = y^4 - y$. Then, $y^2 - 1 = 0$. Factoring, $(y-1)(y+1) = 0$. Solving, $x = -1, 1$

12. Substituting the given points, $(c)(0) = (d)(2)^2 - 4$ and $3c = (d)(16) - 4$. From the 1st equation, $0 = 4d-4$, so $d = 1$. The 2nd equation becomes $3c = 16 - 4$, so $c = 4$

13. A consistent system of equations means their graphs intersect at one point. Since x 2/3k and $y = 6 - 2k$, rewrite the middle equation as $6 - 2k - 6(2/3k) = 6k$. Then, $6 - 2k - 4k = 6k$. Simplifying, $6 = 12k$. So, $k = 1/2$.

14. For $ax^2 + bx + c = 0$ to have 2 real, unequal roots, $b^2 - 4ac > 0$. Thus, for $x^2 + 4x + c = 0$, we need $16 - (4)(1)(c) > 0$. Then, $16 > 4c$, so $c < 4$.

15. $|x-2| < 4$ means $x - 2 < 4$ and $x - 2 > -4$. This means $x < 6$ and $x > -2$, which can be written as $-2 < x < 6$.

16. We note that $x^4 - y^4 = (x^2-y^2)(x^2+y^2) = (5)(13) = 65$

17. Rewrite as $x^2 + y^2 = 5$. The center is located at (0,0). Any circle with the equation $(x-h)^2 + (y-k)^2 = r^2$ has a center at (h,k).

18. If $x^2 - 5x - 14 = 0$, then $(x-7)(x+2) = 0$, leading to x = 7, -2. But since it is also required that x > 5, the only final answer is x = 7 only.

19. If $(x-3)(x+1) > 0$, then either both factors are positive or both are negative. If both are positive, x > 3 and x > -1, which yields x > 3. If both are negative, x < 3 and x < -1, which yields x < -1. Thus, x < -1 or x > 3.

20. The numerator will contain the coefficients of x and the constants on the right side of the equation, whereas the denominator will contain the coefficients of x,y. Thus, the determinant for y is

$$\begin{vmatrix} 2 & 3 \\ 1 & 7 \\ 2 & 1 \\ 1 & 4 \end{vmatrix}$$

21. If $25^X = 5$, then $5^{2X} = 5^1$, so x 1/2 = 3^{x+y} = 81 means $3^{1/2+Y} = 3^4$. So, 1/2 + y = 4. Solving, y = 7/2 or 3 1/2.

22. If $x^2 - x - 1 < x^2 - 1$, then -x < 0; so x > 0.

23. By substitution, -3 = 2m+b and 9 = -6m+b. Subtracting, -12 = 8m. Thus, $m = -\dfrac{12}{8} = -\dfrac{3}{2}$

24. 2, 6, 18, 3x+3,.... As a geometric series, 3x+3 must equal 54. Then, 3x = 51, so x = 17.

25. Note that the slope is (4-0)/(0-3) = -4/3 and the y-intercept 4 is (0,4). The required equation is y= -4/3 x+4, which is equivalent to 3y + 4x = 12

TEST 4

DIRECTIONS: Each question or incomplete statement is followed by several suggested answers or completions. Select the one that BEST answers the question or completes the statement. *PRINT THE LETTER OF THE CORRECT ANSWER IN THE SPACE AT THE RIGHT.*

1. In the arithmetic progression $-\frac{1}{4}, 0, \frac{1}{4}, \frac{1}{2}, \ldots$, what is the 13th term?

   A. $\frac{5}{2}$ B. $\frac{11}{4}$ C. 3 D. $\frac{13}{4}$ E. $\frac{7}{2}$

2. Solve the following system of equations for x:
   $$y = -2x$$
   $$x^2 + 6y^2 = 4$$

   A. $\pm\frac{2}{5}$ B. $\pm\frac{8}{11}$ C. $\pm\frac{2}{13}\sqrt{26}$ D. $\pm\frac{4}{13}\sqrt{13}$ E. $\pm\frac{4}{5}$

3. For what (if any) values of x is it TRUE that
   $$1+\sqrt{x^2+12}=1-\sqrt{62-x^2}\,?$$

   A. None
   B. -5 *only*
   C. 5 *only*
   D. -5 and 5
   E. $4\sqrt{2}$ and $-4\sqrt{2}$

4. The quadratic equation whose roots are 4 and -3 is

   A. $x^2 + x - 12 = 0$
   B. $x^2 - x - 12 = 0$
   C. $x^2 - 7x - 12 = 0$
   D. $4x^2 - x - 12 = 0$
   E. $4x^2 - 3x - 12 = 0$

5. The graphs of two linear equations are distinct and do NOT intersect. How many solutions do these two equations have in common?

   A. None
   B. One
   C. Two
   D. An unlimited number
   E. It cannot be determined from the information given

6. $(-2i)(-2i) =$

   A. $-4i$ B. $4i$ C. -4 D. 4 E. 8

7. If an integer x is divided by another integer y, the quotient is If the sum of the two integers is 75, then x =

   A. 3   B. 8   C. 25   D. 48   E. 72

8. For what value of k will the roots of the equation $x^2 + kx + 9 = 0$ be equal?

   A. 0   B. 3   C. 6   D. 9   E. 18

9. Evaluate $i^2 + i^4 + i^6$, where $i = \sqrt{-1}$.

   A. -3   B. -1   C. 0   D. 1   E. 3

10. $x^3 \cdot x^2 =$

    A. x^6
    D. x^5
    B. $2x^3$
    E. none of the above
    C. $3x^2$

11. Which of these is the equation of a line that is parallel to the line defined by the equation $y = 2x + 5$?

    A. $y = 2x$ B. $y = -\frac{1}{2}x$ C. $y = x-5$ D. $y = -2x+5$

12. $\sqrt{16^3} =$

    A. $4\sqrt{3}$ B. 24   C. 64   D. 512

13. The graph of the equation $3x + y = 6$ crosses the y-axis at what point?

    A. (0,-6)   B. (0,6)   C. (2,0)   D. (3,0)

14. $\sqrt{x^{16}} =$

    A. $x^{\frac{1}{4}}$ B. x^2 C. x^4 D. x^8

15. If $2^{2x} = 64$, then x is

    A. 3   B. 6   C. 12   D. 16   E. 32

16. If $x^3 - 2x^2 - 3$ is multiplied by $2x^2 - 5$, what is the coefficient of x^2 in the product?

    A. -16   B. -4   C. 0   D. 4   E. 16

17. $\frac{1}{a} + \frac{1}{b} =$

    A. $\frac{1}{ab}$ B. $\frac{2}{ab}$ C. $\frac{2}{a+b}$ D. $\frac{a+b}{ab}$

18. $\dfrac{8x^3 - 4x}{4x} =$

   A. $2x^2$ B. $8x^3$ C. $2x^2-1$ D. $8x^3-1$

19. In the Photography Club's membership, the ratio of the number of boys to the number of girls is 3:2. If the Club has a total of 60 members, how many of them are boys?

   A. 20   B. 24   C. 36   D. 40

20. For which value or values of x is the expression $\dfrac{2(x-1)}{x(x+2)}$ NOT a *real* number?

   A. 0 only   B. 1 only   C. 0 and 1   D. 0 and -2

KEY (CORRECT ANSWERS)

1.	B	11.	A
2.	A	12.	C
3.	A	13.	B
4.	B	14.	D
5.	A	15.	A
6.	C	16.	D
7.	E	17.	D
8.	C	18.	C
9.	B	19.	C
10.	D	20.	D

SOLUTIONS TO PROBLEMS

1. The nth term of an arithmetic progression is $a + (n-1)d$, where a = 1st term and d = difference between terms. For this example, the 13th term is $-1/4 + (12)(1/4) = 2\ 3/4 = 11/4$

2. Since $y = 2x$, we have $x^2 + 6(-2x)^2 = 4$. Then, $25x^2 = 4$. So, $x = \pm\sqrt{4/25} = \pm 2/5$

3. $1 + \sqrt{x^2 + 12} = 1 - \sqrt{62 - x^2}$ simplifies to $x + 12 = -\sqrt{62 - x^2}$. Squaring both sides, $x^2 + 24x + 144 = 62 - x^2$, which becomes $2x^2 + 24x + 82 = 0$ or $x^2 + 12x + 41 = 0$. Since $12^2 - (4)(1)(41) = -20$, which is less than 0, no x values will work.

4. If the roots are 4 and -3, then $(x-4)(x+3) = 0$. This can be written as $x^2 - x - 12 = 0$

5. Two linear equation graphs that don't intersect are parallel. There are no common solutions to the equations.

6. $(-2i)(-2i) = 4i^2 = 4(-1) = -4$

7. $x/y = 24$ and $x+y = 75$. The first equation says, $y = \dfrac{x}{24}$. Substituting into the 2nd equation, $x + \dfrac{x}{24} = 75$. Then, $\dfrac{25}{24}x = 75$, so $x = 75 \div \dfrac{25}{24} = 72$

8. For $x^2 + kx + 9 = 0$ to have equal roots, $k^2 - (4)(1)(9) = 0$ Then, $k^2 = 36$, so $k = 6$ or -6

9. $i^2 + i^4 + i^6 = -1 + 1 + (-1) = -1$

10. $x^3 \cdot x^2 = x^5$. When multiplying with like bases, add the exponents.

11. In the form $y = mx + b$, two lines are parallel if the m values are equal. Thus, $y = 2x$ and $y = 2x + 5$ represent parallel lines.

12. $\sqrt{16^3} = 16^{\frac{3}{2}} = 4^3 = 64$

13. On the y-axis, $x=0$. So, $3(0)+y=6$, and $y = 6$. The intersection point is $(0,6)$.

14. $\sqrt{x^{16}} = x^8$, since $x^8 \cdot x^8 = x^{16}$

15. $2^{2x} - 64 = 2^6$. Then, $2x = 6$, so $x = 3$

16. $(x^3 - 2x^2 - 3)(2x^2 - 5)$ will contain a coefficient of x^2 as $(-2)(-5) + (-3)(2) = 10 - 6 = 4$

5 (#4)

17. $\dfrac{1}{a}+\dfrac{1}{b}=\dfrac{b}{ab}+\dfrac{a}{ab}=\dfrac{a+b}{ab}$

18. $(8x^3-4x)/4x = 4x(2x^2-1)/4x = 2x^2-1$

19. Let 3x = number of boys, 2x = number of girls. Then, 3x + 2x = 60. 5x = 60, so x = 12. The number of boys is (3)(12) = 36.

20. A fraction is undefined if the denominator is 0. Here, x(x+2) = 0, so x = 0 or -2

EXAMINATION SECTION
TEST 1

DIRECTIONS: Each question or incomplete statement is followed by several suggested answers or completions. Select the one that BEST answers the question or completes the statement. *PRINT THE LETTER OF THE CORRECT ANSWER IN THE SPACE AT THE RIGHT.*

1. Which ordered pair of numbers (x,y) is the solution of the following system of equations?
    $3x - 2y = 5$
    $2x + 2y = 10$
    A. (1,1) B. (1,2) C. (2,1) D. (2,3) E. (3,2)

    1.____

2. A certain microcomputer's memory contains 16K (K = 1,024) storage locations. If a program being run uses 12,517 storage locations, how many storage locations are still available?
    A. 3,767 B. 3,867 C. 4,867 D. 11,493 E. 16,384

    2.____

3. $(3.5 + 0.3) - 4(0.82 + 1.08) =$
    A. -3.800 B. -0.380 C. 0.304 D. 1.700 E. 4.840

    3.____

4.

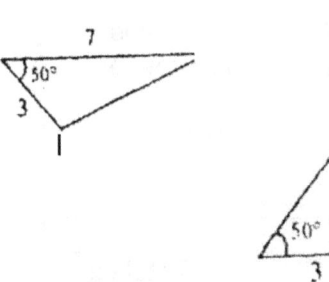

    Which of the above triangles are congruent?
    A. I and II
    B. I and III
    C. II and III
    D. All of the above
    E. No triangle is congruent to any other triangle

    4.____

5. A survey asked a sample of people to choose the better candidate in an upcoming election. Of the people surveyed, 20% said they would vote for Candidate A, 30% for Candidate B, and 50% said they were undecided.
    If 1,000 people said they would vote for Candidate A, how many people said they would vote for Candidate B?
    A. 300 B. 1,100 C. 1,500 D. 2,500 E. 5,000

    5.____

6. Sheila's salary is $110 per day. Due to financial problems in her company, her employer has asked Sheila too take a 10% cut in pay.
How much will Sheila be earning per day if she takes the cut in pay?
  A. $11   B. $99   C. $100   D. $109   E. $121

7. The 6 M. temperature one day last winter was -13°F. From 6 M. until 1 P.M., the temperature rose an average of 3°F per hour.
Which of the following expressions represents the temperature in °F at 1 P.M.?
  A. 7(-13+3)   B. -13-7(3)   C. 7+3(-13)   D. -13+5(3)   E. -13+7(3)

8.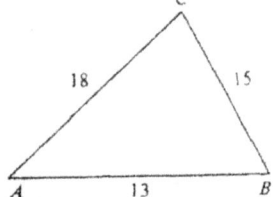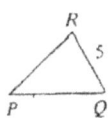

In the figure above, △ABC is similar to △PQR, and the measure of ∠A is equal to the measure of ∠P. The length PR is
  A. 4 1/6   B. 4 1/3   C. 5 10/13   D. 6   E. 8

9. |-5|+|6|+(-5)+6 =
  A. -22   B. -1-   C. 2   D. 10   E. 12

10. A bread recipe calls for 1/2 cup of butter and 3 1/2 cups of flour. Using this recipe to make enough bread for a party, John will need 1 1/2 cups of butter. How many cups of flour will he need?
  A. 4 1/2   B. 5 1/2   C. 7 1/2   D. 9 1/2   E. 10 1/2

11.

\multicolumn{4}{c}{Midland A/V Supply House}
Item	Price Each	Quantity Ordered	Total for Item(s)
8 GB Flash Drive	$4.50	6	
Bluetooth Earbuds	$36.00	1	
CD cases (plastic)	$0.10	25	
		Subtotal	$
		Add 4% Sales Tax	+
		Shipping	+150
		Total	$

What would be the TOTAL cost of the order shown above?
  A. $42.10   B. $65.50   C. $67.00   D. $69.62   E. $69.68

12. The distance, in miles, from an observer to the horizon is 1.35 times the square root of the observer's elevation, in feet.
If an observer's elevation is 16 feet, how many miles away is the horizon?
  A. 5.4   B. 7.0   C. 10.8   D. 11.9   E. 48.6

13. If 3x – 2y = 6, then y equals which of these expressions?
    A. $-\frac{3}{2}x - 3$ B. $-\frac{3}{2}x + 6$ C. $\frac{3}{2}x - 3$ D. $\frac{3}{2}x + 3$ E. 3x-3

14.

Age	Number of Students
14	50
15	180
16	180
17	340
18	210
19	40
Total	1,000

The ages of the students attending City High School this year are listed in the table above.
If a student is picked at random from this school, what is the probability that he or she will be 18 or older?
    A. 1/25   B. 1/4   C. 1/3   D. 1/2   E. 3/4

15.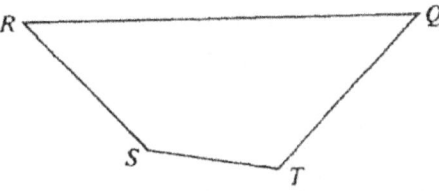

In quadrilateral QRST above, the measures of ∠Q, ∠R, and ∠S are 45°, 45°, and 140°, respectfully.
The measure of ∠T is _____ degrees.
    A. 120   B. 130   C. 135   D. 140   E. 220

16. If x = 3 and y = -2, then the GREATEST value is
    A. |x-y| B. |x|-|y| C. |x|-y   D. x-|y| E. x-y

17.

Name	Height in Inches
Adam	65
Barbara	64
Chris	69
Daniel	64
Ella	65

What is the average (arithmetic mean) height, in inches, of the five people whose heights are listed in the above table?
    A. 65.0   B. 65.2   C. 65.4   D. 66.0   E. 66.5

18. The Jones family wants to buy a refrigerator that costs $750. They agree to pay 15% of the cost initially and the balance in 5 equal monthly payments without interest.
How much will each monthly payment be?
A. $112.50   B. $127.50   C. $129.50   D. $147.00   E. $150.00

19. What is the SMALLEST positive integer that gives a remainder of 1 when divided by any of the integers 12, 18, and 27?
A. 121   B. 109   C. 61   D. 55   E. 37

20. A serving of a certain cereal, with milk, provides 35% of the potassium required daily by the average adult. A serving of this cereal with milk contains 112 milligrams of potassium.
How many milligrams of potassium does the average adult require each day?
A. 35   B. 39   C. 147   D. 320   E. 392

21. Three people share $198 in the ratio 1:3:7.
To the nearest dollar, how much is the LARGEST share?
A. $18   B. $28   C. $54   D. $126   E. $134

22. Which of the following is a factorization of the polynomial $2x^2 + x - 10$?
A. $2(x^2+x-5)$ B. $(2x+2)(x-5)$ C. $(2x+5)(x-2)$
D. $(2x-5)(x+2)$ E. $(2x+10)(x-1)$

23. In the figure at the right, B, E, and C are collinear; A, D, and C ae collinear; E is halfway between B and C; and $\overline{DE}$ and $\overline{AB}$ are each perpendicular to $\overline{BC}$.
If $\overline{BE}$ is 40 units long and $\overline{AB}$ is 60 units long, how many units long is the perimeter of quadrilateral ABED?
A. 100
B. 140
C. 180
D. 200
E. 220

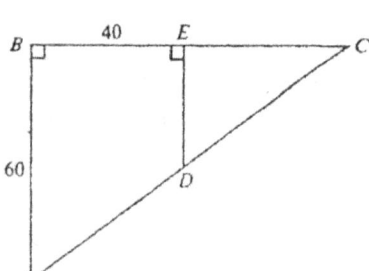

24. The circle graph at the right represents the relative sizes of the sources of a tax dollar. The degree measure of the central angle of the sector labeled *Income* is _____ degrees.
A. 40
B. 72
C. 100
D. 120
E. 144

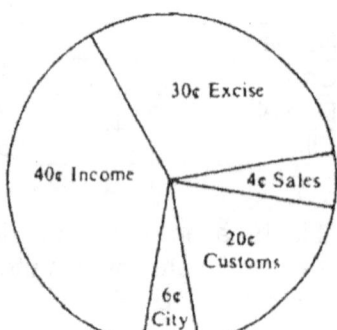

25. $\sqrt{8} + \sqrt{16} + 3\sqrt{2} - \sqrt{3} =$
    A. $4 + 5\sqrt{2} - \sqrt{3}$
    B. $11\sqrt{2} - \sqrt{3}$
    C. $3\sqrt{26} - \sqrt{3}$
    D. $15 - \sqrt{3}$
    E. $3\sqrt{23}$

26. Two lines have the equations $2x + y = 4$ and $x - 2y = 7$, respectively. At what (x,y) point do they intersect?
    A. (3,2)   B. (6,-5)   C. (5,-6)   D. (-3,-2)   E. (-2,3)

27.

x	0	2	4	6	8	10
y	4	7	10	13	16	19

Which of these equations expresses the relationship shown in the above table?
A. $y = 2x$
B. $y = x + 4$
C. $y = x + 9$
D. $2y = 3x + 4$
E. $2y = 3x + 8$

28. A life insurance policy costs $0.75 per month for each $1,000 worth of insurance.
At this rate, how much would someone have to pay in a year for $25,000 worth of this insurance?
A. $225.00   B. $187.50   C. $156.25   D. $75.00   E. $18.75

29. In the circle at the right, which has O as its center, $\overline{OA}$ and $\overline{AB}$ are each 4 units long.
If $\overline{OE}$ is perpendicular to $\overline{AB}$, how many units long is $\overline{OE}$?
    A. $\sqrt{3}$
    B. 2
    C. 3
    D. $2\sqrt{3}$
    E. 4

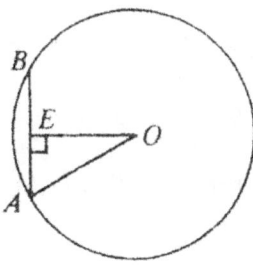

30. If the solutions of the equation $2x^2 - kx + 6 = 0$ are $x = 1$ and $x = 3$, then $k =$
    A. -4   B. 4   C. 7   D. 8   E. 10

31. If $f(x) = x + 3$ and $g(x) = 3 - x$, what is the value of $f[g(3)]$?
    A. 6   B. 3   C. 0   D. -3   E. -6

32. Let x equal the numerator of a certain fraction. The denominator of that fraction is 2 more than the numerator. When 5 is added to both the numerator and the denominator, the resulting fraction equals 5/6.
Which of these equations determines the correct value of x, the numerator of the original fraction?
    A. $\frac{x+5}{x+3} = \frac{5}{6}$
    B. $\frac{x+3}{x+5} = \frac{5}{6}$
    C. $\frac{x+5}{x+7} = \frac{5}{6}$
    D. $\frac{x+5}{2x+5} = \frac{5}{6}$
    E. $\frac{2x+5}{x+5} = \frac{5}{6}$

33. A man throwing darts at a dartboard hit the board on 95% of the throws he made. He hit the board 114 times.
Which equation determines the CORRECT value of x, the number of throws he made?
   A. (0.95)114 = x
   B. 0.95x = 114
   C. 114x = 95
   D. $\frac{x}{95}$ = 114
   E. x = $\frac{0.95}{114}$

34. Which equation determines the line that is parallel to the line with the equation y = 3x + 1 and intersects the line with the equation y = 6x at the y-axis?
   y =
   A. 3x − 1   B. 2x − 1   C. 1/3x − 1   D. 1/3x + 1   E. 1/2x - 1

35.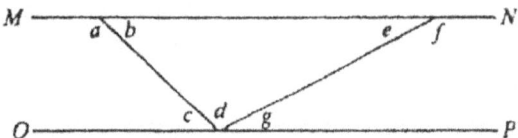

   In the figure above, 2 line segments intersect $\overline{MN}$ and $\overline{OP}$, $\overline{MN}$ is parallel to $\overline{OP}$, and a, b, c, d, e, f, and g are the measures, in degrees, of the indicated angles. Which of these statements is NOT necessarily true?
   A. b = 180° - d − c
   B. e = 180° - d − c
   C. a = 180° - c
   D. f = 180° - g
   E. g = 180° - f

36. If x = 2, y = 3, and z = 5, then the product xyz is how much GREATER than the sum x + y + z?
   A. -34   B. -26   C. 20   D. 26   E. 34

37. If n! = (n)(n-1)(n-2)….(2)(1), then 5! =
   A. 12   B. 15   C. 30   D. 120   E. 54,321

38. For all x, (2x+3)² + 2(2x+4) − 2 equals which of these expressions?
   A. 4x² + 4x + 11
   B. (4x+15)(x+1)
   C. (2x+5)(2x+3)
   D. (2x+5)(2x+2)
   E. (2x+5)(2x-3)

39. What is TRUE about the solutions of the equation x² − 3x = 2?
   They are
   A. real and unequal
   B. real and equal
   C. real and negative
   D. irrational and negative
   E. imaginary

40. If the retail price of a dinette set is 1 1/3 times the wholesale price, and the retail price of a dinette set is $200.00, what is its wholesale price?
   A. $133/33   B. $150.00   C. $166.67   D. $266.67   E. $300.00

KEY (CORRECT ANSWERS)

1. E	11. D	21. D	31. B
2. B	12. A	22. C	32. C
3. A	13. C	23. C	33. B
4. B	14. B	24. E	34. A
5. C	15. B	25. A	35. A
6. B	16. C	26. A	36. E
7. E	17. C	27. E	37. D
8. D	18. B	28. A	38. C
9. E	19. B	29. D	39. A
10. E	20. D	30. D	40. B

8 (#1)

SOLUTIONS TO PROBLEMS

1. Adding the equations, $5x = 15$, so $x = 3$. Substituting this value of x into the first equation, $9 - 2y = 5$. Then, $y = 2$.

2. $(16)(1024) = 16,384$. Then, $16,384 - 12,517 = 3867$.

3. Simplify to $3.8 - 4(1.9) = -3.8$ or 3.800

4. Triangles I and III are congruent by SAS, which refers to two pairs of matching sides and an included equivalent angle.

5. The ratios of votes for Candidate A to votes for Candidate B is 2:3. Then, letting x = number of votes for Candidate B, $2:3 = 1000:x$. Solving, $x = 1500$.

6. Her pay after a 10% cut is $(\$110)(.90) = \$99$

7. Since the temperature rose 3° per hour for 7 hours, the temperature at 1:00 P.M. was $-13° + 7(3°)$

8. $18:PR = 15:5$. Solving, $PR = 6$

9. $|-5|+|6| + (-5) + 6 = +6 - 5 + 6 = 12$

10. Let x = cups of flour. Then, $\frac{1}{2} : 3\frac{1}{2} = 1\frac{1}{2} : x$. This becomes $\frac{1}{2}x = 5\frac{1}{4}$. Solving, $x = 10\frac{1}{2}$

11. Total for items before tax is $6(\$4.50) + 1(\$36.00) + 25(\$0.10) = \$65.50$. Then, $\$65.50 + (.04)(\$65.50) + \$1.50 = \$69.62$.

12. $(1.35)(\sqrt{16}) = (1.35 \times 4) = 5.4$

13. Subtract 3x from both sides of the equation to get $-2y = -3x + 6.3$. Dividing by -2, $y = \frac{3}{2}x - 3$

14. There are 250 students 18 or older out of 1,000 students in the school. Probability of selecting a student 18 or older is $250/1000 = ¼$

15. $\angle T = 360° - 45° - 45° - 140° = 130°$. Note that the sum of the angles in any quadrilateral is 360°

16. Choice C has a value of $|-3|-|(-2)| = 3 + 2 = 5$, which exceeds the value of each of the other choices.

17. Total of heights = 327. Average height is $327/5 = 65'4"$

9 (#1)

18. ($750)(.15) = $112.50. The balance is $637.50. If this is paid in 5 equal installments, each installment is $637.50/5 = $127.50.

19. The number 109 when divided by any of 12, 18, or 27 gives a remainder of 1.

20. The amount of potassium required is 112 ÷ .35 = 320 milligrams

21. Let x, 3x, 7x represent each person's share. Then, x + 3x + x = 198, so x = $18. Then, largest share is 7($18) = $126

22. $2x^2 + x - 10 = (2x+5)(x-2)$, which can be checked by multiplication.

23. Because △GED is similar to △CBA, ED = 1/2(BA) = 30
    Now, AC = $\sqrt{80^2 + 60^2}$ = 100, so AD = 1/2(100) = 50. The perimeter of ABED is
    40 + 60 + 50 + 30 = 180

24. Total of all sources is 100 cents. The central angle for income is, in degrees,
    (40/100)(360) = 144

25. $\sqrt{8} + \sqrt{16} + 3\sqrt{2} - \sqrt{3} = 2\sqrt{2} + 4 + 3\sqrt{2} - \sqrt{3} = 4 + 5\sqrt{2} - \sqrt{3}$

26. Double the 2nd equation to get 2x − 4y = 14. Subtract the 1st equation to get
    -5y = 10, so y = 2. Substitute into the 1st equation to get 2x − 2 = 4. Then, x = 3. The point of intersection is (3,-2).

27. Determine the slope to be (7-4)7(2-0) = 3/2. Then, $y = \frac{3}{2}x + k$, where k is a constant.
    Substituting the point (0,4), $4 = \frac{3}{2}x + 4$ or equivalently 2y = 3x + 8.

28. ($0.75)(25) = $18.75 per month = $225 per year.

29. BE = 1/2(4) = 2. Then, $(QE)^2 + 2^2 = 4^2$. Solving, OE = $\sqrt{12} = 2\sqrt{3}$

30. Substituting x = 1, $2(1^2) - k(1) + 6 = 0$. Simplifying, 8 − k = 0. So, k = 8. Note that if we used x = 3, $2(3^2) - k(3) + 6 = 0$. This would lead to 24 − 3k = 0, and still k = 8.

31. g(3) = 3 − 3 = 0. Then, f[g(3)] = f(0) = 0 + 3 = 3

32. Since x = numerator, x + 2 = denominator. Adding 5 to each makes the new numerator x + 5 and the new denominator X + 7. Thus, (x+5)/(x+7) = 5/6

33. Let x = number of throws. Then, .95x = 114, since his 114 hits represent 95% of his throws.

34. A line parallel to y = 3x + 1 must be of the form y = 3x + k, where k is a constant. The equation y = 6x − 1 crosses the y-axis at (0,-1) and this point must lie on y = 3x + k. By substitution, -1 = 3(0) + k, k = -1. The resulting equation.

35. The statement which is NOT necessarily true is b = 180° - d – c. We know that c + d + g = 180°, but b and g are not necessarily equal.

36. xyz = 30, x + y + z = 4. Then, xyz – (x+y+z) = 34.

37. 5! = (5)(4)(3)(2)(1) – 120

38. $(2x+3)^2$ + 2(2x+4) – 2 = $4x^2$ + 12x + 9 + 4x + 8-2 = $4x^2$ + 16x + 15. This last expression factors as (2x+5)(2x+3).

39. Rewrite as x^2 – 3x + 2 = 0, which becomes (x-2)(x-1) = 0. The solutions are x = 1 and x = 2, which are real and unequal.

40. Let x = wholesale price. Then, $200 = $1\frac{1}{3}$x. Solving, x = $150

www.ingramcontent.com/pod-product-compliance
Lightning Source LLC
Chambersburg PA
CBHW082032300426
44117CB00015B/2456